SAGE | 50 YEARS

SAGE was founded in 1965 by Sara Miller McCune to support the dissemination of usable knowledge by publishing innovative and high-quality research and teaching content. Today, we publish more than 750 journals, including those of more than 300 learned societies, more than 800 new books per year, and a growing range of library products including archives, data, case studies, reports, conference highlights, and video. SAGE remains majority-owned by our founder, and on her passing will become owned by a charitable trust that secures our continued independence.

Los Angeles | London | Washington DC | New Delhi | Singapore

Praise for the Book

"One of the attributes of Huawei is that the company has gone global reaching a relevant position in Europe and addressing the United States. The US government, however, is slowing down the process of Huawei entering the American market on suggestions that Huawei could get access to critical US government information. No question Huawei is the result of the entrepreneurial effort of Ren Zhengfei. The book allows us to get some understanding of the entrepreneur, his philosophy, the culture he wants to establish in Huawei, and the process to do it.

Few of the leading Chinese companies have taken relevant positions internationally. For a high technology company, addressing the international markets is an important challenge. But Huawei has managed to have thousands of employees outside China and satisfy important customers in many countries. The book helps in understanding the approaches followed by Huawei. Mr Ren Zhengfei has been capable of pioneering the development of technology while growing in the world. Obviously, this has required a strict control of information which attaches a flavor of secrecy and even mystery to the behavior of Mr Ren Zhengfei. He has maintained the company as private and his management style has been extremely unconventional.

The book by Tian Tao and Wu Chunbo is an extraordinary research effort, to analyze and describe a very complex reality and a very special entrepreneur. It is a very valuable work to understand entrepreneurship in our complex world."

—Dr Pedro Nueno,
President, Chengwei Ventures Chair Professor
of Entrepreneurship, CEIBS, China

"After years of phenomenal growth, China has arrived at a point where it is a middle-income economy. Its big challenge is to reform the driving forces of the economy so as to be able to continue the upward journey, rather than becoming stuck in the so-called "middle-income trap." A key to success is developing innovative products and solutions, and building global brand recognition and independent marketing structures. Japan and later Korea succeeded in doing this. Can China do the same?

We still don't have the answer. However, the story of Huawei indicates that it can be done. Huawei happened in a time and a place that were unique in the Chinese history. Founder Ren Zhengfei left his job as an army engineer when the Chinese military-industrial complex was radically downsized. He started a small import business in the commercially most liberal place in China, the special economic zone of Shenzhen, just across from the Hong Kong border. He made the most of the opportunity that history provided. He chose an operating model that had never been seen in China, sharing ownership with his employees. Huawei's growth is the result of dedication and pragmatism of Ren and the other early employees.

Reading Tian Tao's account of what has driven Huawei to where it is today provides more insight than anything I have seen before about Huawei. His isn't the traditional type of corporate history that we know well, the ones that start with the family background of the founder, then focus on early challenges, maybe describing some near-death experiences, before moving on to ultimate success. Rather than delving into sales statistics, product development, and so on, Tian Tao focuses on the evolving philosophies and strategies that have guided the company. It is a fascinating inside account that explores the soul of the company.

It is a story told in a Chinese way—there are many metaphors—and from a Chinese perspective, which here and there will surely surprise a Western reader. But this has the great advantage of helping us understand how China sees the world. The many stories about the Chinese corporate landscape are an additional bonus.

A dominant theme is how quickly the wheel turns in business. Firms grow, may become immensely successful but most often then flounder and disappear. The telecom sector has had more than its share of such development. The list of failed ICT giants is long. Huawei itself was close to leaving the ICT sector—in the book I learned that Huawei in

2002 agreed to sell its hardware system to Motorola for 10 billion dollars, investing the proceeds in real estate. A new Motorola chairman turned down the deal at the very last minute. Imagine how it, had it gone through, would have changed the course of both companies!

Awareness of the continuous cycle of growth and death has very much influenced Ren Zhengfei. A constant question in his mind has been how Huawei could succeed when so many others failed. Humility and curiosity have been guiding sentiments. Or to use a rather Chinese term, "self criticism." Ren Zhengfei wrote in 2008: "Without self-criticism, we would have confined ourselves to an enclosure and missed out on the new ideas which have proven essential for us to become a world-class corporation … Our future is dependent on how long we keep the tradition of self-criticism."

One of the answers to the many challenges that have confronted the company has been a willingness to learn from the positive experience of others not just in the area of technology but also in soft matters. Huawei has made a major and multi-year effort to learn and adopt Western management techniques. It also understands that as a global company it needs to integrate into the societies where it is active. A quote from Tian Tao tries to capture this: "Huawei leverages the best from China and the West, and yet it is neither Chinese nor Western."

My personal acquaintance with Huawei is as one of 15–20 foreign senior advisors. We meet Ren Zhengfei and the corporate leadership every year for a polite but frank dialogue of a kind that I doubt takes place anywhere else in the Chinese industry. This willingness to listen to and debate with foreigners with widely varying backgrounds speaks tons of the openness that characterizes the company."

—Mikael Lindstrom,
Senior Advisor, Six Year Plan AB, and former Ambassador to China

"Huawei is a prominent company among the most successful and most internationalized in China. This book offers insights to Western readers, allowing them to truly understand Huawei, its management philosophy and culture, and the special leadership approaches of Ren Zhengfei."

—John A. Quelch,
Charles Edward Wilson Professor of Business Administration,
Harvard Business School

"Over the course of the last quarter century, Huawei has become one of the most important telecommunications companies in the world and, arguably, one of the most powerful Chinese companies in the global economy. Yet, there is much that is not known about Huawei and much that is misunderstood. As the foremost authority on Huawei in the world, Tian Tao brings deep knowledge and unprecedented access to help pull back the veil on one of the world's most enigmatic companies. This book will be essential reading for politicians, pundits, and anyone interested in gaining a deeper understanding of this important company."

—Doug Guthrie,
Professor and Former Dean at the George Washington School of Business, Author of *Dragon in a Three-Piece Suit: The Emergence of Capitalism in China*

"As a long-time observer and friend of China, I have watched with admiration the global growth and innovative strategy of Huawei. This book will give readers a special insight into Huawei's capacity and entrepreneurial drive under the dedicated leadership of Mr Ren Zhengfei."

—**Kerry Matthew Stokes AC,
Executive Chairman, Seven Group Holdings Limited, Australia**

"This is the most complete book about Huawei I have ever read."

—**Liu Chuanzhi, Founder of Lenovo**

"Over the past two decades, Huawei has composed an amazing epic in the business world. It has started from an emerging market and conquered the global market. What is the code of success? This book offers the most reliable answers."

—**Qin Suo, Editor-in-chief, *CBN Daily***

"This book does not present the business history of Huawei only; it also highlights the evolution of the business philosophy of Ren Zhengfei, the boss of the company. Huawei is Mount Everest in the mind's eye of all Chinese businessmen, and Ren Zhengfei has behaved like a hermit living in a cave. He has not created any precept or claimed any truth. As the closest observers of Ren Zhengfei, Tian Tao and Wu Chunbo are the most likely authors to tell us the precepts and truths of Ren Zhengfei."

—**Niu Wenwen, Publisher and Creator, *The Founder Magazine***

"Huawei is a privately owned company. It is highly sensitive to technological changes. It is the real multinational based in China. These facts reflect the alertness, adaptability, and conviction of Ren Zhengfei, the top leader of Huawei. Ren is a unique manager and his speeches have been widely quoted because they offer great philosophical delights. This book is full of such delights, which you cannot miss."

—Liu Zhouwei,
Founder, *21st Century Business Herald*

The Huawei Story

The Huawei Story

Tian Tao
with
Wu Chunbo

www.sagepublications.com
Los Angeles • London • New Delhi • Singapore • Washington DC

First published in 2015 by

SAGE Response
B1/I-1 Mohan Cooperative Industrial Area
Mathura Road, New Delhi 110 044, India

SAGE Publications Inc
2455 Teller Road
Thousand Oaks, California 91320, USA

SAGE Publications Ltd
1 Oliver's Yard, 55 City Road
London EC1Y 1SP, United Kingdom

SAGE Publications Asia-Pacific Pte Ltd
3 Church Street
#10-04 Samsung Hub
Singapore 049483

Published by Vivek Mehra for SAGE Publications India Pvt Ltd, typeset in 11/13 pts Berkeley by RECTO Graphics, Delhi and printed at Sai Print-o-Pack, New Delhi.

Second Printing 2015

Library of Congress Cataloging-in-Publication Data Available

ISBN: 978-93-515-0068-1 (HB)

The SAGE Team: Sachin Sharma, Vandana Gupta, Nand Kumar Jha and Anupama Krishnan

Vision, Will and Integrity—Gifts for
Young Men and Women from Ren Zhengfei

Thank you for choosing a SAGE product! If you have any comment, observation or feedback, I would like to personally hear from you. Please write to me at <u>contactceo@sagepub.in</u>

—Vivek Mehra, Managing Director and CEO,
SAGE Publications India Pvt Ltd, New Delhi

Bulk Sales

SAGE India offers special discounts for purchase of books in bulk. We also make available special imprints and excerpts from our books on demand.

For orders and enquiries, write to us at

Marketing Department
SAGE Publications India Pvt Ltd
B1/I-1, Mohan Cooperative Industrial Area
Mathura Road, Post Bag 7
New Delhi 110044, India
E-mail us at <u>marketing@sagepub.in</u>

Get to know more about SAGE, be invited to SAGE events, get on our mailing list. Write today to <u>marketing@sagepub.in</u>

This book is also available as an e-book.

———————&)C&———————

Contents

Contents

Foreword

by Simon Murray

This is a story not of a company but of a man. A man possessed of all the qualities that we need in our leaders, but so seldom find—vision, courage, determination, honesty, integrity, tolerance, fortitude, and more, much more. This is a compulsory read for all students of life, not those who want to "be" but those who want to "do."

Ren Zhengfei, having left the army as a relatively low-ranking officer with an engineering background, started his business with only RMB20,000 in 1987. The mobile telephone was coming. The big dinosaurs, AT&T, BT, Cable & Wireless, France Telecoms, Deutsche Telecom, and all the rest of them, who had been milking their monopoly status for years, were about to be invaded by ants heralding the arrival of the handheld cellular telephone. One of these in China was Huawei, a private start-up with three employees and a wafer-thin balance sheet, looking for space in a competitive field full of the companies from the United States, Europe, and Japan, and Chinese state-owned companies supported by the Central Government both financially and politically.

Today, with 150,000 staff worldwide, Huawei's 80,000 employees are stockholders in the company, with shares given to them by Mr Ren who has kept only 1.4 percent for himself. This made Huawei a 100 percent employee-owned company. It now has revenues of US$40 billion and operates in over 170 countries around the world.

This book is not only about amazing corporate success and the reasons for it, but also about philosophy, wisdom, humility, and a wonderful culture from which many in the Western world could learn. America accuses Huawei of "listening" to others through their systems, but Mr Ren is far too shrewd to do that, for he knows that if he did and was found to be doing so, even once, his business would die—so stupid he is not. He leaves that to the others!!

We know dinosaurs die—Motorola, Lucent, IBM, and so many others. They get distracted, go down the wrong path, or forget that the priority is not technology but the customers. This book examines some of those. It may sound like a heavy subject, but it is not. It is a racey read, full of the excitement of competition, blended with the quiet philosophy and observations of the wonderful Mr Ren, who makes other business "heroes" look metallic and devoid of warmth, which he has in abundance.

Simon Murray is the Chairman of GEMS Ltd and Gulf Keystone Petroleum. Murray in the past held various high positions on boards, including Group Managing Director of Hutchison Whampoa, Non-Executive Chairman of Glencore International, Executive Chairman Asia/Pacific of the Deutsche Bank Group, and the Vice Chairman of Essar Energy plc. At age 63, he became the oldest man to reach the South Pole unaided, on a 58-day slog during which he lost 50 pounds (23 kilograms).

Foreword

by Admiral William (Bill) A. Owens

The information and communications technology (ICT) sector is fast paced and relentless in transforming its prominence in our everyday lives, and it is causing our lives to be more efficient and fulfilling. Since the invention of the telephone, consumers have benefited greatly from the evolving scale of this technology platform. It is natural for us to instantaneously access information and make important decisions on command. Our reliance on ICT's ubiquity and reliability in this age of the "Internet of Things" has concurrent expectations for speed and content accuracy. Prospects for these elements and the baseline for how we communicate continue to spiral upward. This connectivity is making our world a better place and one of the most significant driving forces behind this swelling technology wave, is Huawei Telecommunications Company.

A book about Huawei is a book about its founder. Ren Zhengfei has made a difference that many will never appreciate in the building of what is likely the most successful private business to come out of post-Mao China. Ren is a humble man with humble beginnings, he is a proud Chinese, a former People's Liberation Army (PLA) soldier, but unlike how the Western press would portray Ren, he is not a career military officer and was not a high ranking "general" as some in the west have wrongly represented him.

I have known Ren Zhengfei for over 10 years and have followed Huawei with a sense of curiosity and respect for their corporate culture, their core values, and their innovation. I competed head on with Huawei while CEO at Nortel Networks and realized early on that Huawei's motivation to succeed in the telecom space was resolute with very specific intentions. Ren led Huawei with a master's blend of hurried patience, innovation, and focus, which moved the company forward in large steadfast steps. Now at the forefront of the telecoms industry on a global scale, Huawei remains fiercely committed to innovation and operational excellence.

My relationship with Ren began in a set of meetings the two of us had concerning the potential merger of Huawei and Nortel, a merger that was not to be; yet, my time with him allowed me to get to know him personally, and our friendship was established. I can remember many meetings in mahogany boardrooms and discussions with Ren relating Chinese folklore about "chicken ribs," but what we didn't lose in translation was a wisdom that he brought to the table; a story of dedication, global strategy, and thoughtfulness that caused me to reflect on the certainty that Huawei under his leadership would one day be the best in the business. Ren has many similarities to some other great people I have known. Outside of Ross Perot Sr.'s office is a stunning picture of an American bald eagle flying solo over a beautiful Pacific Northwest scene with the caption "Eagles Don't Flock." Certainly, Ren has never flocked! This book skillfully points out those elements of folklore and wisdom.

Huawei, the "wolf," has competed fiercely around the world, and alongside Ericsson, has essentially become a formidable market leader in advanced wireless and fiber telecoms equipment. This has been skillfully done, through a unique culture, a dedication to the business (only occasionally seen in the West), a strong management efficiency, precise execution, and individual responsibility and accountability.

I believe that Huawei embodies a new management strategy, the one that is based on culture, a culture of patience and humility, a culture based on doing everything possible to delay an "almost certain failure in the future" and a "go it your own approach." This philosophy and the complete reliance on the Huawei employees and employee ownership also make an IPO difficult, because it would put the destiny of the company in the hands of outside shareholders and an unpredictable marketplace, one that tends to rely on a quarter-to-quarter strategy and results. "Dedication" is a profound word, and Ren has inspired his people with the spirit of unwavering dedication and commitment to the business and their customers. Often to abstraction, he has focused on the business, and caused his people to do the same.

Ren is clearly focused on the future. You can see this from the continued dedication of research and development (R&D) resources to the development of products. He has learned this and other precepts from Western consultants, but I think it is also a part of his natural makeup. He knows this is necessary in order to pursue that dedicated long-term company that will continue to be in the future, one of the two or three most significant telecoms and enterprise technologies companies in the world.

As a military man I have known many clever and truly outstanding strategists. I have rarely come across an individual more strategically oriented than Ren. He studies the world, studies the market, talks with many people with knowledge, and then judges where the pitfalls and minefields live for his business. This has led the company to take great advantage of both the upsides and downsides of this industry. He has forecasted both booms and busts and has been unafraid to take contrarian actions to drive his company through them. After 30 years in the US military, I have some idea of grand strategies. Ren has managed a grand strategy that has continued over the decades of his leadership, and included all elements of politics, finance, markets, and a familiarity with the black swans stalking the business. This book cleverly lays out those elements of brilliance that he has brought to the marketplace and should be another great reminder to many MBA classes about what real strategy can do.

Huawei's impressive performance as a corporation has led some countries, most notably the Great Britain and the United States, to raise concerns over Huawei's alleged capability to collect sensitive information through its network equipment. These contentions have not been proven and are largely wrapped in a political mesh that has excluded Huawei from competing effectively in these markets. Notwithstanding this, under Ren's leadership, Huawei has become a global leader in the telecommunication sector (second only to Sweden's Ericsson). This competitive ranking, while excluded from some of the largest international opportunities, speaks to Huawei's formidable achievement.

I believe, especially, that in the United States there is a growing awareness that in the telecoms equipment industry, Huawei must be allowed to enter our country in a meaningful way to allow us to take advantage of the world-changing technology that they have developed and will continue to develop in the future. The United States is no longer leading the world in telecoms and enterprise equipment build-outs. It's time to put the history of charges and counter charges about Huawei and the Western governments around the world behind us. Huawei possesses technologies

xiv   The Huawei Story

that America needs, and the partnership with Huawei could be profound between them and the technology companies in the United States.

In conclusion, the story of Huawei so well told in this book is about an employee-owned company, a humble founder and leader, and a different philosophy, one that we should all consider as we look toward new approaches to our businesses in an unpredictable world.

Bill Owens *is the Chairman of one of the three largest telecom companies in the United States, and has been a board member of 23 public companies. He was a nuclear submarine officer in the US Navy and retired as a four-star officer, the vice-chairman of the Joint Chiefs of Staff in the United States. Since leaving the Navy, Owens has served in three CEO roles including a fortune 500 company.*

Preface

The sunset's glow is not the color of tomorrow.

We must first declare that this book does not intend to condemn Huawei to failure. We have written it so that the Huawei organism can be rationally and clinically examined, thereby helping us identify the gene for long-term survival and serving to eliminate cells that may harm the organism. We aim to stimulate public discussion around the central topic: Will Huawei be the next to fall?

Will Self-Criticism Help Keep Huawei's Core Values Fresh and Valid?

Prosperity is often achieved at the expense of the future; everything most desirable comes with a trade-off, just as roses come with thorns. A boom does not necessarily lead to a bust; this is not a natural law. However, charcoal turns to dust once it has served its purpose. At the turn of the century, many giants fell, and headlines were filled with big corporations going bankrupt. Huawei is not exactly considered a global leader, but it has achieved a certain level of success. Will it fall someday? Journalists have entertained and flirted with this topic. Although some journalists are bitterly critical and point directly to the company's weaknesses, Huawei continues to grow.

In general, Huawei has kept a clear mind and, through self-criticism, the company has aligned itself, developed a unique self-cleaning mechanism, and formed a system of core values centered on customers and a long-term commitment to hard work. In recent years, however, as older employees become wealthy and new ones join the company, the commitment to self-criticism is weakening and the definitive degree of modesty displayed with customers is fading away. In the meantime, the company has to cope with tough challenges, including changes in technology, customer base, and the economic climate. Past success is no guarantee of a bright future. Can Huawei remain modest and humble? Will the company continue to listen to customers and respond promptly to their needs? Can the company continue the painful tradition of self-criticism? Can the company keep its core values fresh and valid?

Can Huawei Adapt to New Dynamics and Regain Its Flexibility?

Huawei was flexible when it was founded, but as the organization has grown and management intensified, the company has developed a centralized and vertical power hierarchy. Headquarters possess enormous power. Will it regain its flexibility and let those who can hear the gunfire call for support?

When Huawei was a start-up, the frontline teams had enough authority and freedom to make prompt decisions. However, as the company is expanding and applying institutionalized management and control, power is increasingly being centralized and headquarters are becoming a command post that directly controls each business operation in all corners of the world. Will the corporate bureaucrats delegate authority to those who hear the gunfire at the frontline so that they can seize opportunity as it arises? How can the company control risk if headquarters does not perform well in servicing, supporting, and supervising field operations? Will Huawei persuade its departments at headquarters to give up power and adopt a new strategy of positioning that provides services, support, and supervision? This is perhaps the toughest part of Huawei's reform program.

An important part of the agenda is to let those who hear the gunfire call for support. Huawei has 150 regional units and innumerable product and project units, and the particulars for each regional or business unit vary significantly. When situations arise in operations across the globe, which internal and external trade-offs should Huawei consider, and how can it build and allocate expert teams and strategic resources? As the management system remains divided, how should the company harmonize the system to provide timely services and support? Currently, Huawei's annual revenue amounts to US$40 billion, which, according to its own estimates, will rise to US$70 billion in five years. Can Huawei manage such huge business volume on a single platform? The organization, incumbent leaders and their successors, its management philosophy, and management system and structure, based on numbers, are now subject to relentless tests. Of course, we hope that Huawei does not fall, but the company has to face reality itself.

The Test of Huawei's Organizational Competence: Can the Company Build a Sound Business Environment?

First, what kind of internal environment should the company develop? Should the organization be accountable to its leaders or its customers?

Employees should be keenly aware that the most important leaders are customers, not their bosses. Individual incomes are dependent on what employees do for their customers and the value of their contribution, not how close they are to their bosses and colleagues. The income of the team to which they belong is derived from the projects awarded by customers.

Huawei is applauded for its courage to accept criticism, but the reality is that more people are currying favor with their leaders. Management teams have too much power over employee performance evaluation, promotion, compensation, and stock allocation. As such, are employees misled to believe that their career has nothing to do with customers, and they instead need to prioritize gaining favor from leaders? Is the company moving farther away from its customers?

Moreover, Huawei is operating in a sector that is becoming saturated. Will excessive competition damage the company's general competence? Is the proposition of effective and profitable growth acceptable, both internally and externally? As the company gets bigger and bigger, will an air of superiority to that of customers pervade and allow arrogance to creep into the cracks? Will the company lack the patience to listen to its customers? Will the company lose its sensitivity? Will the company eventually fall if such arrogance is not recognized and corrected?

The core issue for the external environment is to identify how Huawei can build a foundation for solid operations amid the surging tide of globalization.

Huawei is based in China. The Chinese origin is a fact that the company cannot change; it must be accepting of this. Then, how will changes to China's policies affect Huawei operations in the global market? Generally, wages are low in China, but Huawei also operates in high-income countries with generous welfare programs. To complicate matters further, telecommunications is a pillar industry in just about every country, very often intertwined with national interests—handling all these international issues is a daunting challenge for Huawei's senior management.

It is essential for Huawei to respect the laws of each locale and win the trust of countries in which it operates if it wishes to expand its global presence. Its relationship with the United States, in particular, is a formidable challenge. Huawei has fallen victim to allegation after allegation from its American competitors. The company did not realize until recently that it—originally a group of Chinese farmers—has suddenly become a global force. In its global rise, Huawei has stepped on other people's toes. It has upset industry incumbents with cutting-edge technologies, and the industry has not yet adapted to that fact—neither has Huawei.

The sunset's glow is not the color of tomorrow, just as a brilliant past does not guarantee a bright future. Every large corporation in the West that has fallen boasts a wonderful past. Therefore, Huawei should cherish but not relish its achievements while continuing to maintain its core values and remain true to its tradition of self-criticism. There is no other way for Huawei to survive in the turbulent global market.

Acknowledgments

After the simplified Chinese edition hit the shelves, the China Critic Press and the authors received a flood of inquires from English, Japanese, Arabic, and other readers who are eager to know when editions in their language would be published. We'd like to thank the China Europe International Business School (CEIBS) and SAGE Publications for their close cooperation in the early publication of the English edition. We also want to take this opportunity to thank Mr Hu Zhifeng from CEIBS, the translator Mr Huang Xie'an, proofreaders from Huawei Translation Services Center, including Mr Wang Kai, Ms Zhang Linyan, Mr Giovanni Valenti, Ms Xu Tiantian, Ms Du Xiaolian, Ms Yu Kaishan, Ms Feng Wenchao, and Ms He Yanghong, and other friends who contributed to this book. The English edition would have been impossible without their diligent efforts and support.

Tian Tao and Wu Chunbo

Special thanks goes to my wife, Ms Yao Baozhen, whose support and encouragement both inspired and compelled me, even when I felt worn out and didn't want to write anymore. At one point I was considering having someone else finish the book according to my narrations, but she strongly objected and made me press on, convincingly persuading me that the book would become "awkward and shallow" without my personal engagement. I want to offer my heartfelt gratitude to my wife upon the publication of the English edition of this book.

Tian Tao

Introduction—Business Management Philosophy

The Mysterious Driver of Huawei's Success

Section I. Time and Destiny: Ren Zhengfei—The Dreamer

In 1987, Ren Zhengfei was abandoned by mainstream society at the age of 44. This is a significant age, because the number 4 sounds the same as the Chinese character for death, but 4 doubled is equal to 8, which sounds like the Chinese character for prosperity in the southern dialect. Four times 4 is 16, which means a smooth road ahead.

This age is, therefore, full of different metaphors concerning fate and marked the beginning of Ren's entrepreneurial journey. In fact, he had spent three years in the business world already before, but the experience had ended in failure.

Since founding Huawei Technologies, a private company, at 44, Ren's fate has become inseparable from that of Huawei. Huawei was dismissed in the early days of the great reform, and Ren Zhengfei was the Chinese Don Quixote who dared to challenge opposition alone.

In the late 1970s, Deng Xiaoping started an economic revolution in China. Within a mere decade, from 1978 to 1988, the Chinese economy and society underwent drastic changes. For thousands of years, China had been dominated by politicians and men of letters, and agriculture was the key or even the sole source of economic power. Merchants had no position in the country, and even the most successful, such as Lü Buwei (292 BC–235 BC) and Hu Xueyan (1823–1885), survived as dependents of politics. Through the reform program, Deng Xiaoping created an opportunity to change this rigid tradition.

Deng Xiaoping is acclaimed for his political courage and foresight because he was the driving force behind the commercial revolution that had far-reaching impact. This reform shone broad beams of hope for merchants in the country who, as a social class, have since gained increasing value.

In the 1980s, the country was stirring and all classes were full of passion and desire. There emerged a number of forerunners and immediate followers of the reform movement, including Bu Xinsheng, Ma Shengli, Mou Qizhong, Nian Guangjiu, Zhang Ruimin, and Liu Chuanzhi. They were rebels against the old system and adventurers in a whirlwind, brought to a new world by a tidal wave.

Former military engineer Ren Zhengfei was also carried by this whirlwind. He became an individual merchant, whether he liked it or not.

At first, Huawei traded telecom equipment and was dismissed as a "minor vendor." Just as surely, however, Ren placed high expectations on the company and himself: to become a world-class telecom equipment manufacturer within two decades.

Heroes are made in an age of turbulence. Who, then, would become the leaders in a world of tumult? Nassir Ghaemi, a professor of psychiatry at Tufts University, says that such leaders are found among the mentally ill or mentally abnormal. In fact, he discovered that all outstanding leaders in times of crisis had psychological problems. This is also true with Ren Zhengfei. He suffered serious depression and anxiety during the darkest days of the company. Twenty years ago, when Ren announced his dream to be world-class, the small audience was divided, as some were convinced, while others suspected their boss had gone mad.

Of course, there were many dreamers like Ren Zhengfei, as his was a passionate and peculiar generation. Liu Chuanzhi, the founder and chairman of Lenovo, was also a dreamer. He dreamed of challenging IBM, and that dream came true. Another dreamer was Mou Qizhong, who declared he would draw water from the Brahmaputra River to the Yellow River through the Himalayas, and who traded China's socks for Russian jets. He ended up in prison, but not even the prison walls or the barbed wire on top of the walls could repress his passion and dreams, according to recent reports.

In the telecom industry, there were also a number of eccentric merchants that emerged with such magnificent names as Great Dragon and Datang. Dragon is a representative symbol of China, while the "tang" in "Datang" refers to the Tang Dynasty, one of the most powerful and prosperous dynasties of China that, to some extent, represents the best of China. Another appealing appellation was provided by Zhongxing Semiconductors (now the ZTE Group)—the name Zhongxing literally means "China is reviving." Last but not the least, the name Huawei means "China is rising and taking action."

These are the most successful telecom manufacturers in China, but they all started with the odds stacked against them, suffering from a lack of capital, technology, and human resources. To make matters even worse, they faced Western giants, most of which had been established for over a century.

They were playing a game of ants versus elephants, and only crazy dreamers could believe that they would eventually see victory. Let's take a look at four middle-aged, but imaginative idealists: Wu Jiangxing of Great Dragon, Zhou Huan of Datang, Hou Weigui of ZTE, and Ren Zhengfei of Huawei. Over the past two decades, they have all played an excellent game in the Chinese and global telecom markets, and created tragic–comic legends full of twists and turns and ups and downs.

Section II. Great Minds Think Alike: The Story of Four Middle-aged Men

Arrogant Multinational Giants

In the 1980s, China was at the forefront of revival. Revitalization was a buzzword in the political and media spheres in a country eager to recover from political tragedy. Revival was the shared aspiration of people at all levels of society.

At that time, economic activity had been suspended for decades and the social system was almost dead. The thundering call of Deng Xiaoping to reform and open up awakened the entire country, releasing its productive power and setting people free from rigid controls. The country had taken on a completely different appearance not long after the reform program started. Economic development was a mega trend, and speed and efficiency were defining the daily life of a billion people.

Lamentably, however, infrastructure projects, such as power, transportation, and telecommunications, lagged far behind, with telecommunications being the most underdeveloped. In 1978, China had only a 4.05 million line switching capacity and 2 million telephone subscribers; the telephone penetration rate was 0.38 percent, ranking over 120 in the world, and lower than the average rate of African countries. A telephone was a luxury, to which only the privileged class in China had access; this being more than a century after Alexander Bell invented the telephone!

The extreme inadequacy of communication facilities was a bottle-neck in the development of China's national economy. It became strategically imperative to build telecom facilities on a large scale; however, the country did not have one decent telecom equipment manufacturer. For this reason, the country adopted a policy of "exchanging the market for technologies," which meant opening up its telecom market to foreign companies. Fortunately, the opening-up policy coincided with a global IT revolution, enabling China to progress rapidly with its telecom infrastructure and acquire the most advanced telecom technologies.

In retrospect, the decision to exchange its market for technologies was timely and visionary. The automotive industry in China, in contrast, has suffered from market protectionism and has never really caught up with the leaders.

It is painful to open the door, of course. When foreign companies entered the Chinese market, they charged high prices but offered little to no service. For example, a private branch exchange (PBX) line is now worth US$10, but in the late 1970s was US$500. Chinese customers also had to wait lengthy periods for the product to be delivered and installed: Sellers were the lords. This is absurd logic in any Western country that boasts a long commercial tradition, but this logic prevailed in the Chinese telecom market in the 1980s. At first, there were eight companies from seven countries, and then nine companies from eight countries in the Chinese telecom market: Fujitsu and NEC from Japan, Ericsson from Sweden, Bell from Belgium, Alcatel from France, Siemens from Germany, AT&T (whose network division later became the independently operated Lucent Technologies) from the United States, Northern Telecom from Canada (later becoming Nortel after market consolidation), and Nokia from Finland. Most of them were already century-old companies at the time, and each acted like a victorious conqueror in China, selling products at high prices.

The Destiny of a Generation

China has rapidly developed its telecom infrastructure at considerable but necessary cost, and policymakers have initiated strategies to develop the communications manufacturing industry at the right time. In the mid-1980s, over 400 Chinese telecom manufacturers sprung up, including private companies, state-owned enterprises (SOEs), and other types.

The dominant SOEs were Great Dragon, Datang, and ZTE. Born in 1953, the former military official Wu Jiangxing founded Great Dragon, later emerging as the "national hero of the telecom sector" and "father of the Chinese large-capacity program control switch" before settling in as the Major General of a military institute. Datang was founded by Zhou Huan. Born in 1944, the former official of the Post and Telecom Ministry of China is now dean of the China Academy of Telecommunication Research under the Ministry of Industry and Information Technology. ZTE was founded in 1985 in Shenzhen by Hou Weigui, who was born in 1942, and previously served as a technology officer of the 691 Factory under the former Ministry of Aviation and Aerospace of China. There is no doubt that each of these SOEs was committed to a national mission: developing China's communications industry to challenge Western giants!

This did not mean that private companies were not aware of this mission. In 1987, Ren Zhengfei founded Huawei, with the aim of becoming the backbone of China's communications industry.

This aim to advance the country is the shared aspiration of his particular generation. Entrepreneurs born in the 1940s and 1950s embody many traits: patriotism, idealism, sense of mission, integrity, desire for leadership, and dedication. They were full of passion inside, with an inclination to break established rules. Whenever they were given a bit of hope, even slim ones, they would choose to challenge the reality. The founders of the four major Chinese telecom manufacturers—Great Dragon, Datang, ZTE, and Huawei—all represent these characteristics and ambitions.

Regretfully, such passion has almost died in China.

Survival of the Fittest

In retrospect, one cannot help but pay tribute to old-school entrepreneurs who acted like Don Quixote. At their inception, the four major Chinese telecom manufacturers were hungry for funding, technology, and talent. Even government-sponsored enterprises ran into difficulty from time to time, as surely did Huawei, a private company with initial working capital of just CNY20,000. Each of these Chinese enterprises had to compete with the toughest rivals in the world.

Eight of the nine international communications manufacturers doing business in China were over a century old at the time. In comparison,

Chinese telecom companies were like newborn calves, far smaller than the Western elephants; however, these calves fought boldly with the elephants. Of course, the law of the jungle is brutal, and the four major Chinese telecom manufacturers grew on the backs of hundreds of smaller peers killed by the Western elephants. Even Great Dragon, the forerunner of Chinese telecom companies, eventually fell.

Nevertheless, the tables have turned. Two decades later, the Chinese telecom industry has ascended to one of the top three, alongside the United States and Europe. During this period, Chinese telecom companies have grown from strength to strength and expanded into the global arena, startling the Western giants. At the same time, many Western giants have either merged or collapsed. Only a few, Ericsson for example, can compete with "Chinese ghosts" like Huawei and ZTE. In 2010, Huawei ranked No. 397 on the list of Fortune 500 companies and was the only privately owned Chinese company to make the register. In the global telecom industry, Huawei was second only to Ericsson and the margin was a mere US$2.8 billion in sales.

"We don't want to become the world's number one, but we have to walk on the road to becoming number one," said Huawei Chairwoman Sun Yafang.

Ren Zhengfei's prediction that Huawei would become one of the world's top three telecom manufacturers has come true. His top priority now is to slow down and create a sound business ecosystem.

Section III. Huawei Rises to Prominence

We have much respect for competitors like Huawei. (Ericsson CEO Hans Vestberg)

The story of Ren Zhengfei would be an amazing success story in the US. (3Com President Bruce Claflin)

The rise of domestic firms such as Huawei is a disaster for the multinationals. (*The Economist*)

This company is on the same road as Ericsson toward becoming a global giant. Now all these telecom giants eye Huawei as the most dangerous competitor. (*Time Magazine*)

Some of these remarks may be a bit exaggerative, but no other Chinese company instills fear into foreign players and creates such awe in the European and American markets.

How then has Huawei been able to do this? It is a combination of being in the right place and at the right time. Twenty-five years ago, Huawei was born in a residential building in Shenzhen as a limited company with five or six founders. This fledgling company had a meager CNY20,000 as initial working capital. According to the regulations of the Shenzhen government at the time, a private technology company must have at least CNY20,000 as registered capital and at least five shareholders. Yet, Ren Zhengfei had only CNY3,000. In order to obtain the business license, he looked for partners and pooled enough capital to satisfy registration procedures. Later, after the company boomed, the original partners were generously rewarded, and Ren Zhengfei began to implement the shareholding scheme for employees. In early 2012, Huawei had 140,000 employees worldwide in more than 150 countries and regions, serving more than one-third of the world's population. In addition, Huawei leads the world in international patent applications.

Huawei's success, in every sense, further proves the success of Deng Xiaoping's reform and opening-up policy.

Things change. How can changes be implemented and which direction should be taken? In the mid-1980s, policymakers in China had no idea about direction. Without any clear blueprint in mind, Deng Xiaoping proposed the idea of "groping stones while crossing the river" and argued that "It doesn't matter whether it's a white cat or a black cat; a cat that catches mice is a good cat." These are general guidelines, but in that specific political climate, they were not particularly operable. It was therefore difficult for anyone without brash adventurism to make up their mind to "plunge into the sea," a slogan of that time, meaning to go into business for oneself.

Luckily, Deng Xiaoping supported trial and error, encouraging everyone to unleash their potential to the fullest extent and contribute to the country's progressive reforms. China has moved from a planned economy to a planned commodity economy, then to a commodity economy, and finally to a market economy. In this process, Chinese entrepreneurs have experienced ups and downs amid changes to systems and regulations. Nevertheless, the goal of China over the past two decades has been clear: implement a market economy.

The twists and turns of the four major telecom equipment manufacturers exemplify the spiral growth story of China.

In the late 1980s, a group of senior-ranking R&D officials from the PLA founded Great Dragon, which became a shining star in the telecom sector. At the same time, Datang and ZTE were established under two central government ministries, and like Great Dragon, they were the "pets" of the country in the age of a planned economy. The government lavished funding and market support policies on these SOEs and also supplied them with a huge amount of talent. At that time, SOEs were the first choice amid job seekers, a trend that still persists among many today; only an enterprise with close ties to the military was considered an even better choice.

As a private company, Huawei was marginalized, with its chances of success considered slim.

Change is inevitable. Twenty years later, Great Dragon collapsed, and Datang lagged far behind due to the rigidity of its decision process, HR policy, and incentive mechanism, which prevented even the most daring and decisive company leaders from turning things around. Moreover, the telecom industry was becoming more liberal and global, and even century-old giants in the West began to suffer from inflexibility and eventually began to gradually fade. A company will fall flat if it is incapable of adapting to change and innovate and improve on a flexible platform.

ZTE was an exception. Even though it was an SOE, ZTE was based in Shenzhen, an experimental zone under China's reform and opening-up policy. As a result, ZTE reaped the benefits of both the old and new market systems, benefiting from as much government support and resources as Great Dragon and Datang. In addition, the company reformed to become a state-owned, private-run company, providing itself with strong motivation.

Huawei is a different story. As a marginalized market player, Huawei would not have survived in the 1980s had it not been based in Shenzhen.

Adopting the principle of trial and error is perhaps the wisest decision made by Chinese reformers 30 years ago because it drove institutional innovations and led to the establishment of a number of innovative and adventurous pilot zones, such as the city of Shenzhen. This city abandoned the planned economy model and replaced dependence on interpersonal connections. A number of SOEs under central government ministries began to build their branches in Shenzhen in the hope of reforming their own institutions. An example is ZTE, which belonged to the former Ministry of Aviation and Aerospace. Private companies, such as Huawei, enjoyed ample freedom in this city.

Huawei's ambitious equity-sharing program could not have been implemented and applied to thousands of employees if it had not been based in Shenzhen. Even in the early 21st century, such a shareholding plan was still defined as illegal fundraising in some of the inland provinces.

The fate of a country determines the fate of each individual and organization. No entity can steer completely clear of sharing in the trials and tribulations of the country, nor can they grow unrestrained from the entanglements thus created. Before China's reform, Lenovo founder Liu Chuanzhi was too flexible to confine himself to China's rigid market system, and the result was a series of frustrations. After the country's reform program was initiated, Liu Chuanzhi maintained his adventurist spirit and flexibility to transform Lenovo into a business miracle.

Huawei is more an example of a miniature study of the country's progress. Founded by a former military engineer without any political background or social connections, Huawei has evolved into a world-class company through 25 years of dedication. There are many ingredients in Huawei's growth story, but the fundamentals are the change of environment and the creativity of people. To some extent, Huawei is a product of China's institutional reform.

Section IV. The Mysterious Power: Ren Zhengfei's Business Management Philosophy

Founder of a Unique Management Genre

Why was Huawei able to succeed? How did it overtake most other Chinese and Western peers to become the second largest player in the world?

China's progress and its institutional reform were critical to the company's success because Huawei could not have achieved success if the environment was not right. In the same age and under the same sky, however, more than 400 telecoms companies have come and gone; even in Shenzhen, a test bed for reform, five out of the six most valuable Chinese brands, except Huawei, started as SOEs.

Over the past three decades of reform and opening-up, there are many examples of the rise and fall of private companies that line the road of transformation with their lifeblood and sweat.

Why, then, has Huawei succeeded? Is there any mysterious power behind it? The West and the press have been trying to pry the box open. In fact, many Huawei employees are curious about the company's success.

Huawei now has 150,000 employees, most of whom are well-educated. What needs to be done to unite all these individuals and encourage them to give full play to their capabilities and potential? Given that Ren Zhengfei, the company's spiritual leader, has only a 1.42 percent stake, how has he established authority and maintained it for two decades? The answer to these questions can help us understand the secret of Huawei's success.

Western media have depicted Ren Zhengfei as the "godfather" of his business empire, who has religionized his company. This is a clever comparison, if it were a neutral comment. Ren Zhengfei has never been an imitator; he has chosen to be a loner. Although he has never explicitly said so, Ren has essentially never fully accepted the management theories presented in conventional textbooks. Rather, he has created a unique management genre. He is fond of meditation, deliberating over an idea for months or even years. Moreover, he is an excellent communicator; he repeatedly talks with his management teams, external advisors, customers, and scholars until his ideas become fully vetted and ripe.

Huawei's Secret Ingredients

Huawei is a company of ideas. Over the past two decades, Ren Zhengfei has expressed numerous ideas about the company's development, formally and informally, openly and privately, systematically and through piecemeal bits. The word count of his articles, speeches, and meeting minutes is of millions. These ideas are weapons with which Huawei has fought through the wilderness and reached the international stage. This is what sets Huawei apart from most other Chinese companies or even multinationals. What is especially noteworthy is that Huawei can always put ideas into action.

There is no exaggeration to the statement that Huawei's success is based on its management philosophy. As Ren Zhengfei said, "Without any special background or resources, we can rely on no one except ourselves; each bit of progress is by our own hands, and our system and culture are crucial." The management philosophy is perhaps the "mysterious power" that helps Huawei succeed. "I can tell you what factor has helped Huawei people unleash our potential: It is our management philosophy. Uranium atoms release devastating nuclear energy with neutron bombardment. Like a tiny atom, every Huawei employee, driven by our corporate core values, can generate enormous energy."

Business management philosophy is the top-level design that applies principles from metaphysics. It is the privilege of Ren Zhengfei and a select few others. They have to think at abstract level and far into the future. All their wild thinking then has to be backed by a system of methods and through proper organizational structures. That is the priority for senior management. The leaders brainstorm, and the management materialize and even institutionalize the abstract ideas of the leaders.

It seems that the fundamental ideas of Ren Zhengfei have not changed for over two decades. Ren once commented:

> What is the driving force behind our rapid growth? It is a management philosophy that is deeply rooted in the minds of our employees, it is customer-centricity, it is treating dedicated employees as our foundation, and it is remaining committed to dedication. Our success does not depend on any special background or supernatural power.

These have always been the core values of Huawei. As time has passed, Huawei has added three concepts that embrace its core values: openness, compromise, and grayness. These core values and management philosophy have been mulled over by Ren Zhengfei and his leadership team, constantly enriched to form a complete system and a cultural stamp that distinguishes Huawei from other companies. They are the secret ingredients of Huawei's growth and success.

Understanding, Preaching, and Practicing the Management Philosophy

Ren Zhengfei develops his business management philosophy in two steps: understanding and mastery. It is difficult to understand a philosophy, yet even more difficult to master. It requires constant reflection on past success and failure, untiring reading, communication, and thinking, and above all, a spiritual purgatory. Of course, he must have enough self-control. Thinkers and psychotics are similar in that they have extremely active brain cells, and the difference is that thinkers can manage their illusions while psychos can never hold themselves back. Ren Zhengfei did it. He has kept himself thinking, but never got psychotic. As his philosophical ideas are implemented, Ren advocates self-criticism as a way to optimize ideas. He believes that everything changes except change itself, so ideas have to change accordingly. Huawei's success can be attributed in large part to the culture of self-criticism, and the whole organization is committed to this culture. Nothing or no one is an exception, from the very top to the very bottom, and Ren Zhengfei himself is a role model.

In the church, the priest shares the revelation after being shown the way. Ren Zhengfei is the "preacher" of Huawei's unique management philosophy. He has written and published many essays, including "My Father and My Mother" and "Spring in the North Country," which have been translated into dozens of languages. Any speech he delivers to internal staff serves to inspire all Huawei employees. Customers, politicians, and business leaders are all equally impressed by him.

Ren Zhengfei does not like running the business with slogans. He would rather lead his team with a system of values. Inside Huawei, core values are reinforced extensively, during new employee training, ad hoc training, retreats, and business meetings. As a result, a team of 100,000 well-educated employees, each with their own unique background and personality, share the same core values. This is a miracle indeed.

Of course, Huawei is not a church, a philosophy salon, or a business school that merely teaches ideas. Its business philosophy must be grounded, take root, and bear fruit. The application of philosophy to actual business operations requires painstaking efforts.

It is a traditional Chinese belief that metaphysical philosophy and practical action complement each other. At Huawei, dedication is advocated as a core value, and at the same time, the company has institutionalized some effective measures to ensure this core value materializes. For instance, employees are granted shares and benefit from the growth of the company. Gradualism is a second key word for Huawei. Ren Zhengfei insists that conservatism is good for an organization that cannot stand repeated changes and grows best in a relatively stable environment. A conservative organization may not be as efficient, but the cost is much lower. Focus is the third key note of Huawei's philosophy. It would help the company a great deal if it can hold onto its own goals regardless of external temptations. This is difficult, of course, in a country suddenly full of opportunities. Therefore, it became a clause in the Huawei Charter to restrain the impulse of its decision makers. Operation mechanisms, including incentives, decision-making procedures, rules and regulations, and corporate culture are essential to transform any business philosophy into deeds. But the leader's commitment, courage, self-motivation, and dedication are also critical. A priest should not confine himself to the altar, contemplating and preaching doctrines; he must get down to the ground to test and practice his revelations, and even sacrifice himself to the fulfillment of the holy creed. Ren Zhengfei has made it. He has identified himself with Huawei and dedicated his life of two decades to building a "Commercial Church." Huawei is therefore successful, but Ren Zhengfei has kept himself in solitude.

Section V. Huawei Is Lonely Also, Not Just Ren Zhengfei

Tearless Grief After Success

Several years ago, when asked by a Chinese leader to briefly describe how she feels about Huawei's success, Huawei Chairwoman Sun Yafang replied without hesitation: "feel like weeping, but found no tears."

The leader was shocked. He could not find his word …

Huawei is a private company from the very start and was never favored by the old system. It has gone along a rough road with hardly any room to hold its feet and one riddled with hidden traps. Ren Zhengfei said time and again, "Failure will come one day, so we must be prepared. I firmly believe this to be a general law of history." He also commented, "What is success? If we can survive after narrow escapes like the Japanese companies, then it is real success. Huawei has not succeeded; we have just been growing."

His comments are in no way exaggerative. As a businessman, Ren Zhengfei must be an adventurer while remaining cautious to avoid violating rules that could topple the company. Adventurism and fear continue to haunt him, placing him under tremendous pressure. Before he was 44, Ren Zhengfei had lived a life considered mainstream of the time. Though the system was closed, his personality was unrestrained. The strong idealism and self-motivation earned him many honors: He was elected as a delegate at the National Science Conference in 1978 and at the 12th National Congress of the Communist Party of China in 1982.

After China began to reform and open up, Ren Zhengfei became a businessman. Unfortunately, he had to navigate the company through institutional barriers, public criticism, unfounded rumors, and attacks from domestic and international competitors—he had to find a way to unshackle the company from its self-imposed chains and set the entity on an upward rotation. Yet fortunately, the harsh environment compelled Ren and Huawei to give up on their illusions and explore their own management philosophy, which has contributed to tremendous growth for the company.

Proof of Identity

Of course, the price of Huawei's tremendous growth has been dear. Ren Zhengfei once recommended a TV series titled *Proof of Identity* to his management team: For years Huawei has been struggling to prove its own identity.

Yes, Huawei is a private company, but its contribution to the country is no less than that of many SOEs. Over the past two decades, Huawei's tax payments have exceeded CNY120 billion and the company has directly and indirectly created several million jobs. Especially noteworthy is that the rise of Chinese telecom companies like Huawei, ZTE, Datang, and Great Dragon has saved the country trillions in expenditures on telecom infrastructure. It is safe to say that Huawei has contributed tremendously to China's information sector, which has evolved into one of the country's pillar industries. Still, Ren Zhengfei wonders why the government has yet to give his company a bit more support, given the many resources or incentives its state-owned or foreign-invested counterparts have enjoyed.

Politicians and media from the West have never ceased to doubt or attack Huawei, alleging its close ties to the military and the government. Some competitors have even publically demonized Huawei as receiving hundred millions of dollars from the Chinese government each year. They cannot believe that a Chinese company without political and other types of connections could win the game right under their noses. They cannot imagine that a Chinese company can go all the way to the top of the world on its own.

Huawei aims to establish its presence in every corner of the world. Naturally, Ren Zhengfei and Huawei have to prove the company's identity time and again. Maybe no other company has faced the same dilemma as Huawei: In the international market, Huawei is seen as a representative of socialism that could threaten the West; in the Chinese market, Huawei, as a private company, might be deemed as the embodiment of capitalism. How could Huawei grow in the face of such conflict?

Adapting to Solitude

The loneliness of Ren Zhengfei and Huawei is apparent. A contemplative man is naturally solitary. For over 20 years, Ren has dedicated himself to Huawei. As an intellectual and a former military engineer, he started the company almost from nothing at the late age of 44. But he is an idealist and born forerunner. From the very beginning, he had set an ambitious goal for himself and the company. This was his personal mission that demanded all his time and energy. He has no hobby, other than reading and contemplating. He has no friends in political, military, or business circles. Indeed, he has made no friends in his school years or during his service as a military engineer, or even as the leader of Huawei. It is surprising, however, that he is an excellent communicator; he is eloquent about domestic and international economic, political, and diplomatic affairs. Above all he is an avid thinker, a contemplator, and a faithful preacher of his own ideas, which are all about the fate of his company.

Ren Zhengfei once said that it is relatively easy to maintain balance in a turbulent external environment, but it is much harder to manage and draw synergy out of over 100,000 people with divergent ideas and interests. This difficulty has troubled Ren and his colleagues for over two decades, and the solutions have added up to the company's management philosophy. This is the determinant factor for Huawei's success and greatness.

Practice Is More Painful than Thinking

Ren Zhengfei and his senior leadership team have to rack and beat their brains in order to push, motivate, or draw 100,000 intellectual workers to take one market after another. Moreover, they have to fight at the very frontline, and to be real leaders and role models. From the age of 44 to 68, Ren Zhengfei has kept his mobile phone on 24/7 and has spent one-third of his time on business trips. Most senior executives of Huawei, either still in office or retired, have a certain depression, anxiety, or other job-related diseases such as diabetes and hypertension. Ren himself once suffered serious depression.

Death is a permanent topic. In the final analysis, the fate of a business or any other organization is how long it can survive or whether it can live longer. Huawei has survived for over two decades, while a lot of its peers have fallen, including some seemingly invincible giants. This is a fast-changing time, and the frequent situation is that one falls, or plummets, without any sign from mid-day glory.

Who is next? Will Huawei follow in their footsteps? When the world is hailing Huawei as the future number one, will Huawei be the next to fall?

Forty-four is a mysterious age. Four times 4 is 16, and this number symbolizes "a smooth road ahead" in Chinese. But ever since Ren Zhengfei started Huawei at the age of 44, smooth sailing has been a rarity for the company, and the road ahead doesn't appear to be any smoother. Can Huawei overcome all its future challenges? Can Huawei retain its strong thinking capacity and the willpower to face any challenge head on?

These are some of the questions this book hopes to answer.

CHAPTER ONE

Common Sense and Truth: Customer Centricity

Section I. Customers: The Only Reason Huawei Exists

Alcatel: The Lost Captain of Industry

One hot June day in the early 21st century, Alcatel Chairman Serge Tchuruk received a Chinese guest at his private chateau in Bordeaux, France. The visitor was Ren Zhengfei, Huawei's CEO. The sun was warm, and the endless estate of grapevines was packed with purple fruit that shone like gemstones. The air was filled with the unique charm of Bordeaux: Quiet, proud, romantic, and dignified. After they sampled two different wines, Serge Tchuruk got serious:

> In my life, I've invested in two companies: Alstom and Alcatel. Alstom is a nuclear power company. The business is very stable. The only variables are coal, electricity, and uranium. The technology does not change quickly and the market is not very competitive. In contrast, Alcatel is in a cut-throat market. You cannot predict what will happen the next day or the next month in the telecom market.

Ren Zhengfei could not agree more. The quiet and intoxicating air turned heavy and somber.

Serge Tchuruk is a widely respected industrialist and investor, and Alcatel was a leading telecom manufacturer at the time. After the 2001 dotcom bubble burst in the United States, Alcatel was considered invincible, as were other European telecom companies such as Ericsson, Nokia, and Siemens. The open and liberal spirit in Europe had also nurtured a number of global telecom operators such as British Telecom, France Telecom, Deutsche Telekom, Telefonica, and Vodafone. While based and operating in Europe, they provided network services across all continents. American, Japanese, and Chinese telecom companies were far behind.

In the early 21st century, Huawei was still struggling to get on track. Ren Zhengfei was shocked when he heard about the troubles of Alcatel, the captain of the industry. After he got back to China, Ren shared Serge Tchuruk's views with Huawei's senior executives and asked them, "Does Huawei have a future? What is the way out?"

A general debate was then conducted across Huawei. A consensus was reached that the company must continue to embrace "customer centricity." The underlying principle that had taken the company so far would remain fundamental to its future. In other words, customers are the only reason for the existence of Huawei, and as a matter of fact, of any company.

Of the four strategic statements Huawei later developed, the first one reads: "Serving customers is the only reason Huawei exists. Customer needs are the fundamental driving force behind Huawei's growth."

Turn Your Eyes to Your Customers and Your Back to Your Boss

On a flight from Shenzhen to Beijing, a passenger about 60 years old sat in the last row of the first-class cabin. Throughout the three-hour journey he was reading quietly. This passenger was Ren Zhengfei. When the plane landed in Beijing, he stood up, picked up his luggage, and joined the crowd just like other travelers. He didn't have an entourage and was not picked up by anyone. When he travels for meetings or other purposes, he usually does not inform people from local offices. He simply takes a taxi straight to the hotel or to the meeting. He is used to taking taxis, but this does occasionally make headlines when he is spotted.

This is also the custom of most other Huawei senior executives.

A deputy chairman of Huawei said, "This custom does not mean that the leaders of Huawei are all more sensible than others; this is not our starting point. What matters is that it represents one of Huawei's core values: Customers are more important than company executives. This is the founding principle and is critical to the company's success." Ren Zhengfei also cautioned many times:

> The atmosphere in the company is that bosses seem to be much more important than customers. Perhaps because management has too much

power, some people care about their bosses more than their customers. They develop fancy PowerPoint slides to present to their bosses, and they make extremely thoughtful arrangements for executives traveling on business. The question is: how much care are we still able to give customers?

Ren, therefore, commanded:

Everyone in the company must turn your eyes to your customers and your back to your bosses. Do not go crazy doing slides to impress your bosses. Do not assume that you will get promoted if you succeed in pleasing your bosses. If this happens, the organization will eventually lose its force.

At a meeting in 2010, Ren Zhengfei proposed:

Huawei should and will promote those who turn their sight to their customers and their back to their bosses, and let go anyone who turns their back to their customers while focusing on their leaders. The former are value creators for the company while the latter are just plotting to gain their own individual benefits. Managers at every level of the organization should recognize the value of employees who turn their backs to you. You may feel uncomfortable at first, but they are the right people for the company.

Huawei is a typical private company in China. It started as a trading company and, therefore, knows very well how to win over customers as a vendor. As such, it is committed to serving its customers and holds the belief that the customer is king. This strong belief has long been in its blood and helped the company tremendously when it transformed into a product development business. Although its products were not as good as those of its competitors at the beginning, Huawei was still able to attract and keep customers because of its excellent services. Later when the products became as good or even better, customer loyalty came naturally. Essentially, over the years, Huawei has relied on the belief that customers always come first.

Who am I? Where do I come from? Where am I going? These are the fundamental questions all companies have to answer. Every successful company is always able to answer them correctly, although the answer may vary in different periods of development. There are some enterprises that put customers in the center of everything they did when they started, but lost their clear vision after initial success. They may sway and wonder about who is the lord: Their shareholders, employees, customers, or managers? The different answers reflect different pursuit and eventually underline different fates.

Magic does not exist, and truth cannot be reversed. The secret of Huawei's growth rests with its core values: Commitment to customer centricity and dedication.

This is a plain statement. However, since Huawei was established, Ren Zhengfei and his colleagues believed this to be the right answer, and the plain statement has been instilled into the company's culture. It is now the tenet for each and every member of the organization.

In December 2010, Ren Zhengfei gave a lecture titled "Embrace Customer Centricity, Value Dedicated Employees, and Remain Long Committed to Dedication" to senior executives of a large European telecom company. He told the audience:

> This is the entire secret as to how Huawei has surpassed its competitors, and this is the guarantee for Huawei's continued success. This is not a message of foresight, but a lesson we have drawn from our experiences. The three pillars are interconnected and support each other. Customer centricity sets the direction for dedication; dedication is the means to customer centricity; and dedicated staff is the source to drive long-term commitment to customer centricity.

Distorted Common Sense

Customer centricity was not invented by Huawei; it is part of the universal business values. "The customer is king," Westerners first said. This remarkable concept has permeated throughout the history of business in the West. The idea is very simple. Businesses are about making money, and companies that fail to generate profit are worthless. Then where does the money come from? Customers, of course. Therefore, you are potentially a great company if you can find a way to make customers give you as much money from their pockets as possible and for as long as possible. The business philosophy of the West has evolved for centuries around a permanent theme: The mission of a company, its managers, and its products is to satisfy customer needs.

This is a plain fact. A business has to pay taxes to the government, pay compensation to its employees, and pay its suppliers for goods it has bought; it gets money only from the customers. Yet, no customer would give the business money for nothing. Customers are not blind charity contributors. They have the right to choose and will only pay companies who provide high-quality and good-value products or services. In this sense, customer centricity is always right.

Therefore, management expert Peter Drucker believes that the purpose of a business is to create customers.

With the rapid development of the securities market, capital has been king of the world for 30 years, and traditional business ethics based on customer centricity have been wildly distorted. In the US market, for example, it is now a common business ethic to maximize shareholder value. Businessmen are focused on the stock market and make business decisions according to the opinions of securities analysts. In consequence, a company may expand rapidly or burst overnight. It could become an industry giant within three to five years or see its market value plummet within days or even hours. The Chinese market is no exception. Industrialists become rising stars in the capital market, but their companies inflate and burst like balloons. They are crazy opportunists, short-lived, or struggling to meet the near-term goals of their shareholders.

Common sense has been distorted. Customer centricity, a common sense in the business universe, has become the lonely pursuit of few leading enterprises.

Truth Is Naked

Huawei is a wonder because it never lost its common sense.

Huawei's management is convinced and has remained true to its faith that the company is part of the value chain of its customers, and its value depends on the whole value chain. In other words, Huawei derives sustenance and vitality from its customers and will die if it does not serve them. Customer centricity is the guideline for the company's efforts to stay alive and prosper.

In July 2001, *Huawei People*, the company's internal publication, carried an essay titled "Serving Customers Is the Only Reason Huawei Exists." The title was originally "Serving Customers Is the Reason Huawei Exists," but Ren Zhengfei revised it. He believed that Huawei had been born to serve its customers, and the company has no other reasons for existence. This is the only reason indeed.

Qian Zhongshu, a renowned Chinese scholar and writer, said, "Truth is naked." Ren Zhengfei said similarly, "We must not complicate the culture of Huawei. Our corporate culture should be archetypal."

Customer centricity is the archetypal character of commercial activities. A company may survive only if its customers are satisfied. This is a plain truth, and although it is so hard to turn this truth into practice, whoever sticks to it will be the winner.

An executive of Huawei once told a story. A group of Executive Master of Business Administration (EMBA) students from the School of Business at Renmin University of China visited Lancaster University in the United Kingdom. They were deeply impressed by the glories of Britain's industrial history and the current development of the United Kingdom. One of them mentioned Huawei to their British professor. The professor said,

> Huawei is walking on a road which some famous companies in the world have once travelled. They were glorious once, because they kept fighting their way on the ground of customer centricity. Still, when they reached the peak they stopped and refused to listen to customers. And then, of course, they declined.

Ren Zhengfei said in a speech in July 2012, "The rise and fall of companies in the West prove that Huawei's commitment to customer centricity and dedication is correct."

Truth is simple and direct. Huawei does not believe in economic magic or short-termism. While competitors such as Ericsson and Motorola plan their development by financial quarter or year, Huawei plans its development by decade. According to Xu Zhijun (Eric Xu), deputy chairman of Huawei, this is one of the secrets why Huawei is able to catch up with and surpass its competitors. If the Ericssons were not public companies and focused entirely on their customers, Huawei would not have been able to get close to them.

Of course, public companies do not necessarily ignore their future or their customers. Apple is a success story. When Steve Jobs died, the whole world lamented the loss of an innovator. However, to be more precise, Jobs was a great listener and resource integrator. Apple's products are characterized by simplicity plus aesthetics, which are exactly the qualities consumers want. A simple life is good, but a bit of art makes life even better.

Apple is successful not because of its technologies or product, but for the humanistic soul of Steve Jobs and his sensitivity to customers. The question is, without Jobs, who will keep the company focused on customers and win their hearts? In a word, Apple's future is still unknown.

Section II. The Fall of Great Companies

The Age of Debacle

The commercial history since the 1990s is bloodily cruel. If the industrial revolution had started with violent robbery and nakedly cruel conquest, the commercial world today, in an age of globalization and informatization, is also engaged in a war which is no less bloody. This war is even larger in scale and more disastrous. In short, the past two decades have been an epic tragedy, a debacle of many participants. The telecom industry, for example, has been basically overturned, and then overturned again. The change is shocking for both participants and witnesses.

Lucent Technologies was named by *MIT Technology Review* the world's best technology company in the telecom field for two consecutive years. In January 1999, the company had a total market value of US$134 billion, and the share price was at a record high of US$84. But in September 2002, the share price was no more than US$1, and the stock was rated as junk. In its peak years, the company had 153,000 employees, but by this time they had been reduced to 35,000. Eventually, Lucent Technologies was merged with Alcatel in 2007. However, the Alcatel–Lucent conglomerate did not fare well. The combined business suffered from declining income and continuous losses for five consecutive years, amounting to US$12.4 billion. It was forced to cut jobs. Even worse yet, the company was implicated in financial scandals and cultural conflicts. The race from the top to the bottom was so quick.

Motorola shares a similar story. The company was once hailed as a money printer in the telecom industry. Established in 1928, Motorola was distinguished as a pioneering innovator. It developed the world's first prototype cellular phone and the first commercially available mobile phone. It is unquestionably the Father of mobile phones. But the market has been relentless. In the peak year of 2001, Motorola had approximately 150,000 employees, but by the end of 2003 this number had dropped to 88,000. At that same time, Huawei had only 30,000 employees. Today, Huawei has just as many employees as Motorola had at its peak. On October 15, 2011, Google bought Motorola Mobility at a price of US$12.5 billion, and almost at the same time, in 2012, Huawei decided to recruit 28,000 new employees.

Does that mean Motorola has reached the end of its history? Will this prestigious brand that amazed so many people in the early days of wireless communications be removed from the radar screen?

There is no secure place in the world. In 2006, Finland's Nokia and Germany's Siemens announced that the companies would merge their telecom equipment businesses to create one of the world's largest network firms, Nokia Siemens Networks. Several years have passed and this mammoth is also suffering the fate of decline. It has already proved that 1 plus 1 is smaller than 2. It has lagged behind its Chinese competitor, Huawei, which is now challenging Ericsson, another time-honored European communications firm.

As a Chinese saying goes, every generation has its heroes, and each may lead the way for decades. In current times, decades are too long, though, and the reality may likely be only a few years. One may be surprised that the blooming spring has barely passed when fallen leaves cover the ground. External changes have outpaced reforming actions.

Genetic Mutation rather than Genes Is Responsible for the Fall

Many analysts believe that the fall of Lucent Technologies was due to the burst of the telecom bubble in 2001. Some scholars attribute the decline of Motorola to its arrogance, which led to bad decisions and the inability to make a comeback.

They are right to some extent, but they haven't touched upon the key question: Where are the company's core values? Should the company be based on customers or something else?

Paul Galvin, the founder of Motorola, has never believed that profit is the sole or highest aim of the company. Instead, he believed that the mission of the company was much nobler than making profit. Likewise, his son, Bob Galvin, also stressed that the company would not focus on efficiency only when it was coping with the challenges of Japanese semiconductor enterprises in the 1980s. He said he cared more about the future. As a result, Motorola was able to turn out a revolutionary product that catered to customer needs: Commercialized mobile phones. According to Bob Galvin, the key to the success of a company is that there are a number of people working toward the same goal and meeting customer needs. This is exactly why Motorola had been able to go from good to great. But when the company deviated from this faith, it was certain that it would slip from greatness.

In 1991, Motorola decided to invest in a global communications system: The Iridium Project. Yet, Iridium Satellite LLC survived for less than a decade. In March 2000, it went into bankruptcy, incurring a loss of US$5 billion to Motorola. Iridium Satellite was once highly acclaimed as a revolutionary communications tool, but was hindered by a lack of subscribers and a prohibitively high tariff. The project had not moved on and this was a watershed for Motorola. Motorola was not only insensitive to customer needs but had also confined itself in a closed ivory tower of its own creation. The company turned down the common sense that the customer is king, instead believing in the omnipotence of technology.

Many other companies which failed or died out had behaved in the same way. Established in 1996, Lucent Technologies is one of them, and its fall is even more shocking. It was formerly a division of AT&T and had been the darling of investors from the very beginning. The influx of investment, however, had pushed the company onto the road of utilitarian expansion. Within six years, the company acquired 36 businesses with the aim of rapid growth. Lucent was engaged in a profit-making rush to satisfy the endless desire of the capital market. The result was a floating organization with diverse and incompatible cultures, and finally the shocking debacle.

Lucent Technologies was torn between utilitarianism and idealism. On the one hand, it had to cater to the stock market, trying its best to keep the pace of expansion. On the other hand, it had the best research lab in the United States and even in the world—Bell Labs. Producing 12 Nobel laureates, the lab has been the pride of the United States and a global leader of scientific and technological research and development since the early 20th century. In 1997, when he visited Bell Labs, Ren Zhengfei was deeply impressed. He said with strong emotion, "I was told more than 10 years ago that Bell Labs could produce one patented invention a day, and now it can produce three inventions every day. That's so amazing. My feeling to Bell Labs is stronger than love."

This glorious organization of Lucent Technologies, however, had suffered serious conflict between the venturist culture of the capital market and the tradition of science and technology. Bell Labs traditionally put great emphasis on basic research, but now, quite inevitably, focuses more on pragmatic, market-oriented inventions. The organization has gradually lost its future-oriented idealism.

In fact, neither profiteering of the capital market nor an idealistic commitment to the future is fitting with the real mission of a business. Neither approach is based on the customer. Therefore, the fall of Lucent Technologies from greatness seems to be all the more logical in the business world.

Opportunism: The Golden Cup of Poisoned Wine

Taking risks is a common characteristic of entrepreneurs. But taking risks does not mean to bet in a gamble, which is an intellectual game depending on intuition and luck as well as intelligence. Ren Zhengfei once said, "Everyone has the inclination to bet, but I must control myself. I must control my desires and learn to manage them." When he was in Las Vegas, he would also visit the casinos, but he never placed any bets. He would just hang around. He said with a smile, "I'm afraid of getting sunk. . . ."

A man called Wu Ying is just the opposite. Ying in Chinese means hawk, and this name reveals his personal disposition. He has sharp eyes, which he uses to find the best opportunities. He bought the Personal Handyphone System (PHS) technology from Japan at the right time when China had opted to open up the communications market to competition. As a result, he won an almost impossible game, and a company called UTStarcom rose in the market to the surprise of almost everyone. As the PHS was considered outdated technology at the time, international leading telecom companies including Huawei did not believe that it had any prospects. However, the Chinese market had a strong demand for this system. The PHS was adopted by China Telecom, which had not yet obtained the license to operate mobile phone services. The PHS, as an extension of the fixed-line connection, fits in well with the ability to provide both fixed and mobile services.

Thanks to its adventurism and speculation, UTStarcom rose to stardom. In 2003, UTStarcom occupied over 70 percent of the device market. When the PHS market slowed down in 2005, it still maintained a 60 percent share of the system market and 50 percent of the device market.

This was a gamble and it caused excitement in the capital market. In 2000, UTStarcom was listed on NASDAQ, and in the same year the company made it into the Fortune 1000. For 17 consecutive months, its performance exceeded the expectations of Wall Street analysts. Sales ballooned, growing by more than 100-fold from day one to its peak year. In October 2003, the company was ranked first by *Business 2.0* magazine among the 100 fastest growing technology companies of the year. Wu Ying, the company founder, suddenly became a celebrity in the telecom sector.

This seemingly good momentum spoiled UTStarcom. Opportunism is like a coin that has two sides, and the negative side is that opportunities usually do not fall on one company or one person again and again. A company will have to depend on its strength and capability. On June 1, 2007, Children's Day, Wu Ying resigned from UTStarcom. A company, which had grown to a size that belied its age, was about to sink.

Market orientation is not the same as customer centricity. A company should not just follow trends or simply cater to temporary market opportunities. Great companies like Apple and IBM have stuck to the faith of customer centricity; they are committed to satisfying both their immediate needs and their potential longer term requirements and, therefore, offer customers the best products and services. Luck in the market is a golden cup that sometimes contains poisoned wine. Anyone drinking from the cup will become short-sighted, lazy, speculative, self-complacent, and insensitive. Their muscles will lose tightness, strength, and flexibility.

A company that pursues excellence and long-term development must not depend on mere luck.

While Stars Fall, Meteors Crowd the Sky

Human society has entered an era when stars continue to fall while meteors crowd the sky. New technologies emerge in waves as the world becomes integrated like a spider web and the Internet turns ubiquitous. All this is destructive to tradition and has caused a global organizational crisis. The system of organizational theory and practice developed over several thousands of years now faces the cliff's edge, with businesses the most affected.

Over the past two decades, companies have emerged and disappeared rapidly. Names such as Wang Laboratories and Yahoo came onto the stage from nowhere, but began to decline before too long. Some time-honored companies, likewise, have turned from stars to meteors in this dramatically changing historical period; AT&T is a perfect example.

AT&T is a truly prestigious player in the global communications sector. Established in 1877 by Alexander Bell, father of the telephone, it has birthed many distinguished organizations, such as Bell Labs, Northern Telecom, and Lucent Technologies. It also nurtured Claude Elwood Shannon, the father of information theory, and a number of Nobel Prize, Turing Award, and Claude E. Shannon Award winners. After two antimonopoly movements in the 20th century, it hadn't lost its edge and had, in fact, become more competitive. Regrettably, it was unable to survive the new technological revolution and tsunami of the capital market that hit in the early 21st century. Almost all members of this prestigious family have withered away, and AT&T now has virtually nothing substantial beneath its beautiful mask.

It seems to be destiny for telecom companies: If they are committed to innovation, they destroy themselves; if they stay away from innovation, others will kill them.

There is yet another fate: Willingly or not, they end up in the slaughterhouse of the capital market. Wall Street, for example, is well known as the butcher of the world's real economy. The financial capital incubates a number of tech startups very quickly, but kills them just as quickly. Not even the business empire of AT&T could escape this fate. It was ripped into three parts and then abandoned after the flesh was gone. The end is as bloody as most other stories of the capital market: Capital and professional managers, or capital alone, are the only winners, and companies are left to suffer or disappear.

In this globalized world, worship of capital and technology has destroyed a number of great companies and entrepreneurs. On the dead or critically ill list are Wang Laboratories, Motorola, Lucent Technologies, Northern Telecom, AT&T, and Yahoo, to mention just a few.

Can Apple, the company with the highest market value in 2012, escape the slaughter? The answer is NO. After its share price peaked at US$700, the rope around its neck began tightening. As one analyst wrote, "This is a toy company. In the long term, no toy company can become the most valuable company in the US. Its performance in the stock market now is crazy, but very fragile. Once a failure occurs, the dream will be all over." These comments forecast Apple's eventual fall, maybe not today, but it won't be long.

Like Apple, many public companies are nothing but puppets pulled by the golden fingers of equity investors. For example, Microsoft, which was once a global leader in the capital market valued at more than US$500 billion, is now being left out in the cold.

Over the past 25 years, Huawei has had quite a number of opportunities to be wed with venture investors, but Ren Zhengfei chose to avoid them. Several years ago, led by Stephen Roach, chief economist for Morgan Stanley, an institutional investor delegation visited the headquarters of Huawei. Ren did not show up. He asked Fei Min, his Executive Vice President In-charge for R&D, to entertain the delegation. Roach said in disappointment, "He was rejecting a team with US$3 trillion."

Ren Zhengfei later replied:

> Roach is not our customer. I don't see any point in meeting with him. I will see any customer in person, no matter how small they are. His investor delegation has nothing to do with me. We are selling equipment and will look for those who buy equipment.

Huawei has not fallen apart into meteors because it has kept a critical distance from the capital market and resisted all the temptations through these years. The capital market can quickly blow up a company or an entrepreneur like a balloon, but can just as quickly destroy and end the illusory success. As the Buddhist precept goes, "Desire is like holding a torch against the wind, and the flame may burn the hand that holds the torch."

In other words, the leadership of Huawei has kept a clear mind: The underlying factor for the company's sustained success is its customers, rather than technologies or capital. This is a core value of the company. What Huawei needs is a customer-oriented culture, not one that appeals to toward capital investment.

Section III. Customer Centricity: The Result of 25 Years of Contemplation

1987–1994: Survival Was Everything

If you travel across the canyons of Mount Wuyi, you will be amazed by the quietness, the chirping birds, and the fresh air. You may also notice countless ants carrying dirt from the bottom of the cliff to a higher cleft to build their nests. They are busy working to prepare for the cold winter or the rainy season. If they fall to the ground, they start over again, but if they happen to fall into the flowing stream, they are washed away.

This is, to some extent, symbolic of the fate of many small- and mid-sized enterprises (SMEs) in China.

SMEs play a significant role in China's economy. There are now over 40 million such enterprises in China, most of which are privately owned. They account for 60 percent of the GDP, 80 percent of all jobs, and 50 percent of China's tax revenue. However, they are rather short-lived. According to statistics, the average lifespan of Chinese enterprises is less than 2.9 years, and each year more than a million go out of business.

As of 2010, the average lifespan of Chinese SMEs was 3.7 years; in Europe and Japan it is 12.5 years, while in the United States it is 8.2 years. Since the start of China's reform and opening-up program, there have been a number of Chinese companies cited as successful cases for MBA students, but by now 80 percent have fallen. In other words, people are rushing toward the glass door regardless of risk, but most end up seriously hurt and some even lose their lives. They have gone through the process from registration to cancelation in a short period of time. Their startup investment has ended in nothing but a mess and scars.

Survival is a tough task for companies, as Huawei Chairwoman Sun Yafang once said. It is especially daunting in their infancy. According to Ren Zhengfei, Huawei's success is attributable more to market opportunities than the company's capabilities.

Huawei started as a trading company with a dozen employees. This was a poorly equipped team: They had neither product nor money. However, they fought through the lines of foreign companies and Chinese state-owned enterprises (SOEs) and found hope of survival. At that time, Huawei's slogan was: We shall drink to our heart's content to celebrate our success, but if we should fail let's fight to our utmost until we all die. In this specific context, success meant survival. Ren Zhengfei was never a mere merchant aiming at making money. Yet, the reality was cruel: He had to make enough money to survive and get stronger.

At Huawei, everyone agrees that it is not terrible to endure pain when they struggle to realize their dreams, but it is terrible if their dreams eventually turn into a joke. At the very start, Ren Zhengfei called on his colleagues to build a world-class enterprise. We would rather believe that this was his real commitment, but he himself was clear that this was a mission impossible. To accomplish world-class repute, the company should first struggle to survive and live long enough. Therefore, from the first day of the company, both Ren and Huawei were scared of death. Survival became the lowest and highest strategic goal, and pragmatism had been its only choice.

A review of Huawei documents and speeches from Ren Zhengfei before 1994 would present such terms as "wolf and jackal spirit," "call for heroes," and "to be shameless" (shameless means to possess the nerve to face customer complaints and the courage to challenge oneself). Customer centricity was hardly mentioned, let alone discussed at length.

During that period, Huawei was still one of millions of ants struggling for survival in the Chinese market. It was a small trading company with ideals but without values. Its ideals were abstract, and it could not define its values because just surviving was a challenge.

A Clear Vision: Customers Are the Soul of Huawei

The vision started to develop in 1994. After groping for stones in the river for seven years, or fighting for seven years in the jungle for survival, Huawei began to put on some muscle. In October 1994, Huawei launched its first telephone switch system, the Huawei C&C08. It was a milestone in the history of Huawei because it marked the end of the firm's trading history as a vendor without its own product or technology. Huawei had entered a new era.

In June 1994, Ren Zhengfei delivered a victory toast in which he said:

We are faced with big price pressures as the market is filled with both good and bad products. But I believe our sincere commitment to customer service will move our "gods." They will know that our products are worth the money they pay. Our difficulties will be eased and we will surely survive.

In a speech from 1997, Ren Zhengfei said:

Huawei is a profit-seeking entity and everything we do is to create commercial value. Therefore, our culture is called corporate culture, not any other culture and certainly not politics. Huawei's culture is a culture of services, as only through services can commercial value be created. Service is a broad term. After-sales services, product research, production, upgrade and evolution are all part of it. It has to steer the way we build our teams. If one day we no longer need to serve, we'll have to close the company. In this sense, service is the lifeline for our company and for us as individuals.

For a long time Huawei meant low prices, poor quality, but excellent services. A Chinese domestic operator still clearly remembers,

In the early years, Huawei switching products were used mostly by county-level telecom operators. They were not very reliable and often broke down. But Huawei did a very good job at services; its people were available around the clock. At that time, the staff of telecom operators made grand gestures. They would often scold Huawei staff, even Ren Zhengfei, the boss of the company. None of the employees would argue with their customers; instead, they would sincerely apologize and get the system up and running again as soon as possible. This was in great contrast to Western companies, who were used to blaming customers and were insensitive to customer needs. Huawei was impressive. How can you refuse anyone who really treats the customers as king? In the 1990s, service was a rare concept in China, but Huawei had provided impeccable services.

Nevertheless, this was still a one-way thinking in the age of trading, an outcome of forced acceptance and cognitive restraints. Huawei did not clearly state until 1997 that "customer orientation is the basis and future orientation is the direction." Ren Zhengfei explained, "If we are not tuned into the needs of our customers, there would be no foundation for us to exist; if we are not oriented toward the future, there would be no traction for us to move ahead, and we then slack off and lag behind."

Since then, with some slight changes to wording, the concept of customer centricity has become the guiding vision for every activity of the company and every stage of its development. In 2002, Ren Zhengfei said:

Customers are the soul of Huawei. As long as the customers are there, Huawei's soul would be there, no matter who leads the company. A company is very fragile and will run into trouble sooner or later if it depends too much on one leader. Business operations of Huawei have now turned self-sustaining, and this is where we find hope.

In 2003, Ren added:

We've always stressed that we must stick to customer orientation. This should be a rational, unequivocal and unforced orientation that represents universal truth in the market. Any forced, vague, or policy-mandated demand is not a real customer need. We must be able to distinguish real needs from opportunistic demand, and hold on to a rational attitude in following customer needs. Different approaches might be taken to suit particular circumstances.

In 2007, Ren Zhengfei further commented:

Huawei was not born an excellent player in the market. So we must be aware of our weaknesses and take action to improve. We must learn how to fight a battle through actually fighting one, and learn to swim by swimming. In many areas, we're symbiotic with our customers because we've established strategic partnerships with them. Opportunities are not allocated by the company; they are given by the customers. And we need proper strategic planning, or otherwise we will not be able to compete.

On the basis of customer centricity, Huawei executives further deepened their understanding of the premise that the company should be oriented, in a "rational, unequivocal and unforced" way toward customer needs, a way that represents universal truth in the market. It was with this understanding that the company gave up on the investment in the PHS and some other market opportunities. This led to a heated debate within the company. Eventually, everyone agreed that Huawei would not pass up any business opportunity, but it was also a company with lofty ideals.

Since 2005, Huawei's relationship with its hundreds of customers has been much more than a transactional one. They are symbiotic and mutually enhancing strategic partnerships. This was a fundamental change for Huawei. But companies at this point are even more likely to lose their common sense. Their concept of customer centricity, as well as their system of values, may become distorted. Some Western companies have spiraled downward when their prospects looked rosy. The decision makers at Huawei have witnessed those declines and come to realize that common sense is always essential and truth will never be reversed. As a result, between 2006 and 2010, Huawei communicated customer centricity extensively within the company and organized various training sessions to reinforce the idea.

The minutes of an Executive Management Team (EMT) meeting in 2010 clearly state:

> Our long-term strategy is to make the company more competitive in the market through improved quality of products and services and enhanced delivery capability and then develop and maintain a balanced position between ourselves and our peers from the West. Competing on price, not on service quality, did not place us further ahead of the strategic competitors. The room for development of Western vendors has also been heavily pressurized.

This is a new interpretation of customer centricity when strategic partnerships have been fostered with the customers. Huawei also changed its approach toward its competitors, and its market space has been extended.

In 2010, "commitment to customer centricity and dedication" were officially incorporated into Huawei's core values.

No Sensation: Identifying with Lions

On May 22, the Chinese magazine *CEOCIO* published the article "Evolution from Wolves into Lions." The author divided telecom manufacturers into three types. The first type is lions. Western companies that boast comprehensive advantages in technologies, products, capital, and management, and having a self-perceived sense of superiority are typical examples. The second type is leopards, referring to Sino-foreign joint ventures. The third type is wolves, or local companies, such as Huawei, that lack advanced technologies and produce poor-quality products but are highly aggressive in the market, trying to survive through natural selection. Wolves are serious threats to lions and leopards.

This was the most insightful article on Huawei so far, but Huawei's management did not agree that they were wolves; they even felt insulted.

Huawei refused to be sentimental. Ren Zhengfei once said, "Our company has succeeded because we have paid much less attention to ourselves than maximizing the value of our customers. It is our goal to create maximum benefits for telecom operators, and we have tried every means to realize it." Concerning how the company has fought in the market, he said, "Huawei has consistently focused on its customers, rather than its competitors." Therefore, Huawei's culture is quiet and simple. It has a single syllabus and a single color. There is no redundancy, ambiguity, bustle, or splendor.

While the lions and leopards have stopped moving forward due to the curse of ample resources, Huawei, the wolf, has gradually evolved into a lion. How has it managed to do so? Ren Zhengfei explained:

> We must adapt to changing circumstances, rather than follow any rigid tenet. The key is to satisfy customer needs. ... We must act like businesspeople. A scientist can choose to be focused throughout his life on one hair on the leg of a spider, but if we do the same, we would starve. Therefore, we must not focus exclusively on spider legs; instead we must study and understand the needs of our customers.

The remarks were made in 2002 when Lucent Technologies, one of the lions, was about to fall, and Motorola, another huge lion, was also sick.

The most essential resource of Lucent Technologies is Bell Labs, which is known for its research on "spider legs," "butterfly wings," "horse tails," and other fundamental research subjects. Bell Labs had been a boost for the growth of Lucent Technologies, but later became a huge burden. Motorola had invested heavily in its Iridium Satellite system. This cutting-edge technology had pulled Motorola toward Waterloo. Like most other lions, both Lucent Technologies and Motorola had actually suffered from the resource curse, or the paradox of plenty, dragged down by excess capital and technology.

Huawei has grown up in hunger, on the other hand. It suffered from resource inadequacy, so its aim has been very simple: satisfy customer needs with good products, low prices, and excellent services. When Huawei grew into a lion after becoming the second largest telecom equipment manufacturer in the world, the company had come to possess enough resources, including capital, technologies, talent, and management expertise. Yet, Ren Zhengfei does not only hold fast to the common sense of customer centricity, but he also gives the concept new meanings.

In 2009, Ren Zhengfei visited the Dujiangyan Irrigation System, an irrigation facility in the Sichuan Province built in 256 BC. During the tour, he was told the story of Li Bing who planned and built this system, and his son. He was greatly inspired, and later wrote the article, "To Dig Deep Channels, and Build Low Weirs," in which he said for the first time, "Competition in the future will be between industry chains. The robustness of the entire industry chain is the key to Huawei's survival."

From 2009 to 2010, Ren Zhengfei continued to elaborate on this idea. In various speeches and essays, he stated:

> To dig deep channels means to tap further into the company's inner potential. The company must ensure sufficient investment in its core competitiveness and its future, even during times of financial crisis. "To build low weirs" means the company must not pursue short-term goals at the expense of long-term ones. We have to share the benefits of growth and create more long-term value for our customers.
>
> We must maintain the attitude of digging deep channels and building low weirs. We must endure the difficulties ourselves and allow others to enjoy the benefits. We must plant fewer thorns and more flowers; make more friends and fewer "enemies." We are not content to be the only blossom, but join hands with as many people as possible to create win-win outcomes.
>
> By digging deep channels and building low weirs, we don't mean to make as much money as possible, but we cannot afford to lose money all the time, either. We need a small profit, and leave the water to overflow the low weirs and reach our customers and the supply chain. In this way, we will be able to survive, and I believe you will be the best if you survive the longest,

because you have to contend with strong competitors in every partnership you try to build.

Clearly, this is a significant extension of customer centricity, a core value at Huawei. These statements describe its further commitment to the industry, and also a new mission Huawei defines for itself: To open up, foster partnerships, continuously improve, and be a hero that can accommodate the world.

Section IV. The Hundred-Year Business and the Thousand-Year Temple

Supernatural Powers: Religion and Values

Recently, a short blog post on *Weibo* has become very popular and widely quoted:

> The Greatest Business Model in the World. The blogger believed that the greatest business model in the world was not created by Steve Jobs, but Buddha. Buddhist temples are the most successful chain stores. They don't sell products, but they have the largest number of loyal customers. Buddhist temples are among the most-visited tourist destinations in the world. They have a consistent visual identity, management system, and culture. They don't need to advertise. Customers come to them in droves. They don't have to pay taxes, either. This is, people believe, because there is a set of highly and widely recognized values. Therefore, this is the greatest business model the world has ever known.

There is a similar short article. Titled "Buddhist Temples Are Real Estate Businesses Superior to Apple," the article argues that Buddhist temples have quite a few advantages:

1. They have a clear and distinctive theme and represent universal values and spiritual authority.
2. They have a huge number of loyal believers. People from all walks of life, from beggars to billionaires to government officials, have strong faith in Buddhism.
3. They have a unique profit-making model. There is no compulsory consumption, yet they still make a lot of money.

4. They can satisfy huge demand with very few resources. They are typically located in remote areas, but they still have many followers.

5. They operate nationwide and pay no taxes yet enjoy government support wherever they are.

Although they may be considered frivolous or even profane, both articles entail quite a few questions that may point to the truth: Why does religion possess such timeless power in communication? Why can religious faiths like Christianity, Islam, and Buddhism last thousands of years? Why are they acceptable to various nations and people of different social classes?

What is the answer to these questions?

As Plato observed, the most real existence in the world is spirit. Religion is great and eternal in that it is a supernatural power rooted in the spiritual world of human beings. Religion points directly to our hearts, enlightening humanity, and guiding our ethics and behavior. More importantly, it answers in the wittiest way the ultimate questions of human beings: Who am I? Where do I come from? Where am I going?

Religion then extends to the concepts of redemption and universal salvation. It allows humanity to understand the meaning of being and develop spiritual faith. To put it metaphorically, religion points out where the river is flowing and at the same time prepares the boat with which to cross the river.

Buddhists believe in the law of karma, with strong punitive and incentive implications: If you practice goodness in this life, you will be blessed in this life and the next; if you are a proponent of evil, you will be punished in this life and go to hell in the next life.

There are many rituals in Buddhism, such as praying, scripture recitation, incense burning, and meditation. A Buddhist temple is also characterized by grand and solemn buildings, slow and pacifying music. These are all physical vehicles of the religion that signify, demonstrate, and pass on its values.

Will religion decline some day? According to Buddha, everything in the world has a life and every life will eventually end. This is also true with any religion. Religion, however, is greater than any human organization because it can adapt to the vagaries of time and circumstance; it is able to find the way into our hearts through its own evolution while maintaining its core values.

Rarely, any political, governmental, or business organization can do this.

Common Sense in Its Extreme Is Religion

To some extent, the most outstanding business leaders in history can be compared to religious leaders. In the first instance, they worship the perfection of religious organizations, and such worship is intuitive and instinctive. As a successful businessman, Steve Jobs was also an artist, a dictator, a priest in the black gown, and a godfather who had stubbornly worked for extreme perfection all his life. During his last years and even after his death, he had billions of fervent followers who have remained loyal to him. He was their godfather or guru. *TIME* magazine listed Steve Jobs as the most celebrated, successful business executive of his generation, stating that he will be remembered for at least a century for he is far greater than any of his contemporaries.

Then how great is Steve Jobs? *Forbes* answered it: Jobs knew what people wanted. But the greatest thing about Jobs is that he knew that people of the 21st century needed to be listened to, and confirmed with a friendly voice Apple's message that machines may not take charge, but Apple takes charge.

In his early years, Jobs was absorbed with innovation and perfect design, but he then turned his attention to simplicity and customer friendliness. Clean, bright, and orderly, Apple stores are his lasting legacy. They are glue joining up technology and consumers in a mild, precise, and patient way. This is the essence of Steve Jobs: The consumer is his first and last concern.

Jobs was considered the consummate genius of the business world because he cared about the potential needs of customers to an extreme. He was born with a sensitive heart. He knew that truth is part of common sense, and common sense in its extreme is religion. The process of transforming ordinary consumers into product addicts and loyal followers of the product designer is like God's creation of human beings. People remain loyal to God, not only because God created them, but also because God has taken good care of them.

So there is the question: Why can religion last so long while businesses die so soon? This is a question that troubles almost every entrepreneur. To be time-honored has seemed an elusive goal. Microsoft, for example, was once hailed as the best in history, but it remained on the top of the world for a mere 50 years. Now this business empire is slipping. We may also wonder how long Apple's glory will last following the demise of Steve Jobs.

STORE INFO

CALIFORNIA

GARDENA STORE
310-532-5010
Pacific Square Mall, 1610 W Redondo Beach
Blvd #E8, Gardena, CA 90247

DEL AMO FASHION CENTER STORE
310-214-4800
21712 Hawthorne Blvd, Torrance, CA 90503

LAKEWOOD MALL STORE
562-634-6000
Lakewood Center Mall, Lakewood, CA 90712

WESTMINSTER MALL STORE
714-897-1800
1025 Westminster Mall, Westminster, CA
92683

COSTA MESA STORE
714-556-1521
2955 Harbor Blvd, Costa Mesa, CA 92626

SANDIEGO STORE
858-627-9600
4240 Kearny Mesa Rd #128 San Diego CA
92111

NEW YORK

49 W 45TH NY STORE
212-685-1410
49 W 45th St, New York, NY 10036

HAWAII

PEARLRIDGE UPTOWN STOR
808-485-0841
98-1005 Moanalua Rd. Aiea, HI 96701

DONQUIJOTE KAHEKA STOR
808-952-9115
801 Kaheka St. Honolulu, HI 96814

FOLLOW US TO CHECK HOLIDAY

 @bookoffusainc

bookoffusainc

GET LOCATIONS ON YOUR PHONE
Scan & Find Your Store

www.bookoffusa.com

On a sunny afternoon, I visited Wenfeng Temple in Lijiang, Yunnan Province, and had a talk with Tian Liang, a secular disciple of Dongbao Zhongba Rinpoche, the Living Buddha. Tian Liang was about 30 years old. He had worked for Hunan Satellite TV as an editor and director, and was once a keen paraglider and mountaineer. He had acquaintance with Wang Shi, the former chairman of Vanke Real Estate, and other entrepreneurs. A year ago, Tian withdrew from all secular activities. He came to Lijiang and became an informal lama, or a secular monk. Tian said:

> Isn't the culture of a company like a religion? You need to motivate every employee. Money is not enough. You need to give them some belief and values so they will be willing to work hard. You need to do the same with your customers. If we compare employees to monks in a temple, customers are believers who come to worship the Buddha and pay their contribution to the temple. If you want them to buy your products, you need to care for their needs.

He uses an Apple phone, and I bet he knows about Steve Jobs.

On a flight from Lijiang to Beijing, I sat in the first row, next to Dongbao Zhongba Rinpoche. After a simple meal, many passengers were waiting to use the restroom. The Living Buddha said to me:

> Everything changes; this is universal truth. A delicious meal turns into foul-smelling waste a few hours later. This is a natural change. You may be glorious now, but sometime later the glory will go. If you want to be blessed for long, you need to practice discipline for that length of time.

This is true with business organizations, as with people.

All Methods Are a Practical Means to an End

Things change; no company will last forever. For any entrepreneur, it is a dream come true to have a company that lasts a century. To that end, business leaders and management experts have engaged in various studies and practices, proposing one theory after another. They raise assumptions on human nature and the concept of product cycle; they apply innovative business models, strategic management, performance appraisals, and team development; they also innovate in management and technology. All such endeavors are useful, but they are only a practical means to an end. Underlying the means is a fundamental Tao that really matters.

What is the Tao for companies? *Customer centricity.* This is a piece of common sense that can stand the test of time and circumstance. Religions are able to last so long because they are built on common sense. The combination of simplicity and aesthetics by Steve Jobs exemplifies the notion that success is based on common sense.

Ren Zhengfei once said, "We will always treat our customers with religious faith." He added, "Serving customers is the only reason Huawei exists. This should be a true belief of our people, and cannot remain a mere slogan. We need all our employees to take action. Huawei has only one clear value proposition: serve our customers."

Ren is an adventurer. No one can become an entrepreneur without a risk-taking proposition. Entrepreneurs are sailors navigating the sea or knights riding through the wilderness. Generally speaking, Ren is not an extremist, but he has been stubborn to a fault when it comes to company values: "One cannot succeed without insane stubbornness." This is a perfect statement to describe Ren on corporate values. He is neither Christian nor Buddhist, but he uses the word "religious faith" toward customers. He has emphasized time and again the value proposition of customer centricity with uncompromising modifiers, such as "the only" and "always."

In our times, capital and technology are worshiped. Huawei is an exception. It worships a god, but that god is not Jesus or Buddha. Huawei's god is its customers: over 700 telecom operators and approximately one-third of the world's population.

Huawei now employs 150,000 people, most of whom are well educated. Before joining Huawei, each had a unique personality and cherished different dreams. Many were romanticists or idealists. However, after they entered the company, they were "brainwashed" repeatedly. They attended various training sessions on the values that drive their daily work. Almost all have been successfully transformed. Every cell of the entire organization is trained to be customer oriented. The people, organization chain, business processes, R&D activities, products, and corporate culture become living cells which continue to live if they serve customers, or would otherwise perish. At Huawei, practices replace fantasies, execution is more important than creation, and performance is more valuable than the process. Nobody or nothing can deviate from customer orientation.

Common sense in its extreme is religion. This is true with Apple and is also true with Huawei.

For over two decades, Huawei has never swayed from its core values. Even after Huawei has become a world-class company, Ren Zhengfei remains vigilant. He said:

> To better serve our customers, we should locate our command posts in places that can hear gunfire. We should delegate planning, budgeting, and accounting rights and the right to make sales decisions to the frontline, and let those who can hear the gunfire make the decisions. The back office decides whether we should engage in a battle, while the frontline decides how to fight the battle. The back office should follow the instructions of the frontline, not vice versa. The headquarters is the support, service, and supervision center; it is not the command center.

He also remarked, "Who shall call for artillery? The decision must be made by people who can hear the gunfire." Ren further stated:

> We have established the Iron Triangle in our account department to identify and seize opportunities, move operational planning out to the field, and summon and organize necessary forces to hit targets. The Iron Triangle is not for checks and balances. Instead, it is a customer-centric joint operating unit where different roles are closely connected and cooperate toward a common goal: meeting customer needs and helping customers to realize their dreams.

Entrepreneurs share a common dream: Growth. But that dream is checked and sometimes eroded by internal and external changes. The leaders of Huawei are well aware of this, and have determined to adapt to changes through organizational restructuring. Regardless of how the environment or the organization changes, the company knows that customers must always remain at the center of everything they do. This is the common sense that has led Huawei so far.

CHAPTER TWO

Soul of Business:
Dedication Is the Key to Success

Section I. We Can Wither a Bit, but We Must Not Fall Apart

Anxiety Sufferers

Ren Zhengfei has great vision for the long-term future. On multiple occasions in early 2009, he repeated that the global economy would again slip into recession, and fluctuations would persist. The macroeconomic environment would be even more challenging than it was in 2008. China, therefore, should cut taxes for businesses, which would have many benefits, including an increased chance of survival for businesses, more jobs for the people, and greater social stability. For instance, he said that if Shanghai cut its tax rates to the level of Hong Kong, the city would be able to attract a greater number of professionals from Wall Street and would, therefore, be able to compete with Hong Kong and London as an international financial center.

In October 2011, when Ren visited a government official, he said:

> The global economy won't take any V-turn or U-turn in the foreseeable future. Instead, deflation will occur in various places and form a downward trend. For instance, first Greece will be hit hard, then Italy, and then the EU. At this moment, the Chinese government should provide significant tax incentives to prevent companies from collapsing one after another. It is high time to do that.

Ren asserted that the global financial crisis would be a disaster for many businesses in the coming years, but it would also bring opportunities to some others. At an executive meeting, he clearly pointed out that the company can wither a bit, but must not fall apart. If it survives the recession, the company would surely turn out to be a leader.

Ren Zhengfei is a typical anxiety sufferer. He has warned company executives and employees on many occasions. He said:

> A crisis is lurking just behind the boom, but the crisis is not an inherent part of the boom; it will arise when one loses alertness in the booming environment. Huawei may drop out if we let our endeavors rest for one day; it will fall behind Ericsson and Alcatel if we stop learning for just three days. I am not kidding. This is the cruel reality.

Only hard workers can survive in this world. This is a belief Huawei has developed through its business endeavors over the past two decades. Manufacturing is a difficult sector to manage, and electronics is the most challenging manufacturing sector. Different from other traditional industries, the electronics industry is one with fast-changing technologies and markets, and it is not subject to the limit of natural resources. For example, the development of the automotive industry is affected by the availability of steel, oil, and roads, while resources necessary for the development of electronics are unlimited. They are not natural resources, but river sand, software codes, and mathematical logic. As a result, competition in the electronics sector is especially fierce and relentless; it is a fight-to-the-death jungle. You must not withdraw; otherwise, you will be killed.

In 1991, Huawei burned its bridges. It invested all its financial and human resources in developing a new telephone switching system. More than 50 R&D engineers lived and worked on the same floor of a rented building. The floor was divided into four departments, a warehouse, and a kitchen. There were also a dozen beds against the wall. They were not enough, so they put foam padding on the floor to make additional beds. During that period the whole company worked day and night, including the leaders. They would take a nap on the makeshift beds or simply on desks and continue to work as soon as they woke up. One engineer worked so hard that his cornea fell out. He was hospitalized and, fortunately, his eyesight was saved.

In late December, a test run of the system was successful. Huawei had finally developed its own product! Huawei would surely have gone bankrupt if the development process had lasted any longer because the company had virtually run out of cash.

This was a narrow escape and a hard-won battle. The pioneers had a common revelation: There is no ready-made panacea for survival and further development; you must take the most "silly" road—in a word—hard work. Huawei had no other choice but to put up a difficult fight in order to change its fate.

In its history, Huawei has endured numerous crises. As Sun Yafang puts it, the company has gone through almost as many ordeals as Tang Sanzang during his journey to the West. But Huawei has been able to turn around, when it was on the verge of collapse.

Journey of Sweat, Blood, and Death

Yes, Huawei has won one victory after another, but the price it has paid is hefty. Following are some battle stories.

The first story occurred in November in Siberia. The weather was miserable, as the temperature was –50°C, and it was snowing heavily. It was then Ye Shu and his colleagues from Huawei arrived in Norilsk, the world's northernmost city and the second largest city north of the Arctic Circle, because Huawei had won a contract to build a GSM facility there. When they first arrived, daylight lasted about four hours, but soon the dark night got longer and longer. This was during the time of polar nights, which lasts from December through mid-January, where there is no sun for roughly six weeks. Nevertheless, they managed to work from 10 am to 8 or 9 pm every day.

Daily meals were a big problem. They cooked rice with an electric pot. At first, they put in too much water and ended up suffering from diarrhea. They then tried to cook the rice a little drier, but it would easily burn. Anyway, it was all right so long as there was rice, some sausage, and hot sauce.

The installation and test run were completed in two months. This was the first GSM network within the Arctic Circle, and it was built by Huawei.

The second story comes from Africa in 2002. Lü Xiaofeng, a GSM product manager for Huawei, took an EgyptAir flight from Cairo to Tunisia. Due to poor visibility, the airliner crashed into a hill just 6 kilometers before reaching the airport. Lü was seated near the break. He hurt his eyelid in the violent shock. But he was still sensible enough to unfasten his seatbelt as quickly as possible. After he rushed out of the plane, he did not go straight to the safe zone. Instead, together with a British national, Lü carried several injured women from the hillside to a safe piece of flat land. Later, he took off his coat and wrapped it around a two-year-old Tunisian toddler.

In the crash, out of 65 passengers and crew members, 15 died and many passengers were injured.

Unlike Lü Xiaofeng who luckily survived, three local Huawei employees in Ghana died in another air crash on October 25, 2005. It was a Nigerian airliner, and 117 passengers and crew members were killed, including the three African employees of Huawei. They died very young: one was 23, another was 25, and the oldest was 27 years old.

Still another story took place in Tibet. Shen Yibin was responsible for building and installing an intelligent network in the autonomous region. He wrote about his experience in the article, "Footprint on the Roof of the World." Shen said:

> During the first days, I suffered serious headache and had not been able to fall asleep. My lips turned purple and cracked from lack of oxygen. I had to drink a lot of water and apply heavy amounts of lip cream. My heart would beat very fast whenever I carried any equipment on my back. I had to take deep breaths. For two weeks, I had been working while my head felt heavy and my feet were weak.

He went on to write:

> There is an area in Tibet called Ngari Sanai, nicknamed the Third Pole of the Earth. It is 4,500 meters above sea level, and the conditions for existence were not much better than in the Arctic or Antarctic. One night, it was –20°C, but I was still working in the equipment room. We had to install the equipment to meet the schedule. When I inhaled the dry and icy air, my lungs shivered, and my heart jumped violently whenever I moved a machine. I sometimes felt dizzy. Then I had to sit down and take some deep breaths from the oxygen bag. It took quite some time for me to recover, and then I continued to work.

In 2006, *Huawei People*, the company's internal publication, printed another article titled "Heaven Rewards Diligent People," which said, "Huawei people can be seen almost everywhere in the world, including Africa stricken by epidemic, Iraq in war, Indonesia hit by tsunami, or Algeria after earthquake. ... The past 19 years have witnessed an internationalization process for Huawei that has been full of sweat, tears, and even death. We have had quite a journey. Of course, we still have a long way to go, but we won't change our heart or our course."

Their Phones Have Been Kept on 24 Hours a Day for Over 20 Years

Ren Zhengfei himself has also met with several near misses in the air. He once took a flight together with his wife and daughter. Just 12 minutes after take-off, the airliner started to rock violently. The plane nearly entered a dive straight to the ground. The passengers could see mountain peaks flying by the windows. Ren Zhengfei was scared, because his wife and daughter were right beside him. At this time, an air hostess announced that the aircraft had a problem and they were returning to the airport.

Several minutes later, the airliner landed at Beijing Capital International Airport. On the apron, a dozen police cars and fire engines had been waiting for them. Their sirens were blaring, which further intensified the atmosphere. "Thank God! We are alive!" Ren Zhengfei said to himself. But he was still extremely nervous; his face was pale. Yet, his daughter, to his amazement, was rather thrilled. She seemed to enjoy the spine-tingling drama.

About 10 days later, Ren met with another near miss. This time, it was a flight from Cairo to Doha. All of a sudden the aircraft seemed to bump into something and began to experience severe turbulence. Every passenger was caught in horror. Luckily, the aircraft finally landed at Cairo Airport. Sitting on a bench in the airport terminal after the shock, Ren Zhengfei asked another passenger whether she had been afraid. "No," the passenger said, "I have seen patients dying in hospitals. Life is fragile. We must enjoy every day while we're still alive." Ren had thought of canceling the journey, but he was greatly inspired by the answer. Two hours later he was on another flight to Doha.

Ren later said with strong emotion,

> Every day, hundreds of people from Huawei take flights. We are in the same dangerous game. Perhaps this is destined because Huawei is a business enterprise. We have to fight; otherwise, we will die. Sacrifices are inevitable for a fighting organization. If we don't fight, we will end up with nothing.

Besides traveling on planes, Huawei's executives have kept their mobile phones on 24 hours a day for over 20 years. Wherever they are, in China or other parts of the world, they must be ready to answer their phone calls. Huawei is present in more than 100 countries and now has more than 100,000 employees. Things happen every day. Ren said, "I don't want to hear good news. I don't care much about it. But whenever something bad happens, I must know it, especially those things concerning the safety of our people. They are our valued strivers." When he said this, his eyes were full of tears.

According to his close colleagues, Ren Zhengfei takes approximately 100 flights each year, and other Huawei senior executives, such as Sun Yafang, Hu Houkun (Ken Hu), Eric Xu, Guo Ping, Xu Wenwei (William Xu), and Chen Lifang take more than 150 flights each year. At the same time, about two-thirds of Huawei's Board and EMT members have suffered from stress-related diseases. Anxiety is the most common illness, which is followed by hypertension, diabetes, and depression. Of note is that Guo Ping suffers from a very strange condition. When he is sick, his blood platelet drops to an extremely low level, but after he takes some rest for a while, everything is fine again. No one knows what he has been suffering from.

Ren Zhengfei said:

> If we don't strive hard, the company will collapse. Of course, even if we work very hard, the company may still decline. Huawei is not afraid of decline. We know that the macro environment is tough, and many companies have died or are dying. Just being able to survive is good enough.

Section II. Soul of Business: The Culture of Dedication

Dedication Based on Customer Centricity

In August 2007, Huawei was contracted to build two mobile communication base stations for China Mobile Communications Corporation on Mount Qomolangma (Mt. Everest) at two altitudes: 5,200 meters and 6,500 meters. According to the contract, the base stations needed to be deployed by the end of November 2007, but the circumstances were extremely challenging. One could barely do anything due to the extreme and changeable weather, and the air was extremely thin. Oxygen at an altitude of 5,200 meters was 50 percent lower than on the plain, and it was even thinner at 6,500 meters. Four engineers from Huawei, together with one driver, nevertheless, made it onto this "roof of the world," with protective clothing and footgear in addition to special mountaineering equipment and food suited to the harsh environment. Dizziness, headache, swollen lips, ulcers, and sleeplessness were commonplace. And one of them suffered nosebleeds for two days. When camping at 6,500 meters, they would awaken in the middle of the night to find their hair had frozen.

Huawei completed its 3002E base stations at 1 pm on November 13, 2007. Since then, all camps and mountaineering routes on Qomolangma have had access to a mobile communication network. Huawei had built the highest wireless communication base station in the world.

On the eve of the Spring Festival in 2011, Huawei headquarters received a text message from its office in Egypt: "Gunshots are loud outside. They sound like firecrackers celebrating the New Year in our motherland. At this happy moment, we wish China and Huawei a prosperous and happy new year! We will stay here and fulfill our mission."

In 2011, Libya was engulfed in civil war, and almost all foreigners, including tourists and merchants, fled the country. The Chinese government evacuated more than 10,000 people, which was making headlines in media reports around the world. However, Huawei employees in Libya remained.

On May 21, 2003, Algeria was hit by a 6.8 magnitude earthquake, killing more than 3,000 people. Soon after the earthquake, all expatriate staff of Western companies left the country. In contrast, Huawei's staff stayed and continued in their duties. Three days after the quake, the engineering team completed an intelligent network cutover as scheduled, which ensured local access to the communications network.

The last story occurred in Bombay, India. One day, the city was struck by a terrorist explosion. The streets soon emptied and all shops closed down. Rarely could any vehicle be spotted on the roads. Even so, Huawei engineers rushed to the customer's site despite the danger and upgraded the communications facility before 5:30 am. As a Huawei executive said:

> What is customer centricity? It is not about bowing and scraping to customers; it means accountability to the network and loyalty to our job. When our customers choose to build their networks with our equipment, we must make timely, accurate, high-quality, and low-cost delivery, and provide the best service. Under extreme circumstances, such as earthquakes and civil unrest, we must stay and assist our customers through the difficulty because the network is most vulnerable at such times.

Customer centricity is the basis of dedication. Ren Zhengfei stated:

> What is dedication? One is dedicated if they create value for our customers, · no matter how insignificant the value might be. You are dedicated if you try to improve and advance yourself in order to better serve customers; otherwise, you cannot say that you are dedicated, no matter how hard you are working.

In 2010, Ren again elaborated on the same idea:

> We believe in customer centricity and believe that dedication is the key to our success. This belief is based on our experience and is the core of our corporate culture. We are committed to providing timely, accurate, high-quality, and low-cost services to our customers, and this is the aim of everything we do. Customer centricity is common sense. Without our customers, we would have starved. Having dedicated employees as our foundation is in essence being customer-centric. If whoever serves our customers well is considered the backbone of Huawei, and if they share the benefits from the company's growth, then we are fostering customer intimacy and a customer-philic force in the company. Long-term dedication is also customer centricity. Let's say every cent we spend comes from the pockets of our customers, and they won't allow us to spend their money for nothing. If you are afraid of working in a difficult environment or performing a difficult job, if you don't focus on our customers, you won't be accepted and your life won't get any better.

This value statement explains why thousands of Huawei employees and managers have reached various corners of the world and shed their sweat and blood for customers over the past decade.

The Mattress Culture: A Unique Scene of Dedication

In the early years of the company, every new employee was given a blanket and a mattress. During the noon break they would take a nap on the pads. When working late into the night, many of them would rather stay in their office and sleep on their pads instead of going back to their dormitory. It was convenient because they would get up at midnight and continue to work. As many employees of Huawei said, "The pads meant a great deal to us. They represented relentless hard work in the old days, and now this habit has turned into the spirit of dedication. This is a unique glimpse into Huawei."

In 2008, a few Huawei employees committed suicide. These tragedies triggered a thunderstorm in the domestic media. Media outlets collectively lashed out at the company's "mattress culture." Even dedication had become an evil idea. One Huawei executive explained:

> When we started the business, we had only five or six engineers in the R&D team. They had been working with almost nothing but their bare hands. What they drew inspiration from was the tough and unwavering spirit of Chinese scientists in developing China's own atom bomb and satellites in the 1960s. These scientists are our best examples. Our engineers worked day and night on their R&D projects, developing, testing, and validating our products. They enjoyed no holidays and even gave up their weekends quite often. For them, there was no difference between day and night; whenever they felt the need to rest, they would take a nap on the floor and would wake up rolling their sleeves again. This is how the "mattress culture" got started. We now use mattress pads mostly for naps at noontime. In some sense, this bedding represents the hard work of the early generation of Huawei people. This is their spiritual legacy, a legacy we highly value across the company.

Two years later, Ren Zhengfei said with much emotion at a market conference:

> Some people are blaming us for dedication! I wonder, what has gone wrong? This is the tradition of the Communist Party of China (CPC). Every CPC member vows to dedicate their whole life to the communist cause and to the drive of four modernizations. They are also committed to making their hometown as beautiful as Beijing. This is the banner of the CPC, and we are following this banner.

Remembering some scholars who urged China to turn the image from "Made in China" to "Created in China," Ren said:

> People tend to neglect or ignore the fact that creativity grows over a long period of time and at terrible cost. Many companies will have to die before a handful of others may emerge and shine. We have gone through purgatory over the past decades, and only we ourselves and our families can know how tough these years have been for us. We have not worked 40-hour weeks. In our early years I worked 16 hours a day. I had no house of my own; I had to live and work in the same rented apartment. I had no weekends or holidays. I wonder if you can imagine that all our employees, over 100,000 of them, have been dedicating themselves to the company over the past 20 years.

This is true not only with our current employees, but our past employees as well. Industrial transformation is no easy job; it cannot be accomplished very soon, or by working only 40 hours a week. Forty-hour weeks will only get you common workers, but you'll never get musicians, dancers, scientists, engineers, or merchants.

There is another question: Would dedication to a company, or any hard work, necessarily lead to suicide? The answer is not that simple. Work conditions in Huawei were extremely poor during its early years, but people were filled with idealism, passion, and entrepreneurial spirit. No one committed suicide. In recent years, however, there have been reports of students or teachers committing suicide, even at prestigious universities. According to an essay published in *The Lancet*, the world's leading general medical journal, the annual suicide rate in China is 23 per 100,000, which is 2.3 times the global average of 10 per 100,000. The number of suicides per year in China accounts for one-third of the world's total. There are now thousands of suicide websites on the Internet, and the Doomsday 2012 prediction pervades throughout the world.

Is this an age of pessimistic collective unconsciousness?

This is certainly a hard time for companies.

Wolves Born in a Narrow Space

Whoever can endure what other people cannot endure will become the leader. This is a universally acknowledged logic that applies equally well to personal growth and company development. The people at Huawei have always believed there is no free lunch. In 1994, Huawei participated in the PT/Expo Comm China exhibition for the first time and wrote a message in its pavilion: "There is No savior in the world. Do not count on immortals or emperors. We have to create a new life with our own hands." This message aptly describes the past and present status of the company.

In 2006, when reflecting on the past 19 years of Huawei, Ren Zhengfei said:

> Huawei had no background or connections or any other resources. We could not depend on anything but our own dedication, our open mind, and our tough hands. ...This is all what we have relied on to narrow the gap with our competitors. The joint efforts and dedication of all the people at Huawei have taken the company to its current position.

He went on to say:

> We have invested over a billion in developing our GSM system. And I cannot clearly count how many engineers have toiled with sweat, tears, and even blood trying to bring this system to the market. In 1998, we finally obtained the network access license for our system. Eight years have passed, but we have not gained any visible share in the domestic wireless communication market. We can hardly recover the cost. ... China is the biggest emerging market in the world, but it was dominated by foreign giants when Huawei was founded. We were thrown into the most intensive competition, and we had to seek chances for survival in a narrow space. When we started to explore the international market, all the fertile lands had been occupied by Western companies. We could only see hope in remote areas, countries or regions in turbulence, and places with harsh natural conditions. These locations were our last hope because Western companies were hesitant to make bigger investment there. To seize this last hope, countless Huawei employees left their families behind to work overseas.

Huawei had been moving forward in this narrow space. It had no choice but to fight for survival in this seemingly impossible war. The key was resilience and die-hard persistence. It was in such a pressed environment that the so-called wolf culture began to take shape. In a 1997 article titled "Developing Organizational Mechanisms Suitable for the Company to Survive and Grow," Ren Zhengfei cited the concept of wolves, saying that the organization should create an environment where wolves may live well and keep their aggressiveness. He said that business managers with strong drive should be developed and motivated to be as keen and united as wolves while the company worked to expand its market. They should be able to sense and seize every opportunity to expand the company's product portfolio and market presence. At the same time, the organization should have a group of jackals, or back-end administration officials, who are able to provide the frontline wolves with enough support.

The following year, Ren Zhengfei wrote another article titled "How Long Will Huawei Hold Its Banner?" which proposed for the first time that the company should develop a "wolf culture." He said:

> A company needs to develop a bunch of wolves. A wolf has three features: a sharp nose, persistent aggressiveness, and an inclination for collective struggle. These are essential for a business to expand. Therefore, we need to offer a relatively flexible environment in which people are motivated to struggle for success and to catch every new opportunity that may arise. The marketing

department has developed a wolf and jackal organization plan which aims to balance the aggressiveness with sound administration of the organization. Of course, this plan applies to departments responsible for business expansion. Other departments may select their managers fitting with their own goals and missions.

As was written in the press article "Evolution from Wolves into Lions,"

> What are wolves in the eyes of a lion? They are eating into the territory of the lion from the very periphery to the core. Attacking the lion in a pack of 100 to 1, the wolves offer unbelievable prices until the profitability of the lion plummets. The strategy of wolves is to use various unconventional tools in competition and navigate through complex relationships, depending on their unmatched adaptability and market understanding, to render the technical advantages of the lion irrelevant.

This is a vivid picture of Huawei 10 years ago. It may not be complete, but it largely portrays the organization. Since 2002, Huawei has acquired first-class products and technologies and has withdrawn from the price war. Yet another picture painted in that article presents Huawei in a new light:

> Wolves are eager to win, but they are extremely resilient in the face of any resistance or frustration. They adapt themselves perfectly to the environment, and they tend to fight for survival in packs regardless of price. In a word, they are fierce and tough threats to lions.

Huawei is not just a local wolf; it has become a "giant wolf" in the global market. To a large extent, it has evolved into a "lion" itself. What preoccupies the leaders of Huawei is that once the company becomes a "lion," the spirit of the wolves and the spirit of dedication may get lost. They know very well that there are pitfalls to success and prosperity. At any time, what drags down a company are surely the company itself and its owners.

Section III. Clocks That Do Not Swing in Rome

Stars Are Burning Out?

One day I greeted Zeinal Bava, the CEO of Portugal Telecom, and his colleagues in Beijing and offered dinner at the Chang An Club. During dinner, Mr Bava mentioned Huawei and Ren Zhengfei. He said Ren had once asked him a question: "Why had Portugal lost its prominence in most of the world and confined itself to a small corner in Europe?" This question shocked CEO Bava and his colleagues. Yes, in the 16th century Portuguese adventurers and navigators reached almost every part of the world, and a large proportion of the world's territory belonged to Portugal, a small country of several million people. Most Portuguese stopped adventuring after they had come to enjoy a luxurious life with the gold and silver they had gained from Latin America. Rulers and ordinary people of the empire had turned speculative and lazy. Navigation and industry withered and eventually died out. The wealth that had flowed in like water flown away just as quickly.

Italian clocks and watches are famous around the world. In public places in Venice, Florence, and particularly Rome, clocks are seen everywhere, in shops, hotels, cafés, churches, and street squares. They look exquisite and elegant. But people are often surprised to find that those clocks are not precise, and some do not swing at all. They are mere decorations, and time turns out immensely abundant for the Italians. But the question is: Had the Italians really taken time so lightly? If you visit the Colosseum built 2,000 years ago, the churches and museums that have been cherished for centuries, the mercantilist city of Venice, and if you see the water taps in Rome that have been used for 2,000 years, you will be amazed by the achievements of this country, and you certainly wouldn't think that all these achievements could have been made if people had viewed time in such a frivolous way.

In 2003, Ren Zhengfei predicted that Europe would be ruined in the end by its welfare culture. He was also prompted to ponder: Would Huawei fall in comfort as well?

The crisis began in Iceland, spreading to Spain and Portugal, and then to Greece and Italy. France, Germany, and the United Kingdom were also subject to doubts. Among them, Greece is especially tragic. This ancient country, famous for its history and myths, produces half the GDP per capita of Germany, but their welfare system is at par with Germany. In other words, Greece does not create wealth as a member of the Eurozone, but rather consumes wealth without restraint. As Adrian Vrettos wrote in "Live in Greece," *SDX Life Weekly*, 47th issue of 2011.:

> The people [in Greece] are consuming as if Doomsday is coming. Thanks to low labor cost, most families have their own housemaid or laborer. ...For many people, there is no difference between an office and a café. They drink

expensive coffee, 4.5 euros a cup, in their office while lazily talking about some implausible business. For the people of Greece, life is easy if other people do all the jobs for them. Meanwhile, they spend or waste trillions of euros. This is the Greek lifestyle. They care first about themselves, then their families, relatives, friends, and then. ...

Now, Greece is near bankruptcy. Its sovereign debt is 140 percent of its GDP. But Greece is not the only failing country in Europe; the whole continent is near collapse. As of the end of 2011, the national debt of Italy amounted to 1.9 trillion euros, which was 120 percent of its GDP. The seemingly strong country of France also had a total debt of 1.7 trillion euros.

After decades of peaceful and stable development, Europe appears prosperous, but this prosperity has been sustained by debt in most countries, except Germany and the United Kingdom. The people have been spoiled. Laziness has become a common character over the last one or two generations. When the crisis comes, will they give up the free lunch they have enjoyed for decades?

Recent times have been witness to strikes, demonstrations, and even radical and violent protests. The old continent, once separate before being united, is being torn apart. Will the situation become more dangerous? The answer is yes. Europe will inevitably slip into the quagmire of turbulence because the people have a strong faith in welfarism and have acquired a natural resistance to the puritanical values of drive and hard work. Europe may have hope if its people regain their traditional spirit, but the collective unconscious inclination toward comfort is irreversible. Collective unconsciousness would not change into reason unless there is a devastating change or revolution. Angela Merkel, a German Chancellor, spoke quite frankly at the coalition parliament in October 2011:

> Nobody should take for granted another 50 years of peace and prosperity in Europe. ...We have a historical obligation: to protect by all means Europe's unification process begun by our forefathers after centuries of hatred and blood spill. None of us can foresee what the consequences would be if we were to fail.

Bava, however, was confident and optimistic. He said, "Portugal is a different country. We are a more resilient nation. Our young people are more aggressive." When we bid farewell to each other after dinner, he gave me a souvenir: A plate imprinted with an atlas of Portugal as it was

300 years ago. The atlas covered more than half of the world, including Macau of China.

Sleep Is Guilt

On Thanksgiving Day 2008, every American was enjoying their turkey at home. Few imagined that the rope around their necks was beginning to tighten. The news headlines talked about the Portuguese on strike, protesting against the austerity policy. At that time, crisis had hit Italy, France, and other parts of Europe, and was threatening to reach the United States. Did America have the necessary immunity to fend off the epidemic?

The United States was not any better off. It was suffering from mounting debt, excessive liquidity and welfare, and a declining real economy. The United States was caught in the most difficult situation they faced in the 21st century. To make things even worse, it was showing its military power throughout the world.

It does not mean, however, that the United States is slipping from its edge. It is still able to strike a balance between economic recovery and social welfare. It is still the leader of high-tech sectors, such as IT, renewable energy, nanotechnology, and medical equipment. Although its government is "poor," its businesses are rich. The dollar, legal tender of the United States, enjoys predominance in the global money market. All this means that the United States will emerge from the financial crisis ahead of other Western countries.

In addition, no one can ignore the hard work of the American people and the creativity of the entire country. In 2000, Ren Zhengfei recommended an article to his colleagues in Huawei titled "Sleepless in Silicon Valley." One can truly understand from the article the core competitiveness of the United States. The article says:

> All those programmers, software developers, salespeople, and project managers believe that if you fall asleep you will fail and drop out. Supported by their great expectations, and stimulated by big cups of coffee, they have been able to stay awake before their PCs, focusing their eyes on their fluorescent screens until 4, 5, or even 6 in the early morning. They have never spent such hours on their comfortable beds. This is the price they have had to pay for playing in the international market that spans different time zones. They have a new starting point each day, and they are fervently pushing the frontier of Internet technology forward.

It is the uniform lifestyle of about 200,000 hi-tech workers in Silicon Valley. Almost all of them stay up late. In traditional industries there are two or three shifts a day, but in hi-tech parks, the car park would be still crowded until 3 am. Some hi-tech workers may stay home at night, but they are typically connected to their office system with their PCs.

The hi-tech sector, like sports, belongs to young people, but that also depends on how fast the people age. Statistics show that most hi-tech workers are single, male, under the age of 35. Some try to squeeze as many products from their brains as possible to get more from their employers before their minds turn slow.

Of interest is that the mattress culture is not a unique creation of Huawei. It has precedents in Silicon Valley. For instance, the same article says:

At first, Netscape arranged rooms with carpeting in the office, where its employees used to sleep when they worked late at night. The company later called it off and encouraged people to go home and sleep in their own beds. But the employees kept asking the company to set up the rooms again.

Similarly, at Huawei, has anyone heard complaints about the mattress culture? Today, mattress pads of different colors are still found under desks in Huawei offices.

"Sleep is guilt," said Bill Owens, a four-star admiral in the US Navy, who served as the Vice Chairman of the Joint Chiefs of Staff; Deputy Chief of Naval Operations for Resources, Warfare Requirements, and Assessments; Commander of the US Sixth Fleet; and senior military assistant to secretaries of defense Frank Carlucci and Dick Cheney. After he retired from the US Navy, Owens had a stint with Nortel as its CEO and the Vice Chairman. He joined AEA Holdings in 2006 and now chairs the firm's Asia operations.

Bill Owens only sleeps three to four hours a day; the rest of the time he often travels between the Eastern and Western Hemisphere. As a Navy admiral, Owens once spent 2,000 consecutive days on a submarine in the deep sea. There he was considered god, as the captain kept watch over 100 soldiers around-the-clock, and was responsible for telling them whether it was day or night. Since retiring from the Navy, he has been spending his time at the same tempo, although he is now engaged in a different battlefield. Business is battle; this is likely an unquestionable truth in Owens' eyes, as he said in a puritanical tone, "Work is life."

150,000 Solitary Fighters

In 2007, Jason Matheny, Open Source Indicators (OSI) program manager of the Intelligence Advanced Research Projects Activity (IARPA), wrote an essay titled "Reducing the Risk of Human Extinction" for *Risk Analysis* magazine. Matheny writes:

> In one billion years, the sun will begin its red giant stage, increasing terrestrial temperatures above 1,000 degrees, boiling off our atmosphere and eventually forming a planetary nebula, making Earth inhospitable to life. If we colonize other solar systems, we could survive longer than our sun, perhaps another 100 trillion years, when all stars begin burning out. We might survive even longer if we exploit non-stellar energy sources.

This is incredible imagination and crazy optimism. This is the blend of crisis awareness and fantasy, without which the human race would not have gone so far. This is also the source of all the courage we need to face uncertainties in the future. Do you say that stars are burning out? Well, let's exploit nonstellar energy sources!

Facing the upcoming global recession, Ren Zhengfei is also cautiously optimistic. He believes that recessions are circular, and they are unlikely to hit the whole world at the same time. This means Huawei would still have enough space and opportunities for survival and expansion. At this point, Huawei has built up its presence in every corner of the world and has enough resources and courage to cope with any crisis. Of critical importance is that Huawei's culture of dedication will remain a tremendous boost to its continued operation.

Just imagine 150,000 people from different family, education, national, and religious backgrounds with different personal characters and beliefs, all running together toward the same goal in all five inhabited continents of the world under the leadership of a handful of Chinese entrepreneurs who represent a common set of core values. This is rarely seen in the commercial history of China.

Huawei has now more than 30,000 foreign employees, so it is a question whether they can understand the core values of the company. Ren Zhengfei said:

> People often say that foreigners cannot understand the culture of Huawei, but I just wonder why. Customer centricity is one of our core values, and it

is a universal value as well. This idea was first put forward by foreign companies. They insisted on developing solutions according to customer needs because they won't get any contracts if they fail to do so. So our foreign employees should understand the idea better. Why can't they understand it? They should be able to understand the message that dedicated people are our foundation as well. The idea is also very simple. Why are they paid more? Because they work and contribute more to the company. This is the common balance: more work for more pay. Recognition of hard work and contribution is the message we try to get across, and I see no reason why our foreign employees cannot get it.

In short, customer centricity is a basic common sense and a truth; it is also a basic human logic to value hard work. How about the recent European economic and social crisis? Did it not arise from the Europeans' excessive welfare and their comfort and laziness?

Germany, of course, is part of Europe, but its situation fares much better. This is a nation of discipline, efficiency, order, diligence, and social cohesion. The whole country has a sense of urgency and precaution against crisis; this is their cultural gene. It explains why it has been able to produce a number of great thinkers, musicians, scientists, and entrepreneurs. Even more impressively, Germany boasts an excellent balance: rich companies, rich government, and a welfare system that matches its national power. As a result, the country has become the only safe haven in Europe, and together with the weak France, a savior for the whole Eurozone.

In Greek mythology there is a god called Sisyphus, who was condemned to an eternity of hard labor. His assignment was to roll a great boulder to the top of a hill. Every time Sisyphus was about to reach the summit, with the greatest of exertion and toil, the rock rolled back down again. Sisyphus then had to start it all over again and push it up again toward the summit. The tenacious man kept moving on with a heavy yet measured step toward the torment for which he would never know the end, yet he never gave up.

This Greek myth tells a universal law: We are always caught in the paradoxical balance of glory and pain. This paradox exists in every country, every nation, every company, every family, and every individual.

Huawei certainly is no exception.

Section IV. Sharing the Benefits of Dedication

Employee Shareholding and Its Nuclear Power Effects

Commenting on the United States in the 1940s, Winston Churchill said, "The United States is like a giant boiler. Once the fire is lit under it, there's no limit to the power it can generate."

It is true. More than 300 years ago, the Mayflower brought a group of people with courage and dreams to the new continent. These forefathers of the United States have culminated in a sound social system of democracy, the spirit of contract, and the rule of law, which was based on Puritanism and valued individual gain and personal value. This system includes all necessary incentives for the country's growth and prosperity. For example, they have introduced a variety of employee-reward schemes, including stock options, which have played a significant role in the rapid growth of hi-tech companies in the United States. There is now general agreement that Silicon Valley has been driven by two engines: One is the stock option scheme, and the other is its innovative culture; one provides material force, and the other provides spiritual force.

The whole world is learning from the United States, and now China's hi-tech, financial, and cultural companies are learning from their American counterparts.

Since its establishment, Huawei has placed a silver handcuff on its employees—the Employee Shareholding Scheme. It is called the silver handcuff because it is different from the stock option arrangement, termed the golden handcuff. To be honest, however, Huawei did not borrow its shareholding scheme from the West. This scheme was designed and implemented because it was the only choice for the company.

In an article titled "The Spring River Flows East," Ren Zhengfei explained why and how Huawei developed its employee shareholding scheme:

> I designed the employee shareholding scheme soon after I founded Huawei. I had intended to knit all my colleagues together by a certain means of benefit sharing. At that time I had no idea about stock options. I did not know that this had been a popular form of incentive for employees in the West, and there are a lot of variations. The frustrations in my life made me feel that I had to share both responsibilities and benefits with my colleagues. I discussed this with my father who had learned economics in the 1930s. He was very supportive. But no one had expected that this shareholding scheme,

which came into being by chance more than by design, would have played such a big role in making the company a success.

The scheme was the only choice for Huawei, or its only source of power to compete with international giants and Chinese SOEs. It had no connections or resources as a private company and lacked funding. Everyone had to fight arm in arm with each other. Everyone must act like the boss. Ren Zhengfei said:

> Please don't assume that I was a sage or a saint. If I had started a real estate business, I would have taken it for granted that everything was mine because I got the land and loans through my own connections. Why should I share anything with anyone else? I should enjoy all the benefits as I assumed all the risk. But my company, Huawei, was established as a technology company. I needed more smart people, more people with lofty ideals, to work hand-in-hand and to share wealth and woes. Everyone had to take their own share of duty, particularly for the older generation and the senior managers. Only when they diluted their equity can more people be engaged in the battle.

Ren Zhengfei is the largest shareholder of Huawei, but he has only 1.42 percent of the total equity. The rest is held by its employees. According to an internal source, after an upcoming round of share dilution, his share will probably be further reduced. At the end of 2011, among the 146,000 employees of Huawei, 65,596 had a stake in the company. This is the most scattered share structure in the world and a rare phenomenon in commercial history.

Dedicated employees are much valued at Huawei, which is an essential part of its corporate culture. In 2007, this value proposition was stated as follows: "We will continue to reward high-performing employees, and everyone will be evaluated by their duty and contribution." In the early years, Ren Zhengfei repeated time and again that the company must not "let Lei Feng wear worn-out socks." Lei Feng was a special hero during the Red Era of China and the spiritual totem of a whole generation. He was portrayed as a cow that eats grass and produces milk. Almost the entire nation, 800 million Chinese at the time, had been moved by his diary and altruistic deeds. They were fervent about helping other people, cherished extremely pure hearts, and had committed themselves to a lofty communist cause.

But that proved to be a utopian dream. History, in fact, is a drama where desire is strong and immense. Dreams are beautiful but short and false. The real story is about explosion, satisfaction, and the restraint of desire.

Having served as a soldier in the 1970s, Ren Zhengfei has many labels for Lei Feng: dedicated, passionate, self-disciplined, and perseverant. But he knew at the same time that, without continued fire, water does not keep boiling in the pot. It is especially true in the age of the market economy.

Ren is more of a conscious thinker than a rebel against the old times. He said,

> We must dare to break away from old practices and customs. We must have the courage to favor high-performing people with dedication and successful track record. For those of them who have a sense of mission and who are truly capable, we must set the stage to let them run a bit faster.

Huawei, therefore, is committed to letting every worker have a stake in the company. Of course, it is just a parlance easier to communicate, but most people at Huawei do have a certain share of the company's equity. Yet this scheme is not the communistic Big Pot in the age of the market economy, because only those who perform well enough qualify to participate. Ren Zhengfei said:

> Difference creates motive. There would be no wind if there was no temperature difference, and there is no stream if water is at the exact same level. We do not tolerate seniority, inaction, playing it safe, or any once-and-for-all value distribution. We must organize our 100,000 talented employees into a dynamic and ambitious team. We must let dedicated people share the fruits of our success and slack managers feel the pressure of dropping out of the race.

It is difficult enough for an individual or an organization to stay dynamic and motivated for even three years. So it is nearly impossible to remain the same for 20 years or longer. The statement "customer centricity and dedication is the key to our success" has not gone empty and alone. It is substantiated by a set of practical approaches to motivate its employees. This is definitely no easy task, and the human resources department of Huawei has done a tremendous job.

Lao Zi, the founder of Taoism and author of *Tao Te Ching*, the Taoist bible, said, "All things are produced by the Tao and nourished by its outflowing operation. They receive their forms according to the nature of each and are completed according to the circumstances of their condition."

Huawei's 150,000 employees are all solitary fighters with burning desire and passion. Together, they form a great army of collective heroes. They have tried to make a decent life for themselves and their families, but indeed they are making great contributions to the company and even to the country. They are dedicated fighters and are entitled to the benefits of dedication.

Why Won't Huawei Go Public?

At a luncheon in a famous club in New York, Ren Zhengfei met with a dozen top American businessmen, including Maurice Greenberg, the former chairman of AIG, and Vincent Mai, chairman and CEO of AEA Investors. He was asked why Huawei had not gone public. Ren answered:

> ... Technology companies need motivated employees. If a company goes public, a bunch of its employees will instantly get very rich. They will become millionaires or even billionaires. And then they will most likely lose their motivation. This is not good for Huawei; this is not good for our employees, either. The company will stop growing at such a pace, and the people will lose their collective drive. If employees get rich too young they will become lazy, which is a curse to their personal development.

Huawei advocates that in an organization top management should have a sense of mission, mid-level managers should have a sense of crisis, and grassroots workers should have a sense of hunger. The top executives are highly paid and enjoy more dividends. To some extent, wealth is no more than a symbol to them. They are not motivated by material gain. They have already completed their "primitive accumulation." What they need to go further is a sense of mission and passion for their career. In short, the elite at the top of the pyramid must be driven by a spiritual power.

On the other hand, the mid-level managers who were once grassroots workers can often get promoted because they have shown dedication throughout their years of work for the company. For the overwhelming majority of employees, more work for more pay is the basic and most realistic motive.

This is a universal law of humanity that reflects human desire, a law Huawei understands and follows in its compensation design.

Huawei believes that mid-level managers should have a sense of crisis. If they fail to organize and drive their team to fulfill its goals or if they are selfish and self-complacent, they will be quickly replaced or demoted. They will be promoted again if they regain their passion and meet all qualifications. "Grassroots workers should have a sense of hunger," for bonuses, company shares, promotion, and success. Such hunger breeds wolf-like aggressiveness. Without it, any spiritual appeal will be pointless.

Around 1997, Huawei had been at par with its Western counterparts in terms of employee compensation. The company had no choice because it had to attract and retain talent. This is also why, soon after it was established, Huawei adopted the employee shareholding scheme. The shares were not worth much at first, and during the early years no dividends were paid. But they have now become the most valuable assets of its employees, since the company has kept growing and the dividends paid each year are more than their salary and bonus combined. Ren Zhengfei once said:

> Huawei has survived by virtue of hard work and technical innovation. Does technical innovation have no limit? Is Moore's Law always right? Can we keep our market with a certain technology? I believe that technology innovation will slow down when the bandwidth and coverage of wired and wireless access reaches a certain level. At that time, only companies with extensive market penetration and excellent management that can provide high-quality services at low cost will be able to survive the cut-throat competition. So, Huawei should try to reach this level before it dies. Within the coming decade, we will try to learn from Western companies how to manage the business, how to improve its efficiency, and adopt a fitting human resources management system to motivate our people to fight for survival.

Ren has told the truth of the global IT industry. It is a cruel reality. Unlike other industries, IT is engaged in a death race that started very early on and will last far into the future. The law, however, is that the one who lasts the longest wins, no matter how fast they are running. Then how can a company avoid premature death? There is no choice but to fight. And how can a company turn its employees into motivated fighters? The answer is having a reasonable and superior human resources regime.

It seems a natural law that people run fast if they turn rich in measured steps, but they stumble if they get wealthy overnight. A lot of companies, both Chinese and foreign, are promising and robust before they go public, but they suffer from organizational shock quite soon after they get listed. And that primarily rests with the people who get rich too quickly. They stop pushing forward the frontier or leave their company and join their competitors for even more money. Some sell their share of the company and set up their own operation; worse still, they poach people from their former company and become the bitter enemy. Clearly, this is a poor human resources regime.

Ren Zhengfei once asserted on an informal occasion, "If we do not go public, we might someday conquer the entire world." The assertion has at least three meanings. The first is the collective fighting spirit. Abundance weakens an individual or organization. With too many "pies," a team will ultimately lose its muscle, and the worst scenario is cell or organism necrosis. If the company remains private and pays as much compensation as the global industry captains, plus yearly dividends, it will not only attract and retain talented people but also maintain their fighting power and aggressiveness. Up to now, Huawei has struck a perfect balance.

The second is that the decision power should be under control. Given the scattered share structure of the company, any private equity investor may easily gain relative control over Huawei. And should the company become controlled by any investor seeking only short-term returns, Huawei would not be very far away from collapse.

The third is with respect to the goals of Huawei people. Huawei has been able to reach so far and overtake most of its Western counterparts because it has a long-term vision. The company has worked on its 10-year plans, while its competitors struggle to follow near-term fluctuations of the capital market. The capital market, so to speak, is a cold-blooded and impatient animal, and the industry is constantly running out of patience. From 2G to 3G, and then to 4G, from mobile Internet to cloud computing, the industry is busy renewing itself. In this context, a company will die sooner than later if it cannot plan for the future in light of the upcoming changes.

So when will Huawei go public? Perhaps when the threefold challenge just elaborated on gets sorted out mentally and organizationally. After all, the company needs more capital to expand its global presence. According to China's Corporation Law and Securities Law, a company must not exceed 200 shareholders before it may go public. This is an impossible hurdle for Huawei, which is held by more than 70,000 employees. Huawei certainly won't go public until the law is amended.

Spinning Top: The Wooden Monkey That Never Rests

Ren Zhengfei once said at a casual meeting with employees:

> If you believe you are born to die, why then were you born at all? Since you can bathe in the sunshine without doing anything, why should you work hard to enjoy the sunshine? If you believe your life will end in nothingness, you can stop any efforts to improve it. But in this way you will be much too pessimistic. We live an average of 70 or 80 years, and I am convinced that life becomes completely different if some measure of effort is put into it. The process of making life more beautiful and enjoyable could be full of pain. A farmer reaps nothing if he has not tilled the land, and a city won't be any better without construction workers toiling under the scorching sun; a country won't have any steel or iron if none of its people endure the heat of furnaces, and Marine Corps soldiers won't get to the beach if they haven't trained hard enough. "No pain, no gain," as the English proverb says. I believe you have taken great pains to get into university. You deserve everything you have earned. Each pain you have experienced is the price you have paid for a wonderful life.

Success, or the sense of success, is the personal perception or sense of value that each person possesses and is dependent on. Without this sense of value, people feel empty. Emptiness is a dark force that can destroy a person. In human history, prominent and successful people have substituted social commitment and lofty values to replace the perception of emptiness. They are destined to lead a difficult life, filled with solitude and pain.

Ren Zhengfei and other leaders of Huawei carry the same cross on their backs. They are obliged to drive the express train of Huawei to every corner of the world, and to keep it in perpetual motion. This seems to be a national value. Ren belongs to a special generation that identify with the country, and for his generation, personal and business success belongs to the country. Needless to say, every successful business leader is full of national pride when they are conquering the world.

The greater the underlying desire, the stronger the sense of mission. If it is going to live long and thrive, Huawei needs to ensure the organization has enough motivation. The company should therefore develop more extensive and effective incentives to resist or offset (because it is impossible to eliminate) organizational fatigue. This is a big challenge for its leaders and all of management. Although a perpetual motion machine is only hypothetical, Huawei's leaders must keep themselves in perpetual motion. And while they try to resist "leadership fatigue," they must lead the organization out of fatigue as well.

In this sense, not everyone can be a good leader, as it is one of the most painful jobs. It is not a mere issue of competence, personal integrity, or charisma. The key is how to keep the motivation always fresh to counteract laziness and boredom. That simply makes being a leader the most uncomfortable and inhuman job in the world.

This reminds me of my childhood. When I was about seven or eight years old, I loved to make paper boats, and when it rained I would go out front and launch a few on the stream that would form by the gate. I would then watch the paper boats bobbing up and down until they floated out of my sight. These boats carried away the dreams of a boy who had not traveled farther than 10 kilometers. I have now traveled throughout the world, but I still clearly remember these dreams today as vividly as they were 40 years ago.

In my childhood, I also loved to play with wooden balls. Wooden balls are also called spinning tops, and it was our favorite game. During the game, each of us would put a wooden ball on the ground and whip it into perpetual spinning, and the winner was the one who could keep his ball spinning the longest. We were all very excited. And when any ball slowed down, we would whip it until it regained its speed.

This is a philosophical game. In northern China, a spinning top is called a wooden monkey. This name more aptly reveals the philosophical implications. Aren't we all wooden monkeys, since we are spinning all our life, driven or pulled by a certain power? Every member of an organization is also a wooden monkey. He is spun by a force that takes different forms, including incentives and punishments, but the goal is the same: to keep the organization strong and dynamic.

Of course, there are a few people in the world who are ready to spin without any whip. They are exceptional wooden monkeys because they have been born with that power that drives up around. They are born to be leaders.

CHAPTER THREE

Openness: A Matter of Life and Death

Section I. Open Up or Die

Ups and Downs of Wang Laboratories, and the Warnings

One day in 1993, Ren Zhengfei was strolling around Zhong Guan Cun, a technology hub in Beijing and often referred to as China's Silicon Valley. Someone asked him, "How do you like Founder?" He answered, "Founder has excellent technology, but its management is poor." At that time, Founder Electronics' Chinese Ideograms Coded Character Set was hailed as the terminator of Chinese traditional typesetting technology, one of the four greatest inventions of China. "How do you like Legend (later renamed Lenovo)?" He was asked again. "Legend has excellent management but lacks advanced technology," he answered. The inquirer went on, "How about Huawei?" Ren Zhengfei said, "We have neither advanced technology nor good management."

Ren Zhengfei told the truth. This was the reality of Chinese IT companies at that time. Since then, however, they have taken big strides after the global industry leaders. The year 1993 is a very important year. Of course, it does not mean any global event had occurred, but a milestone was laid down this year for the IT industry. The Clinton administration announced the plan to build its National Information Infrastructure (NII), a network of information highways. NII marked the beginning of a new era, an era of creativity and disruption. History has proven that any innovation or creation is made at the expense of old things being destroyed.

By 1993, Huawei was barely six years old. With less than 400 employees, its sales in the first half of the year barely exceeded CNY100 million. In that year, Huawei developed and launched its JK1000 analog switching system, but its market performance was a disaster. In the same year, Huawei's C&C08 2000-line switch was placed into trial for the first time by the Post and Telecom Bureau of Yiwu County, Zhejiang Province. At the same time, it started R&D on a new C&C08 switching system with a capacity of 10,000 lines.

The year 1993 was the real starting point for Huawei, because it had begun to open up itself to the outside world. Over the past six years, the company's goal had been to overtake Stone, one of the leading Chinese IT companies in the 1990s. After 1993, however, Huawei began to vie for a place in the top-three list of the global telecom equipment providers. At that time, Lenovo CEO Liu Chuanzhi also dreamed of challenging IBM.

At the end of 1997, Ren Zhengfei led a delegation of Huawei's senior executives to the United States. They traveled across the country to visit a number of American companies, including IBM, Bell Labs, and HP. The history of the American IT industry, especially the frequent rise and fall of companies, was an unprecedented revelation to all of them. Ren Zhengfei said,

> The history is like a cycle. One large corporation after another is caught up in trouble and then dies; small firms mushroom and grow into large corporations. The cycle then repeats itself. It is almost as if the 500 years of warring states in China transpires in the US within one day.

Nevertheless, he clearly felt the enormous power of the open culture and innovative system of the United States. This is a country of heroes, each of whom may take the lead for as long as decades or as short as several years, and who have inspired entrepreneurship and innovative power that underpin the strength of the nation.

On Christmas Eve, every family in the United States was having a happy reunion. But Ren Zhengfei and his colleagues shut themselves in a small inn in Silicon Valley. They had a meeting behind the closed door for three days and turned out a document of more than 100 pages. IBM's management transformation was a great inspiration for Huawei: A small company lacks competitiveness, while large companies collapse if they are not effectively managed. Hard work in the American high-tech industry also resonated strongly with Ren. Most people worked very hard, especially those successful entrepreneurs and senior executives. Dedicated hard workers, in the millions, have been the engine of technology and management advancement. They are also the cornerstone that great companies in the United States have been built on. Ren Zhengfei felt exactly the same: Hadn't Huawei grown up on the basis of the unwavering diligence of its people?

Huawei's management was also shocked by the dramatic rise and fall of Wang Laboratories established by Dr An Wang, a Chinese-born American. In 1971, Wang Laboratories launched the world's most advanced word processor, the 1200 BASIC. By 1978, Wang Laboratories became the largest information product supplier, yielding US$2 billion in personal wealth for An Wang. In 1985, An Wang ranked eighth on the *Forbes* list of 400 richest Americans. But in 1992, he filed for bankruptcy protection, and the company's share price plummeted from an all-time high of US$43 to 75 cents.

What went wrong? It was not open enough. Wang Laboratories had enviable R&D capabilities, but the problem is no single company or individual can cope with rapid technology shifts alone in an open age. In the case of Wang Laboratories, a closed model for technology development partly explained the company's collapse. The fundamental cause though was its closed culture. In its heyday, Wang Laboratories had a great number of tech geniuses, but the company had been managed exclusively by the Wang family. Dr Wang handed power over to his son, and management soon became enmeshed in family politics. Eventually, the company suffered from a mass exodus of its tech leaders.

The lesson from the fall of Wang Laboratories is both philosophical and practical—in this age of rapid technological and social changes, one cannot stay the course if they keep themselves in a closed space; they won't grow or even survive unless they are open enough. Practically speaking, a closed company has no prospect. In 1999 in a message to his new recruits, Ren Zhengfei clearly stated, "Huawei must keep learning from the outside world if we want to survive. We must open our door if we want to catch up with the world. We have developed each and every major product through open partnerships."

In 2012, to sum up the company's experience over the past decade, Ren Zhengfei said:

> Huawei must hold on to the open policy. We must not waver under any circumstance. If we do not open our door to obtain energy from the outside world, we won't get any stronger. At the same time, we must examine ourselves critically in this process; otherwise, we won't be open for long.

In short, openness is the basis of Huawei's survival and growth.

Learning from American Companies: Where Is the Brake?

One funny story about Ren Zhengfei is widely known among the older employees of Huawei. Near the end of 1997, Ren Zhengfei sold his second-hand Peugeot and bought a BMW. Whenever he was free he would drive his BMW along Shennan Avenue, a main artery in the city of Shenzhen. He would open the sun roof and the windows, enjoying the cityscape and listening to English lessons along the way. One day, he drove past an old car that was moving rather slowly. He turned his head and found it was Louis Gerstner, IBM chairman. Without saying hello to Gerstner, Ren Zhengfei asked, "Have you ever driven a BMW?" Gerstner did not answer. Sometime later, when he drove back and past Gerstner again, he asked, "Have you driven a BMW?" He still got no reply. When Ren asked the same question a third time, Gerstner was a bit upset and said: "What do you mean?" Ren explained: "Do you know where the brake is on a BMW?"

This may be a joke rather than a true story, but it had an interesting message. In 1997, Huawei was growing very fast. It had learned to accelerate the car so to speak, but it did not know how to slow it down. In other words, it knew how to grow but did not know how to manage its growth properly.

This may not be completely true, though. Back in 1997, Huawei needed the knowhow of acceleration more than any braking system. It needed a complete system that included acceleration and control, but it certainly required the acceleration part most. Huawei still needed to grow up fast enough to expand its presence in the global market; it was not yet time for Huawei to step on the brake.

The 1997 tour around the United States proved to be a pivotal event for the company. Since then, Huawei has introduced the process-based management of IBM and the experience of American companies has played a great part in its strategic design. A learning organization grows better; this has been proven time and again. Ren Zhengfei said: "It is good to borrow and transplant the advanced management philosophies and technologies of the West. Why should we resist anything that has proven successful? Huawei should first borrow them, then adapt them, and then institutionalize them. This is the inevitable process."

Ren Zhengfei has repeatedly said, "We must learn from the US in order to overtake our American counterparts. In this process, we must separate a few politicians from the great American people. We must not resist their successful experience simply because some politicians don't like us."

The United States protects its citizenship rights; it has a reliable legal system; it advocates academic freedom and innovative education; it develops a dynamic free market economy; it implements a sound social welfare system; it boasts an inclusive and diversified culture; and heroes appear whenever the country needs them. This all explains why the United States is so strong.

A sound social system is instrumental to productivity, and it is precisely for this reason that the American people are able to create the greatest wealth. This social system has also helped the United States attract elites from other parts of the world. For example, Albert Einstein, a German scientist, chose to become an American, under growing animosity of the Nazis. Similarly, Andrew Grove, the founder of Intel, was born to a Jewish family in Hungary, but fled to the United States as a refugee. And many other people who have made great contributions to the United States were also been born outside the new continent.

Reliable guarantee of property rights, scientific reason, mature capital markets, and advanced infrastructure have spurred the prosperity of the country and placed it at the top of the world. At the same time, the United States is a "militant" country: It "creates" enemies, which serves to keep the country dynamic and vigilant.

In short, the United States has a nurturing environment that produces great people, such as Steve Jobs and Bill Gates.

For this reason, Huawei has tried to learn from the United States. To this end, Ren Zhengfei and other senior executives have made frequent visits. No doubt, Huawei has been a faithful student. So then, why has the "master" recently seen the "student" as his enemy? What is the matter with the United States? And what is wrong with Huawei?

Some Western media outlets and politicians have consistently blamed China and Chinese companies for being conservative, closed, or mysterious. It is a pity, however, that they are ill-informed or their accusations are ill-intended. Over the past three decades, Chinese companies, as a whole, have made huge progress, because the country is opening itself up and the business community has also acquired an open mindset. This is an apparent fact in China.

Merchants in China have historically been belittled. Business trade was the least dignified or even an illegal profession. Therefore, China does not have a commercial system or culture like the West, and the so-called

Chinese way of business management is no more than a shaky stunt. China has borrowed some business concepts from the West and integrated them to a certain extent, but even the most successful companies, including Huawei, Lenovo, and Haier, have not yet created any system of their own on top of imported tenets. This is a tough truth that people of insight in China's business community are keenly aware.

While it could be a joke that Ren Zhengfei has no idea where the brake is on a BMW, this joke carries profound implications. Huawei was open, but it was still groping for stones in the river, and that was risky; it stood to lose everything should it spin out of control. So to speak, during this period Huawei was going through the "Death Valley" that many Chinese companies have trodden. They have completed their primitive accumulation but remained fragile while trying to metamorphose into a modern corporation. Can Huawei navigate through this valley? Then, the next questions would be: If Huawei should learn to get better, who should it learn from? And what should it learn? By 1997, Huawei had developed its own management system, with some concepts and models, based on its own experience, its acquired knowledge, and the wisdom of its leaders. Yet this system was simple and locally oriented, and the concepts and models were merely slogans. It proved unfit for the company's further growth, especially when it was going global. Huawei needed a new system badly. It had to learn from leaders, in particular its American counterparts.

In late 1997, Arleta Chen, a senior executive of IBM, gave Ren Zhengfei a book about integrated product development (IPD) transformation, which marked the start of Huawei's learning from an American company. Since then, IBM has helped Huawei build up a complete modern business management system, including management processes and corporate culture. In this way, IBM has earned a considerable amount of service revenues and promoted its own corporate culture and organization philosophy. Of course, Huawei has benefited even more. With the clues and instructions from IBM, Huawei has undergone dramatic organizational transformation and learned how to control the power and braking system of the BMW. It has eliminated disorder in the organization and laid solid ground for an organizational and corporate culture that is more East than the West and even more West than the West.

This is exactly the power of openness. Without strong courage and the determination to open up, Huawei could not have become what it is today. In contrast, a lot of Chinese companies have also bought advisory services from leading American consulting companies, such as McKinsey and Accenture, at a high cost, but few have reaped the benefits. Some of them, as the joke goes, have died even sooner after taking the pills prescribed by their foreign doctors. Why? There is the problem of cultural differences, but the key problem is their leaders are not really committed to openness. They would lose their heart midway when trouble arises. Of course, they may not possess the necessary wisdom to manage the reform and opening-up process.

Hunting Huawei: What's Wrong with the United States?

A special briefing took place at the US House of Representatives, and Ken Hu, Deputy Chairman of Huawei, appeared before the panel to answer their inquiries:

Interrogator: Is Ren Zhengfei a member of the Communist Party of China?

Ken Hu: Yes. Just as some American businessmen are Democrat or Republican.

Interrogator: Did Ren Zhengfei serve in the People's Liberation Army?

Ken Hu: Yes, sir, just as many American businessmen once served in the US Army.

On February 25, 2011, Ken Hu published an open letter addressed to the US government to clarify false allegations by some Western media and politicians, including "close connections with the Chinese military," "financial support from the Chinese government," "disputes over intellectual property rights," and "threats to the national security of the United States." The open letter also invited the US authorities to conduct a formal investigation into any concerns they may have about Huawei.

The allegation of military ties is nothing new. These claims lay their entire basis on the fact that Huawei's founder and CEO, Ren Zhengfei, once served in the PLA in a position equivalent to that of a deputy regimental chief, yet his position had no actual military rank. This "coming up from the military" is not rare in the United States, where about two-thirds of chairmen and vice-chairmen of Fortune 500 companies, and one-third of their CEOs, have graduated from West Point. West Point is not only a military academy but also an incubator for business leaders: It has produced as many industry captains as all business schools in the United States combined. After World War II, the three major military academies, West Point, the United States Naval Academy, and the United States Air Force Academy, have turned out over 1,500 CEOs, 2,000 presidents, and 5,000 vice presidents at Fortune 500 companies, as well as thousands of SME leaders. Does that mean their companies are connected with the US Army?

In response to the allegation of financial support, or more specifically US$30 billion each year from the Chinese government, Huawei explained, "For the past decade, Huawei has engaged KPMG, a US-based global accounting firm, to audit its financial statements. We would like to know, as people do, where the US$30 billion came from and where it has been spent." Huawei had also issued similar statements through some European media outlets.

From 1993 to 2012, the world has undergone unprecedented changes. It is a revolution indeed. And the United States, by virtue of its open and innovative culture, has brought the human race into the irre coverable past and the unpredictable future. In the past 20 years, through creative disruptions, the United States has produced a number of legendary companies such as Google, Yahoo, Microsoft, Cisco, Apple, and Facebook, and the strength of the country is derived from hundreds of super corporations that are richer than some countries.

The American community believes that the country's core competitiveness rests with its businesses. Meanwhile, the American people, who hold strong faith in empirical and pragmatic philosophy, also believe in the law of natural selection, or the jungle law of survival of the fittest. Therefore, over the past two decades, innumerable American businesses, including some giants, have fallen, collapsed, or disappeared amid stormy technological changes.

Like Cisco and Apple, Huawei is an emerging company that rose above the horizon just 20 years ago. It has risen through learning from American companies, and in this process, it has witnessed one American giant after another falling down and out.

Since 2003, however, a number of American companies have taken shots at Huawei, while the American government and media have accused the company of posing a national security threat and engaging in unfair competition. Later their fire against Huawei intensified, and the aim was clear: They wanted to fend Huawei off the American territory. The plot behind these allegations is observable: They are masking protectionism agendas amid concerns over national security in order to defend the market position of American companies.

Since 2007, Huawei has fallen victim to a continuous onslaught of false allegations from Western media. The most common story starts with Huawei's dubious background and its sales of equipment to Iraq and Iran that threaten the national security of the United States. One of the most absurd claims was from the *Wall Street Journal* asserting Huawei had assisted the Iranian government in tracking dissidents. Huawei had issued an official statement of denial condemning the report as false, deliberately misleading, and materially untrue.

In 2007, 3Com Corporation announced a definitive agreement to be acquired by Bain Capital, a leading global private investment firm. As part of the transaction, Huawei would acquire a minority interest of 16.45 percent in the company and become a commercial and strategic partner of 3Com. But this deal was resisted by several congressmen and denied by a very high-ranking official of the Federal Government. In 2010, Huawei again planned to buy out a small American company at the price of US$2 million, but this small deal had been vetoed by the American government as well.

Once again in 2010, Huawei offered to buy the wireless network business of Motorola at a premium over the leading contender, but this bid was denied by some people in the US Congress. In fact, Huawei had been the original equipment manufacturer (OEM) of Motorola's wireless products, where proprietary technologies of Huawei were being used.

In the same year, five US senators tried to bar Huawei's bid to supply equipment to American operator Sprint.

In this process, the mainstream US media had fanned the flames.

What's wrong with Huawei? As a retired senior American politician admitted, Huawei has cast terror on its competitors for its sweeping success around the world.

One morning in August 2012, I was having breakfast with Ren Zhengfei at the Ritz-Carlton in Beijing when a middle-aged man in a neat suit approached us. He presented his business card, saying that he was an executive with Citigroup China and that he was discussing a financial deal with Huawei and he needed the support of Mr Ren. CEO Ren replied: "Sure, but I suggest you go to Guo Ping directly. He is responsible for all financial affairs. But you guys in the US are sometimes too closed and political. In comparison, the UK is much more open."

Section II. Openness Is a Choice, But There Is No Other Choice

Openness Is a Way of Thinking

In 1954, Albert Einstein pessimistically predicted: "The unleashed power of the atom has changed everything save our modes of thinking, and thus we drift toward unparalleled catastrophe." In retrospect, his prediction has been partially right. Over the past 60 years, the human world has gone through quite a few major crises, including two financial crises triggered by the United States. Yet we have survived. Why? Because we have changed our way of thinking. Einstein had not predicted that our way of thinking may change according to external circumstances, and we are always able to detect opportunities even in a crisis-stricken world. That gives us the capacity to always move forward.

Huawei has grown by leaps and bounds in the past two decades because it has an open mind to embrace changes. On the other hand, some large and established companies have clung to their glorious tradition and behaved in a fixed, proud, and conceited manner. They don't care about change. As a result, they have been overtaken by new startups, such as Google, Apple, and Huawei, who do not have a long history or tradition. A company may be underprivileged if it has no root in tradition, but this lack of tradition may turn out an advantage in an age when external changes outpace internal reforming efforts. Free from any restraint, it can easily break away from old rules and participate in the formulation of new rules. With an open mind, Huawei has developed a unique culture that combines both Western and Eastern characteristics. This is a secret to its rapid growth.

Ren Zhengfei is also an open business thinker who embraces the West and the East, the modern and the traditional. He has developed great insights through learning. When he watched a TV series, *The Qin Empire*, Ren Zhengfei was deeply impressed by Shang Yang, one of the most tragic reformers in the history of China. He was awestruck but also felt regretful. He believed that Shang Yang had followed the right direction, but his approaches to reform had been too radical. Radical reforms often come with a dear cost.

Among foreign politicians, Ren appreciates Yitzhak Rabin the most, and claims that he is a student of the former prime minister of Israel. On the other hand, Ren regards Ariel Sharon as a short-sighted politician with his hawkish diplomacy. Ren Zhengfei believes that the policy of giving "land for peace" proves the wisdom and vision of Yitzhak Rabin, and the thinking behind it has become a principle for corporate governance at Huawei.

In 2009, Ren Zhengfei told the story of the Last Supper at the Pentagon. Then he said,

> Now the financial crisis is roiling the market, and the future is unknown. But I don't want our boat to sink. Now that we have chosen to ride on just one boat, we have to stick to our direction and row the boat hard enough.

The Last Supper at the Pentagon refers to a famous dinner offered by the then Deputy Secretary of Defense William Perry to the bosses of arms suppliers in 1993. During the dinner, William Perry warned his guests that the budget was going to shrink and consolidation was essential for their survival. This dinner led to a rash of industry-wide mergers in the United States beginning in the mid-1990s. Of the 50 major weapon vendors in the 1980s, only 5 survived in 2002, including Boeing and Lockheed Martin, which are multisector conglomerates.

Ren Zhengfei has always been an excellent learner. Thirty years ago, he won the title of Model Learner of Chairman Mao's Works, and the writings have certainly inspired him ever since. Some critics are saying that Huawei's management philosophy has clear Maoist features. This is true, but it is totally wrong that Ren Zhengfei is running the company with the thoughts of Mao Zedong.

Among Chinese political leaders, Ren Zhengfei has the greatest respect for Deng Xiaoping. He has asserted many times that Deng Xiaoping is the greatest reformer in the history of China and that Deng's ideological legacy consists of two key words: "Reform" and "open." These words are precisely the recipe for Huawei's success.

Since it was established, Huawei has defined itself as an open organization. Ren Zhengfei strongly felt that Huawei would not survive as an enclosure. He said: "Openness is the basis for the company's survival. If we do not open up, we will die. We must open up while we grow our core capabilities and develop partnerships. Anyway, Huawei must not sway, because to open up is our only choice."

He also said:

> Openness is one of Huawei's core values, which has been the subject of some dispute. People doubted whether openness really matters to such an innovative company. As a result of our past success, the employees, and even the whole organization, have become very confident, proud, and self-conceited,

and they are shutting themselves up. So we have to open up and open up even further, and try to learn from others; this is a must for us to have self-renewing goals, examine ourselves critically, and develop a sense of urgency.

He went on to say:

> We must not force foreign employees to identify with the Chinese way. Perhaps we are not very clear about our own culture. In fact, Huawei's culture is like an onion with many layers; one layer is the British culture, another layer is Chinese, and still another is American. So I believe ours is an open and inclusive culture. We'd rather not ask them to follow the Chinese way, but use their gift with an open mind to enrich our culture.

In 2001, someone proposed to set up a society of doctors; it was unequivocally denied by Ren Zhengfei. He said that this would be a retrogressive organization, and the company should rather set up an Open Society.

Openness is an easy word, but it is a difficult goal. China's road to openness over the past three decades has been bumpy. And the word was not even in Huawei's dictionary for its first 10 years. The company had to manage to survive. It had to win enough contracts and market share, and the company had struggled like a pack of wolves, for which each was a hero and able to strike independently. This was the period of primitive accumulation, when survival was the most important task. The company had to grow up fast or get slaughtered in the market, where cut-throat competition had forced out more than 400 market players.

As Huawei grew larger, openness became a matter of life and death. The company was born as an underprivileged competitor: It was a private company without abundant capital, or a proud history or political background, and none of its founders had ever managed any other company before they started at Huawei. Under this backdrop, Huawei had no choice but to open up, especially in the international market where a closed mindset would be a game ender.

Daniel Chamovitz has an interesting comment on plants, *What a Plant Knows*:

> People have to realize that plants are complex organisms that live rich, sensual lives. But if we realize that all of plant biology arises from the evolutionary constriction of the "rootedness" that keep plants immobile, then we can start to appreciate the very sophisticated biology going on in leaves and flowers. If you think about it, rootedness is a huge evolutionary constraint.

It means that plants can't escape a bad environment, can't migrate in the search of food or a mate. So plants had to develop incredibly sensitive and complex sensory mechanisms that would let them survive in ever changing environments.

This paragraph fits in perfectly to explain why Huawei had to open up: It had to survive amid inherent constraints and the ever-changing environment.

Opening up Is a Forced Choice

Huawei has been closely scrutinized as it pushes forward into the global market, especially in the United States, where the company has been repeatedly "interrogated" by customers and even government officials.

A Chinese official once asked Ren Zhengfei: "Could you please share with other Chinese companies your experience in the international market?" Ren Zhengfei answered:

> The key is to abide by laws. We must observe the laws of countries where we operate and the conventions of the United Nations. In particular, we'd better treat the domestic laws of the US as international laws, because the country is so powerful that its domestic laws have to be followed just about anywhere in the world. On the other hand, China's legal system is not yet complete, and enforcement tends to be a bit arbitrary and randomized. As a result, solid governance and self-discipline are missing at some Chinese companies. They thought they could easily acclimate and succeed in the international market, but they would often end up in trouble instead.

Ren Zhengfei has often cautioned his colleagues in the managing board that Huawei must not live with the perceptions its competitors impose. Circumstances change, and the concern is that leaders' minds become too static and nonaccepting of this fact. For the company not to be labeled as a "mysterious Black Widow" or a "brash gladiator," it has to stay open in all spheres, and it should open up even wider although the company may believe it has always been; otherwise growth would not be possible. But if Huawei is still criticized as being "closed off" or "nonmainstream," it is certainly because the company is not open enough. To illustrate his point, Ren Zhengfei provided an analogy: Imagine you are invited to a friend's home. The host will loathe you if you kick off your shoes and scratch your toes in the living room. Huawei must not behave rudely like this.

We must prove with an even more open attitude that this is a company that plays by international rules.

In 2010, when examining what Huawei had done to achieve openness, Ren Zhengfei was both affirmative and critical. He said:

> Any strong man is balanced. We can be extremely strong, but can we last if we have no friends? No. So why should we defeat everyone else and take the whole world in our hands? Genghis Khan and Adolf Hitler had wanted to conquer the world, but in the end they had perished before their goal was achieved. Huawei will surely fail if we attempt to do the same. Why shouldn't we work with partners, especially strong ones? Our relationship with them should be a blend of competition and cooperation, and we should be satisfied if we enjoy some benefits.

He further commented:

> When we work with others, we cannot act like a black widow. It is a spider one can find in Latin America known for its sexual cannibalism. After mating, the female spider eats its male partner in order to provide nutrition for their offspring. Huawei used to eat up or dump its partners one or two years after the partnership was formed. Now that we have grown stronger, we should not do the same. We must be more open, modest, and broadminded. We must develop better partnerships to achieve mutual wins. Our R&D teams are quite open, but they need to open up further, both internally and externally.

Huawei has been growing fast. Some people may love it, while some others may hate it, because we may have robbed many smaller companies of their business. We need to change this situation; we need to create a win-win outcome through open partnerships. If we have turned many friends into enemies during the past 20 years, we will turn our enemies into our friends in the next 20 years. When the value chain is full of our friends, we will surely go from success to even bigger success.

Section III. Openness: All Roads Lead to Rome

Reinventing the Wheel Versus Using External Resources

On January 27, 2009, the World Intellectual Property Organization (WIPO) published the following news on its website announcing the number of international applications filed under the PCT in 2008:

For the first time, a Chinese company topped the list of PCT applicants in 2008—Huawei Technologies Co. Ltd., a major international telecommunications company based in Shenzhen, filed 1,737 PCT applications in 2008.

Huawei's rise to the world's number 1 led to exultant media coverage in China at a time when independent innovation was hailed as a national priority, although some international media remained cautious and doubtful. Within the company, however, this title brought no jubilation. At an EMT meeting, some senior executives soberly emphasized the downside of such a large number of patents: "The number of patents does not ensure quality. How much royalty have you earned?"

Following a decade of quiet transformation, Huawei has developed a unique culture of composure, rationality, self-restraint, and self-criticism. When the company made its way into the list of Fortune 500 companies for the first time, an executive walked into the meeting room and said, "I have some bad news. We have become a Fortune 500 company." No one applauded or proposed having a celebration. In fact, Huawei had been trying to postpone its entry onto the list.

From 1987 to 2011, Huawei has invested at least 10 percent of its sales revenue into R&D each year. In recent years, more than 50,000 employees and an annual spend of over CNY10 billion have been put in R&D. The outcome of such huge efforts has not pleased the management, however. As a senior executive said at an internal meeting:

> Up to now, Huawei has not produced a single original invention. We have merely enhanced existing product functions or features, or made them more integrated. In other words, our technology achievement has been primarily on the engineering side. We are still far behind our competitors who have been there for decades or even centuries, because we still lack core technologies. We have paid high prices to acquire or license core technologies, and that allowed us access to the international market and to survive in a competitive marketplace. At the same time, this approach costs much less than reinventing the wheel, and we have bought peace with Western companies with paid use of their technologies.

At the China National Science and Technology Congress in 2006, Sun Yafang expressed similar ideas:

> In the past, we have defined intellectual property rights as an issue of international trade to address trading frictions. Most people believed that this

issue was raised by the West as a barrier to contain the development of China. We have therefore tried to defend ourselves from the paws of the Western powers by clarifying that we have not misused any proprietary technology. We have not really understood the strategic importance of intellectual property rights to China's future development. Now we believe we must consider intellectual property rights as a necessary component of our national strategy. We must change the defensive position, and take an active approach by establishing our own system of intellectual property rights. We must attach greater importance to IPR development, accumulation, commercialization, and protection. If no rigorous IPR system is in place to protect the interests of original inventors, we cannot expect anyone to be committed to technology exploration or expect any new original inventions to be made in China. Without a considerable amount of original inventions, China will never reach the technology highland, and we will always be held back by barriers others erect. Chinese companies, rather than our Western competitors, will suffer in the end.

In 2010, Huawei paid US$222 million in patent royalties to its Western counterparts, while its total payout to Qualcomm has exceeded US$600 million, which undoubtedly is the largest royalty any Chinese company has ever paid. As huge as these royalties are, they earned Huawei over US$20 billion worth of contracts.

When an R&D executive reported their engineering achievements, Ren said with a smile: "Brag to me when we stop paying US$200 million a year."

Ren Zhengfei believes that Huawei has to embrace an open mind in its R&D if the company hopes to meet customer needs. This is imperative. Ren explained with a metaphor:

Huawei has managed to carry its banner uphill and planted it on the top. But then it finds out that it has been surrounded by its enemies. Virtually all essential patents in the telecom industry belong to Western companies. After 10 years of technology accumulation, Huawei has been caught in an unpleasant situation: yes, it is on the top of the hill, but it has been barricaded by enemies who occupy the foot of the hill and the hill side.

What can Huawei do? It will starve if it remains on the hill top, but if it goes down it has to buy "passes" or pay for "tolls." In other words, it has to pay royalties for patented technologies or exchange patents. It cannot steal or rob any patent, and it can hardly win a head-on fight.

Since the early 21st century, Huawei has encountered more than a dozen patent disputes or lawsuits each year. From time to time, Ren Zhengfei receives letters from CEOs of Western companies claiming that they would sue Huawei unless he pays them a hefty price for the alleged patent infringements. While earlier cases seemed like dramatic events back then, such patent lawsuits have become routine affairs for the company, and it has also taken legal action against other companies over IPR infringements. This is a common occurrence in the global telecom industry in which the arena may seem overcast with intense hostility at times, but then the dark clouds suddenly disperse as quickly as they appear. Almost all lawsuits in the telecom industry are ultimately settled peacefully out of court. Why? "That's the rule of the world," as Huawei's Deputy Chairman Guo Ping puts it. He said:

> If you hope to enter the "international club," you must pay a certain price for what you get from others according to international rules. How can you expect to use the proprietary technologies of other companies for free? They have acquired their intellectual properties at a high price as well. They have to pay us if they use our proprietary technologies. Or perhaps we can exchange patents. This is fair play.

In the past two years, Huawei has made peace with its Western counterparts, although there are still some flare-ups over patents. This improved relationship is the result of openness, as well as the balance of power. As Ren Zhengfei predicts, in the coming three or five years, there will be a world war over patents, and China could only engage in a defensive war. Chinese companies, including Huawei, should be forewarned.

The good news is that Huawei has gained enough strength and experience through its battles with the West. Most importantly, Huawei has developed its open strategy and open mindset, which is the key to the company's ongoing success.

Dancing with Wolves but No Alliance

Lawsuits prompted Huawei to become more open.

Huawei has ever since reflected on its strategic positioning: It is apparently not realistic to depend solely on itself, although it has become stronger after a decade of development and able to stand up to the storms.

During its first 10 years of existence, Huawei behaved like a noisy, furious, fearless, and aggressive wolf that seized every chance to grow. But during the second decade, it became much quieter and refrained as it transformed and expanded in peace. Now, Huawei has emerged as a world-class corporation, a gigantic ship that can sail through turbulent currents. It has turned the table around, or at least it is at par with its Western counterparts. Therefore, Huawei can afford to open up its door wider and with more courage. Now Huawei has given up the tradition of fighting alone; its new principles are mutual benefit, compromise, and cooperation, but no alliance.

Ren Zhengfei believed that, in this new world, technologies are renewing rapidly, and the market is changeable. Huawei cannot afford to always reinvent the wheel, and it does not possess the capacity to dominate the market. Neither does any top player in the West. In this context, Huawei should foster partnerships with its competitors in order to build up its strength and presence.

In 2005, Ren Zhengfei emphasized partnerships with competitors as a strategic priority of its future development. He said:

> Seven or eight years ago, we proposed to give land for peace, and to build up partnerships with our counterparts to complement each other's strengths and create more value for our customers. Now, we have been recognized by more people, and our competitors have come to treat us as their friends. While we compete to provide better customer services, we work together to lower development costs. This change in the paradigm has fueled our growth momentum and reshaped the development trajectory of Huawei.

In recent years, Huawei has built worldwide partnerships for technology and market development. The company has set up joint labs with Texas Instruments, Motorola, IBM, Intel, and Lucent Technologies, and established research institutes in India, Switzerland, and Russia. It has also set up over a dozen joint innovation centers with its customers in order to better understand customer needs. Meanwhile, Huawei has built joint ventures with Siemens, 3Com, and Symantec to complement technology and market strengths. Ren Zhengfei said, "These years we have been trying to work with our international peers to share resources and create mutual success. We would like to see a symbiotic market where all players depend on and help each other. This is an ancient philosophy in the East." Of course, partnership is not equal to alliance. Any alliance, in essence, is a close-end system that runs counter to openness. If it enters into an alliance, Huawei would confine itself in a new closed circle or even become the prey of its allies. In history, numerous alliances between countries or between companies have ended in tragedy. China has been committed to nonalliance in its foreign relations policy, and this has proven to be the right choice.

In 2005, Microsoft CEO Steve Ballmer visited Huawei headquarters and met with Ren Zhengfei. Without much courtesy, he directly requested Huawei not to join the antimonopoly movement against Microsoft. Ren said: "It is the responsibility of the government to prevent monopoly in the market. Huawei does not have the duty or necessary competence to stop any monopoly, although open competition is helpful for technology innovation and social progress and serves the benefits of consumers." Ren Zhengfei, of course, knew very well that Huawei had forced back some of its competitors with antitrust appeals, and open competition is critical to its survival. But Huawei would not choose to launch any antimonopoly movement. He said:

> Isn't it good for Huawei to stay under the umbrellas of industry captains? We would still make a very good life if we sell at lower prices while the giants sell the same at higher prices. If we tore down the umbrellas, we would be exposed to the scorching sun and our sweat would nourish the grass which would take away the ground from under our feet at even lower prices. So why should we bother?

A Cup of Coffee: Communicate with World Leaders

One afternoon in October 2011, Ren Zhengfei met with Eric Schmidt, Executive Chairman of Google, at the head office of Google in Beijing.

Schmidt greeted Ren: "Huawei is the most successful story of China. You're changing the world. You're a great magician." Ren Zhengfei replied:

> We are still in the 18th or 19th century of the West, the age of cost plus quality. We have entered this industry because we were not smart enough. We have depended on cheap labor for two decades, but as the cost of labor rises in China we will gradually lose our advantages. In five years, we expect our sales to reach US$70 billion, but we cannot count simply on continuous expansion. We have survived by driving up the scale to lower the unit variable cost. This won't work anymore in the future.

Eric Schmidt said: "All my life I've dreamt of connecting the entire world. Google has developed close partnerships with many companies. We're convinced that Huawei will be a leader in the future."

Ren Zhengfei said: "The flood in 2012 will not subside. It will get even bigger. Of course this flood refers to the deluge of data. Google provides the water, and we provide the pipelines. We always believe that this world is full of enormous opportunities."

Eric Schmidt could not agree more.

Ren Zhengfei, now 68 years old, is always keen on thinking, and his mind is open to ideas. He takes great interest in reading books on politics, economy, society, humanity, literature, and the arts. He reads history books the most, while fiction and management books are least read. He explained: "Fiction is just invented stories; they are too far from reality. Management books are produced by professors behind closed doors. They would restrict your imagination and inspirations. Corporate management cannot be boiled down into just a few tenets."

Communicating with the people of various kinds is one of his most important jobs. Over the past two decades, he has visited most countries in the world, from the most developed to the least developed. He has broadened his vision having talked with hundreds of politicians, business leaders, scholars, competitors, scientists, artists, and monks. Perhaps Ren Zhengfei is the best informed business leader, and a most outstanding business thinker in China.

Ren Zhengfei encourages and requests his colleagues on the managing board to communicate with world leaders. The global village, in some sense, is an open college full of information and knowledge.

According to Ren, coffee breaks are an opportunity for people to hang out and talk with others over a cup of coffee. Then why not a cup of tea? He believes that tea is something of the East, while coffee is a global drink and a symbol of global culture. Ren Zhengfei argues that Huawei is part of the world and must stand firm at the forefront of the world.

Often mocking himself as a bumpkin, Ren Zhengfei is honest and candid. He never beats around the bush. After a meeting with Ren, Texas Governor Rick Perry said: "Mr. Ren is a very interesting man. He is as straightforward as a Texan. He won't just say what you would love to hear. … To some extent, Huawei represents a high standard. …

Unlike Ren Zhengfei, Sun Yafang is more elegant. As a Harvard Business School graduate, she speaks fluent English and behaves with propriety. Therefore, Ren Zhengfei nicknamed her Huawei's image ambassador. Unlike Ren Zhengfei, who easily dominates the conversation with his charisma and is able to create "creative frictions" from time to time, Sun Yafang is more patient and skillful in communicating with bigger potatoes.

Ken Hu, Huawei's Deputy Chairman and rotating CEO who was once in charge of the company's global sales, exudes a peaceful power. At various global summit meetings, such as the World Economic Forum in Davos, Ken Hu meets with world leaders in a very casual manner and chats in the lobby over a cup of coffee. In recent years, as Huawei's ambition in the US market is defeated, Ken Hu has often traveled to the country and met with politicians, business leaders, think tanks, and public relations agencies, having candid conversations and answering their inquiries without reserve.

Guo Ping, another Deputy Chairman and rotating CEO of Huawei, has also earned a reputation in the American IT and legal communities, for his central role in combating lawsuits filed against Huawei in the United States.

As one American said, "[T]he West is not a monolith." There are divided opinions between the European Union (EU) and the United States, and even between the United Kingdom and the United States. American companies do not speak with the same voice, either. Therefore, it is right for Huawei to communicate openly and extensively. The US market will accept Huawei one day; it is only a matter of time.

Huawei believes similarly that the world is not dark all over, and Huawei will see sunshine in every corner of the world someday. At this moment, however, Huawei still needs strategic patience. Well, Huawei has developed it because it has been growing through patient waits and aggressive attacks. For Huawei, according to Ren Zhengfei, it is important that the company opens up its mind's eyes, and embrace the whole world. He said, "Do not focus exclusively on ME, but think about the world at large. Everyone should consider how we can help make the world better, and we should feel proud if someday we do. That's good enough."

Section IV. Openness Is an Art of Mind

Destruction Is Easier than Creation

The contemporary people seem to be afraid of quietness. Huawei was born in the grassroots, and to many people its rise has been astonishing.

The company had awed its Western counterparts in its first 10 years and has soared in just two decades to the world's number 2 spot, second only to Ericsson. At first, few believed that this is the result of market competition, and some even invented stories about the company's background. Now there are still quite a few people, both inside and outside the industry, who argue that Huawei's success is credited to nonmarket factors, or otherwise, as they would ask:

Why wouldn't Huawei go public?
Why does Huawei avoid contact with the media?
Why does Ren Zhengfei reject media interviews?

Most Chinese entrepreneurs are caught in a dilemma: Being vocal would be criticized as ostentatious, while keeping quiet would be viewed as disguising dark secrets. They are always under microscopes and even distorting mirrors that will not leave them alone until they finally fall and die.

For quite some time, Huawei has had an almost morbid fear of the media because Ren Zhengfei has seen so many tragic heroes fall in this age of the Internet when a drop of spit may cause a tsunami. The top 10 entrepreneurs in the 1990s have fallen, and the top 10 in the first decade of the 20th century have essentially disappeared. Among the business celebrities who made headlines and stood in the spotlight, how many are still on stage?

Since the reform and opening-up program started in China, a number of business adventurers have reached center stage, including Nian Guangjiu, who made a fortune selling fried melon seeds; Bu Xinsheng, who broke up the Iron Bowl on which the employees of his factory had been fed comfortably; Ma Shengli, who was the first businessman in China to be granted rights to run a company through a lease contract; Lu Guanqiu, who changed from a farmer into a large corporation owner; Chu Shijian, who championed SOE reform; Ni Runfeng, who turned Changhong into a leading producer of televisions; Mou Qizhong, who trod the line between politics and commerce; Shi Yuzhu, who occupied the market through tidal waves of advertisements; Zhang Ruimin, who created the legendary Haier model; and Liu Chuanzhi, who guided Lenovo's transformation from a technology-led company to a sales-led conglomerate.

Sadly, many of these adventurers had failed to resist temptations and had lost themselves in the arms of the media when their companies were at the most critical pass. As a result, many stars had fallen like short-lived meteor. This is the tragedy of the Chinese business community and a miserable page in the history of Chinese businesses.

To climb uphill is tough, while falling downhill is much easier and faster. The most tragic part of the story is when businessmen opt out of their original role and are enticed by the lure of the limelight, putting on dancing shoes and makeup. They may not realize that the same people who cheered the loudest are also the first ones to denounce them and eventually dig the grave for them. They would lose their luster someday, and then find themselves in the corner of oblivion.

As a Chinese saying goes, a building may fall just days after it is built. During the 30 years of China's reform and opening-up, numerous business stars rose to take center stage only to quickly fade away. This short history seems very much like a tragic comedy. One may wonder why. The reason is very simple: Danger is near when one is exposed. The mission of a merchant is to make profits, and it is taboo to seek fame. In this diverse world, everyone or every trade plays a definite role, and the title of "stars" is for performers, politicians, and some other circles. Entrepreneurs and merchants, on the other hand, should keep themselves as far away from this stage as possible. No one can attain both profit and fame at the same time. Merchants should refrain from fame as politicians should not seek for profits. Over the past three decades, too many Chinese business leaders have jumped into the limelight to taste their victory, but they had not expected that they were like moths jumping at the flames. The end is tragic, of course. This sweet taste of fame is transient, and worse still, their companies may also fail in no time. On the contrary, those who have held themselves back from the carnival can most likely survive and become real leaders. Quiet in the shade for now, they could be tomorrow's lasting stars who build enduring world-class business empires.

1998–2008: A Decade of Being Open and Closed

Opinions concerning Huawei's openness differ greatly.

The company's management believes Huawei is open. As Ren Zhengfei said:

> Huawei must embrace globalization and avoid the narrow mindset of nationalism and protectionism. Therefore, we have tried from the very beginning

to create an open culture. Through competition with Western companies, Huawei has learned to compete and improved its technology and management. We believe that Huawei may not become a globalized and professional company unless it gets rid of a narrow sense of pride, and it may not mature until it gives up its narrow brand awareness.

The decade from 1998 to 2008 is the most open period of Huawei; it has learned the most from Western companies. During this period, Huawei established partnerships with more than 700 telecom operators worldwide and worked with more than a dozen consulting firms from the United States, Europe, and Japan on IPD and integrated supply chain (ISC) transformation in developing a management platform tuned for the international market. Huawei once hired a German as its vice president for procurement, and during the two years he was in charge, the procurement system had modernized a great deal. Even in the hardest years after the IT bubble burst, procurement was able to save more than 2 billion a year. Huawei now employs 29,700 non-Chinese nationals, 20.19 percent of the total workforce, including 7.56 percent from other Asian countries, 4.92 percent from Europe, 2.93 percent from South America, 2.85 percent from Africa, and 1.72 percent from North America. The presidents or chairmen of Huawei's subsidiaries in the United States, Europe, and Japan are mostly foreigners. Last but not least, Huawei's relationship with international peers is also very special: They are partners as well as competitors.

Isn't that sufficient to prove Huawei is an open company? Perhaps not, because the key rests with its media strategy.

Openness is an art of mind. It takes great deliberation to decide as to when the company should open its window? When should it open its door? When to open both? To whom? And how wide?

In fact, Huawei has been inspired by China's progressive opening-up program. The company must open up across the board. This was the mega trend of the 1980s. But the company may still control how and when it could be opened up. It could decide the level of opening-up according to its own strength and maturity.

In 1998, Huawei started its adaptive reform program. The top management of the company understood that this radical process transformation to westernize the whole company would surely trigger cultural clashes or even extensive resistance. In the worst scenario, the reform might abort and the company might collapse. After all, this was a large-scale organizational reform that would substitute processes for man, automation for personal will, and cold rules for interpersonal emotions. This had been unprecedented, and even now we have not seen many successful cases. Therefore, it was especially important to rule out any internal or external interference, especially from the media. According to Eric Xu, Huawei's Deputy Chairman and rotating CEO, this was a critical program that would decide the fate of the company, so the company should be left alone to make its own decisions. Moreover, since the internal and external environments were uncertain, the chance of success would reduce further if the media meddled in. Fortunately, Huawei had been able to remain level-headed and shy away from the media for nearly a decade. Otherwise, the company might have fallen already. Huawei had been able to fend off the media because it was and still is a private company without any obligation of disclosure. Of course, the company is different now from what it was 10 years ago, as its transformation has been essentially completed, and it is much stronger to survive any odds.

Nevertheless, the media and general public hold a different argument. Huawei is portrayed as a closed and mysterious company. Few seem to have noticed Huawei's open strategy for market and technology development, and the increased openness of its operations and management.

In China, on the contrary, there are companies that take a welcoming approach with the media but, in fact, they lack the nerve to open up their R&D, market, and organization in the real sense. This contrast deserves attention.

Huawei's estrangement from the media began in 1998 when its sales totaled CNY89 billion, the highest among the four major Chinese telecom equipment companies. Huawei had reached its first peak: No. 1 in China. But at that moment, Ren Zhengfei and his company were not thrilled or proud; instead, they felt unprecedentedly lonely, anxious, lost, and terrified.

They were wondering what Huawei's next step would be. Huawei had to plan its future and were aware that they had to undergo a metamorphic organizational and cultural change. Since then, Huawei had opted for silence, shunning interviews and forums, and dodging awards like an ostrich hiding its head in the sand.

This silence has lasted for a whole decade. According to Ren Zhengfei, the company had kept silent because he, his team, and his organization had to focus on their own transformation and development. The success, or more exactly the sense of victory, would fetter their progress.

Without external disruptions, they could move forward with lighter but firmer steps.

In 2005, *TIME* magazine included Ren Zhengfei in its list of 100 Most Influential People of the Year. This should have been a great honor, but Ren Zhengfei told his colleagues:

> Don't care too much about external comments. We'd better focus on our job. I won't care a bit about the list. I will be as light-hearted and forgetful as you are, and work as hard for the company's future. I have tried to keep away from the media, because I don't know what I can tell them. If I speak too highly of ourselves, I would feel deceptive, but if I say we are no good nobody would believe me. They would even say I am a hypocrite. The only choice is to avoid them and remain silent. I know I have more shortcomings than merits. But people love to pour all the success on one person, so the story won't appear dry. But it is false.

During the decade from 1998 to 2008, Huawei and Ren Zhengfei had kept silent, and the company had completed a historic transformation. Huawei did it because it had remained reasonable, quiet, firm, and persistent. But it had met with the real problem, a crisis this time.

Crisis Led to Complete Openness

In a sense, the history of Huawei is a history of crisis management. Since its establishment, the company has faced many intense predicaments, including crises of capital, talent, and management in its early years, besieging and obstruction from its competitors, the institutional conflicts with the Chinese market system, as well as emergencies that seemingly occurred almost every month. During the past 25 years, Huawei has suffered a great deal, but it has survived and grown up. It is just like a tree. The tree takes root in the earth, but this "rootedness" is a huge evolutionary constraint. The tree, therefore, cannot grow unless it has a strong will against all the foul weather, absorbs nutrients from the earth to enhance its roots and stem, and stretches its canopy to reach upwards.

On May 28, 2005, yet another crisis hit Huawei. Hu Xinyu, a 24-year-old employee, died from viral encephalitis. It aroused a carnival of criticism among the media, and Huawei was denounced as a sweatshop that had worked its employee to death. They went further to criticize the mattress culture, which had supported the survival and growth of the company. On the Internet, especially on some Bulletin Board System sites like *tianya.cn*, there were a flood of bitter messages against Huawei arguing that Huawei was a closed and mysterious paramilitary organization. Most of the messages were apparently posted by Huawei's own employees.

At first, Ren Zhengfei, Sun Yafang, and other Huawei executives were enraged and bewildered. They gave instructions to find out who started the whirlwind and wanted to hold the media accountable for their "false reports." This was surely an unprecedented crisis for the company.

To be fair, Huawei was an open company, and Ren Zhengfei was a highly enlightened entrepreneur. Ever since its establishment, Ren had firmly held the belief that "openness is critical to the fate of the company" and "the company will die if it is not open." In fact, Huawei had always been open in corporate management, R&D, and market penetration, and had taken bold steps to westernize its organizational structure. To some extent, Huawei was already different from its Chinese peers because it was more open than any other Chinese company.

The reality, however, is that Huawei was still not open enough. Its organizational culture, in particular, was closed and rigid.

In the history of corporate management, military concepts have played a significant role. They have found their way into the modern organizations that have tried to improve their structure and efficiency. Ren Zhengfei loved to read the book *The Whiz Kids: The Founding Fathers of American Business*, which includes the stories of 10 veterans who reformed Ford Motors and brought the company around. This is a very good example. A former soldier himself, Ren had transplanted military tenets into the corporate culture of Huawei, including discipline, order, obedience, aggressiveness, unwavering courage, uniform will, and team spirit. These had been proudly labeled as the organizational characters of Huawei. At a casual meeting, an employee asked Ren Zhengfei, "What is the most important lesson you learned from your military experience?" Ren Zhengfei replied, "Obedience." Obedience is a natural and unquestioned obligation of soldiers, but the problem is whether it is the same for corporate employees? The answer is both "yes" and "no." It is true that modern corporate management is inspired by rules of the military. A business organization with a clear goal must have a definite authority to hold everyone together and lead them toward the goal and must have a definite hierarchy where everyone does their own job strictly according to rules. Otherwise, it may not survive in the competitive business world. It is especially true in the standardized assembly-line-based manufacturing sector. It is also true for a start-up company. Apparently, Huawei had acquired its organizational power and competitiveness in its first 10 years, by virtue of an absolute authority that led the company through one crisis after another. It had grown on the basis of a definitively designed hierarchy.

After 2005, however, the internal and external circumstances have changed. First, Huawei started to employ a new generation of intellectual workers, the post-1980 or the Internet generation. They were bound in personality; they were rebellious but they would follow the crowd; they were independent but they would rather depend on others; they were open but they would often shut themselves up in their own world. This is the ME generation. Would the traditional management concepts remain valid?

The ripples caused by the death of Hu Xinyu revealed that Huawei was faced with a dual crisis: That of culture and that of the system.

Success is sometimes very fragile, and frustrations always come in waves. If the death of Hu Xinyu was an isolated case and the media had wronged the management and the company, the suicides of several post-1980 employees certainly deserved the management's serious attention.

In some sense, crises had forced Huawei open. The progress of Huawei over the past two decades has, to a large extent, come from the sensitivity of its leaders to crisis and their strong adaptability to the changing circumstances. This has a lot to do with the company-wide inclination of self-criticism championed by Ren Zhengfei. When the company started its IPD transformation, Ren Zhengfei had reiterated that Huawei must break away from dependence and break down the authority of its leaders, especially its founders. From 2005 to 2008, Huawei had undergone an organizational self-criticism and confrontation. Questions were raised and debated in light of a more transparent media environment and a changing demographic mix of the workforce. Should the company change its corporate culture? Should the company become softer? Among the key elements of the corporate culture, which should be changed and which should be retained? Should Huawei create a more democratic and liberal organizational environment?

As 19th-century critic Walter Bagehot described the British monarchy: "Its mystery is its life. We must not let in daylight upon magic." But is it necessary for Huawei to keep such mystery? Some media took it for granted, or would rather believe, that Ren Zhengfei was the King of Huawei and that Huawei was the incarnation of the will of the state. If they were wrong, why had Huawei and its boss tried so hard to evade them? Why had Huawei refused to let in daylight upon its magic of success?

Ren Zhengfei said, "Time has changed. It is time for Huawei to change. We must become internationalized and more open. Why should we avoid any disagreement? The sky won't fall down, anyway."

The launch of Huawei's internal online forum was a landmark event. All its employees can express their opinions on the online forum about the company or even criticize managers, including Ren Zhengfei. New polices that involve the interests of employees are posted for comment before they are officially endorsed. Forum users are not subject to any taboo; their opinions can be correct, mistaken, fair, prejudiced, negative, or affirmative. Some discussions even turn into animated debates or confrontations.

Once, an employee criticized a regional executive, who later asked the forum moderator for the corporate ID of the employee. When he knew this, Ren Zhengfei said, "Give them my employee ID if it happens again."

Ren Zhengfei explained:

> The more we discuss it, the clearer the truth will be. We should embrace different opinions, because I believe most employees are committed to the company. This is a strategic reserve. We thought at first there would be some risk with it, and now we realize we were wrong. Moreover, if our employees could reach any agreement, things would be easier for management. We can hear more constructive suggestions from our employees, and they are more likely to align their thoughts if our decisions are more transparent. If we make decisions behind closed doors, we will end up in trouble someday.

In late 2010, more than 60,000 Huawei shareholders from over 100 countries and regions gathered at over 300 polling stations and elected 51 representatives who then voted to elect a new board of directors. The whole process was open and democratic without any interference, and the event was rather smooth.

For years, Huawei has convened brainstorming sessions, which are dubbed "meetings of sages," before any major decision gets executed. Since 2010, such sessions have turned even more frequent, and they are conducted in a freer and more democratic way.

Huawei's relationship with the media has also greatly improved. In 2010, Ren Zhengfei said in an unusual tone, "Before the media, we used to act like an ostrich that buried its head in the sand. I believe I can do that, but the company cannot. The company should be more aggressive, but it should also tolerate criticism." The company then made the announcement that any employee may take interviews at their own will and that it would not matter what they express as long as their opinions were based on facts. The company also encouraged its senior executives to meet with the media, and no one would be held liable to any personal opinions. According to Ren Zhengfei, the public relations manager should not claim that he had done a good job if he did not make one or two mistakes each year. He said:

> The media relations manager should speak boldly. The company will not collapse because he or she makes an incorrect statement. If we stumble over any one misstatement, we don't deserve anything in this world. Huawei must tolerate criticism. As you see, I've been calling on our colleagues to speak out loud, even if they don't agree with me or other senior executives. We may not always be right, or at least I may not always be right. Therefore, I must reassure everyone in the company that no one will be punished for speaking their mind. Of course, if a wrong statement is made, we must discuss it and try to avoid it. But no punishment or retaliation should be allowed. No one should be hurt or suffer from free expression. We're not living in a forbidden city.

However, Ren Zhengfei was still cautious and drew a bottom line: "Don't attempt to befriend the media for any utilitarian purpose. Yes, we should improve our relationship with the media, but we should never attempt to use them." Since 2010, Huawei has invited a number of domestic and international media representatives to visit its head office and has proceeded to give many interviews.

CHAPTER FOUR

Compromise: The Law of the Jungle

Section I. Transforming from Warrior to Judo Master

The Historian's Visit to Huawei

On November 24, 2003, Qian Chengdan, Professor at Peking University and a distinguished scholar of British history, gave a lecture at the Political Bureau of the CPC Central Committee on the "History and Development of Major Countries Since the 15th Century." His lecture aroused great sensation, not because the lecture was presented to the top leaders of China but because he had revealed an unusual historical perspective.

Half a month later, Professor Qian visited Huawei and gave a lecture on essentially the same subject. His audience was over 300 mid-level managers and senior executives of the company, including Ren Zhengfei and Sun Yafang. Before he started, Professor Qian requested that none of the listeners record the lecture, take any notes, or disseminate his ideas.

About a decade has since passed, and the ideological climate of China has been completely transformed. Professor Qian lectures in public, much more often, and his ideas have received mainstream recognition and approval. With the academic advice and instructions of Professor Qian, CCTV produced a documentary titled *The Rise of the Great Nations* in 2007, which became a nationwide topic soon after it was aired. Ren Zhengfei bought 200 copies of the documentary and asked Huawei senior executives to discuss it after they had all watched it through.

It was at the end of 2013, when Huawei reached a critical juncture in its march to the international market as a new entrant. And a lawsuit was turning this strange face into a familiar one throughout the global community. Huawei was faced with many tough issues, particularly cultural conflicts. Would the world accept this Chinese company, which was already being dubbed a rule breaker? And how would Huawei participate in the international business arena, a game predominated by the West?

Professor Qian provided Huawei a historical and cultural perspective that allowed the company to envision its future. The leadership realized that studying the West, visiting Western countries, and communicating with Westerners would fall far short of the international skills needed if the company was to break into global markets, especially in Europe and America. Huawei had to acquire a systematic understanding of Western culture and institutions and develop the right way of thinking that could guide the company through challenges abroad.

One may wonder how Spain and Portugal had risen to power. Both of them were small countries in the 15th and 16th centuries: Spain had only a land area of 500,000 square kilometers and a population of six million; the land area of Portugal was not more than 90,000 square kilometers and its population was merely two million. But they had virtually occupied the whole world. Why? Their strength had come from their mercantilist agenda. They had navigated all the oceans and traveled far throughout the world. "They would attempt to profit first through trade, and then plunder—and whenever business was not good, they would loot." They had, in short, taken the world through undisguised robbery and armed adventure guided by a uniform national will and a strong primitive desire for expansion.

In the 17th century, an even smaller country took the place of Spain and Portugal. The Netherlands, which had only 45,000 square kilometers of land and a population of one million, grew to become one of the major economic powers of the time. By 1700, the Dutch owned more than 10,000 merchant ships at numerous ports, transporting just about every good from and to each locale the world over. They also created the earliest credit and financial system, and most importantly, the earliest banks. In this sense, mercantilism was very mature in the Netherlands.

The Netherlands remained the center of the world until its decline in the 18th century, when it was replaced by the United Kingdom and France as world powers. According to Professor Qian, both the United Kingdom and France had taken two steps in developing their capitalism: moving from early mercantilism to late mercantilism, and shifting from mercantilism to industrialism. Both were critical steps of modernization.

The United Kingdom, in particular, had ensured its lasting power and prosperity through industrialization, which was a new form of capitalism.

In the 17th century, the British population was only four million, about half that of Spain and a quarter that of France. But the United Kingdom became a global empire, the empire where the sun never sets. With a still rather small population of 40 million in its prime time, the British Empire controlled 50 colonies with a total population of 345 million and total land area of 11.6 million square kilometers (96 times more than the land of the United Kingdom).

What inspired the senior management of Huawei the most was the Glorious Revolution. As Professor Qian said, "The Glorious Revolution of England in 1688 avoided violence and war, and avoided involvement of the people in the change of the monarch. And the revolution established the supremacy of parliament over the crown, setting Britain on the path toward a parliamentary democracy." This is the last revolution in British history, but there was no bloodshed or loss of life. What was the secret? The key was rational negotiation and compromise. All interested parties, including the king and the lords, had quarreled, bargained, threatened, and induced one another until they finally reached an agreement that would benefit all in the country. So to speak, they had substituted their tongues for guns and exchange of words for bloodshed. Compromise is a derogatory word for Chinese people, but it had inspired the capitalist ideology and nurtured the strongest capitalist country—the United States. Commenting on the congressional system of the United States, Hendrik Willem van Loon, an American author and journalist, said, "Compromise has saved a nation and founded an empire."

In the eyes of the media, especially the Western media, Huawei was depicted as a predatory, autocratic, and intolerant company. Apparently, such a perception would hold the company back in penetrating the international markets. It is true that, for over a decade since its establishment, Huawei had acted aggressively like a hungry wolf or a pirate, in order to survive in the cut-throat jungle. Huawei had been, to some extent, characterized by offensive and even suicidal competition, and this character was restricting its further progress. On the other hand, while its highly centralized governance had been a solid guarantee for efficient operations and rapid growth, many mistakes had been made, especially in staffing management positions.

Huawei's Chairwoman Sun Yafang said, "Huawei has been too rigid for years, and we are turning stiff. We must now change."

So, how would the rise and fall of Western powers inspire an Eastern company?

Must East Wind Really Prevail over the West Wind?

Huawei has been making compromises during each stage of its development. Ren Zhengfei founded the company, but he has continued to dilute his interest to make Huawei an employee-owned company. Isn't that a compromise? Ren Zhengfei has compromised with tens of thousands of his colleagues, exchanging his interests for the unity, motivation, and stable progress of the company over the years. This is a rare case among Chinese entrepreneurs, and even the global business community.

Some scholars compare Ren Zhengfei's compromise to a policy of redemption. They argue that Ren is trying to lure everyone in the organization onto the same boat by giving them material incentives, and he acts as the captain to lead the boat toward a certain destination. His destination is becoming a world-class telecom equipment provider, and he intends to accomplish the goal by upholding the corporate core values of customer centricity and dedication.

Ren Zhengfei has never disguised his intention. He compares this practice to the division of the spoils. He is the chief of a gang of pirates who would capture every boat on the sea and share the loot. Whoever seizes the most trophies could enjoy the biggest share of the gains. As the commander of all pirates and a courageous fighter, the pirate chief is also in charge of distributing the bounty. Fairness would be realized only if the gains are shared on the basis of contribution. This would be especially attractive to the hungry and the needy, and followers would gather in a bigger and bigger crowd. Indeed, for about 20 years, Huawei has built up an "army" of more than 100,000 employees.

Excellent leaders must possess such will to share gains and make compromises. But such primitive culture of compromise and sharing "wine and meat" is likely to create superstitious faith in the leader and dictatorship, and the organizational nerve would turn oppressive and tense. Of course, without a tense nerve an organization is vulnerable, but it would break if it gets too tense. In the several years before and after 2000, Huawei was a highly stressed company almost dictated by Ren Zhengfei alone. During this period, Ren was also extremely nervous and fearful. He recalled, "I was thinking about failure every day, and ignored any success we had made." He was anxious about the fate of the company in case it failed.

Ren Zhengfei, however, was capable of self-reflection and self-criticism. That is what sets him apart from others. In 2000, being aware of the dictating approach across the company concerning the promotion and selection of managers, Ren Zhengfei proposed that compromise was necessary when considering a certain candidate. This was more of a requirement he set for himself than advice to the other senior executives. He once said, "We cannot insist strongly on our own opinions; we should listen to more voices."

In 2001, in an essay titled "Huawei's Winter," Ren Zhengfei argued that Huawei should learn from Yitzhak Rabin, Israel's Prime Minister, who proposed to exchange "land for peace." He believed that the company should make certain compromises to ensure its future.

After Professor Qian's lecture at Huawei, the middle-ranking and senior executives started to learn about Western history, reading books and essays and watching TV programs on the modern history of Western powers. They found that Spain and Portugal had fallen from their peak so easily because they had lost their adventurous pirate culture after they got rich enough. And the Netherlands failed because the country had depended too much on trade and finance that were not supported by the real economy. In other words, the country had suffered from excessive speculation. The United Kingdom rose to power and took their place, dominating the oceans and expanding across the world. It had been able to do this because of its industrialization and, in particular, the Glorious Revolution, which substituted compromise for violence and started the modern capitalist system. As Lord Acton of Cambridge University said, "Democracy is gray, while compromise is gold. Compromise is the soul of politics, if not all." Generally speaking, politics would start with controversy and end with compromise, and the Constitution of the United States is the very result of compromise made 200 years ago. Today, the American people are still amazed by the rationality of the Constitution drafters.

Is compromise the soul of business as well? At least partly so. "In the business community, there are no enemies; there are only counterparts and competitors," said Guo Ping, Deputy Chairman of Huawei, who is versed in negotiation with the West. Since 2011, Huawei has started to call its competitors "peer vendors" in its public and internal documents. Compromise is prevalent in business deals, negotiations, collaborations, conflicts, disputes, and agreements, and it is the basis of mutual wins.

Compromise also exists within any company or business team because it may prevent the organization from breaking up due to in-fighting or dictatorship.

For Ren Zhengfei, compromise is the means to unite his team and create the necessary synergy that has driven Huawei's rapid growth. In this process, through self-reflection and self-criticism, he has come to understand "compromise" better: Compromise is more a way of thinking than a means or tool; it means more division of rights than the distribution of gains; it refers to both cooperative competition in the market and team work among colleagues, especially senior executives.

In a speech titled "Openness, Compromise, and Grayness," Ren Zhengfei said:

> For some people, compromise may mean weakness and indetermination, and any hero is uncompromising. This is a typical excluded middle way of thinking. They believe people must be divided into the conqueror and the conquered, and there is no middle ground.
>
> Compromise is in fact a very pragmatic and flexible wisdom of the jungle. Anyone who survives in the jungle knows very well that they should accept offers of compromise or give such offers when necessary or appropriate. One survives through reason rather than passion, after all.
>
> Compromise is an agreement reached under a certain circumstance. It is not the best solution, perhaps, but it is the best before the real best appears. It has a lot of benefits. To compromise does not mean to give up principles. A wise compromise is an appropriate exchange. In order to achieve our primary goals, we can give up some secondary goals. Such a compromise is not an expression of weakness. Instead it ensures that a certain goal is fulfilled through a certain exchange of interests. Of course, any compromise is unwise if it lacks proper balance or misses the primary goal or incurs unnecessary cost in reaching the goal. A wise compromise is an act of art, a virtue, and an essential skill of any manager.
>
> Compromise is indispensable to achieving mutual wins. If we reject compromise, we will face confrontations and may end up in a lose–lose situation.

Several years ago when we drank tea together, Ren Zhengfei said to me, "Should the east wind prevail over the west wind? Or should the west wind prevail over the east wind? Why don't we embrace wind from any direction?"

Huawei had been a rigid warrior, but it is learning to become a Judo master since it acquired the "gene" of compromise.

Section II. The Dialectics of War and Peace

Yitzhak Rabin or Ariel Sharon?

Politics rejects extremes. So does business.

In March 2001, in the essay "Huawei's Winter," Ren Zhengfei commented on Israel's Prime Minister election:

> What is a leader? What is a politician? The election of Israel shows us the myopia of the Jewish people. Yitzhak Rabin was aware that Israel was a small country surrounded by Arabs, and although it had won several Middle East wars, it could not ensure a permanent future because the Arabs were still likely to rise and overwhelm them 50 or 100 years later. He believed that the Israelis would again be forced away from their land if they refused to trade land for peace to achieve harmony with their Arabian neighbors. Should they lose their land, they might not be able to regain it for another two thousand years. Most other politicians, like Ariel Sharon, were too tough and cared too much about their short-term benefits; yet, the Israeli people supported them all the same. I realize for the first time that the Jewish people could be as nearsighted as us.

Who is a good leader? A good leader is an outstanding person who is able to lead a country or organization out of crisis with independent thinking, great vision, and the ability to master trends. Yitzhak Rabin was a good leader, so he had been highly acclaimed by most media throughout the world. At a gathering to mark the 10th anniversary of his assassination, Bill Clinton, former president of the United States, spoke with moving sentiment that he had thought of Yitzhak Rabin almost every week over the past decade. He said if Yitzhak Rabin had not died, Israel would have a great chance to attain complete and lasting peace with Palestine.

What is myopia? When he met with Ren Zhengfei, Simon Murray, British adventurer and businessman, said, "The largest human migration in history took place after the Second World War. About three million Jewish people migrated from the former Soviet Union and Poland to the Middle East and the United States."

The Jewish people are a tough nation that has suffered from frequent oppression and persecution. During the Holocaust, approximately six million Jewish people were killed by Hitler and Nazi Germany. The total Jewish population in the United States, Russia, and Israel is not more than 13 million, but they are a very special ethnic group. One-third of the millionaires in the United States are Jewish; they control a considerable share of the global capital market; they play a prominent role in the political, military, economic, and technology sectors of the United States; 22 percent of Nobel Prize laureates are Jewish, as are half of the 200 most influential Americans; half of the 100 American Nobel laureates are Jewish; one-third of professors at Ivy League universities in the United States are Jewish; one-fourth of the lawyers in the United States are Jewish; 60 percent of leading literary, drama, and music figures in the United States are Jewish; 40 percent of partners at leading law firms in Washington and New York are Jewish; half of the richest entrepreneurs in the world are Jewish; among the Forbes 40 Richest People in America, 18 are Jewish; 37 Jewish-Americans hold office in the US Congress and another 10 in the Senate; and a great many famous figures from history and modern times are of Jewish decent, including Albert Einstein, Karl Marx, Sigmund Freud, Vladimir Lenin, Alan Greenspan, George Soros, and Warren Buffett.

The Jewish people were once banished from Israel, their spiritual homeland, for 2000 years. Therefore, it is understandable that those people in Israel and in other parts of the world are determined to defend their homeland at any cost. This is the goal none of them are willing to compromise and for which Israel has been fighting with its Arab neighbors, including the Palestinians, for decades.

Yitzhak Rabin made a compromise: land for peace. As the descendant of a Zionist, Yitzhak Rabin would rather secure lasting peace for Israel than capture and retain a certain town. But he was assassinated, and his place was taken over by Ariel Sharon, who some have described as being rather shortsighted and hawkish. Sharon is good at pleasing the public and is known as the Modern Blood Libel. After a series of frustrations, however, Ariel Sharon was forced to make compromises in his final years in office, accepting the Middle East Peace Roadmap and acknowledging that "Israel will not occupy the land of Palestine forever." In the end, Ariel Sharon proved to be essentially a pragmatic opportunist, although he did not possess the vision of Yitzhak Rabin.

Should we learn from Yitzhak Rabin, or follow the steps of Ariel Sharon? Ren Zhengfei said, "I am a student of Yitzhak Rabin." Although he has only 1.42 percent share of the company, Ren Zhengfei considers Huawei as his life-long pursuit. In a certain way, Huawei is the testing ground for his corporate ideas. He has been trying to draw inspiration and lessons from the history of China and the world and apply his ideas to the operations and the organizational development of Huawei.

One could learn from Yitzhak Rabin his vision and from Ariel Sharon his pragmatism. But no matter how visionary or pragmatic a politician or a business leader is, he/she needs to make compromises. A famous entrepreneur once said, "If it would help my company, I would rather kneel down." One may find it miserable to kneel down before anyone else, but he/she is still a great man if he/she can get up straight later.

It is especially true in China. When Liu Chuanzhi, the founder of Lenovo, lectures with his back as stiffly straight as a soldier, few people in his audience would know how many miseries he has suffered on his entrepreneurial journey.

The Dialectics of War and Peace

When two armies meet, they have but two choices: Fight or make peace. How they choose in the end depends on their strategies and approaches to fulfill the goal. Zero-sum games are the most common in sports, but in real military situations and in the business environment, fighting is an alternative diplomacy. Most would choose to fight only when no chance of peace is in sight, with the hope of forcing the other party to accept peaceful terms. To challenge or to meet the challenge, one would want to gain the upper hand in the ensuing negotiations. West Point's motto includes "No Compromise," but that applies mostly to soldiers. Of course, in the battlefield, soldiers must go all out when they get the order to charge, and never stop until they secure final victory. They will be evaluated and rewarded for the number of enemies they have killed. The single principle for frontline soldiers is to go unswervingly ahead. This is also true with the business world. The sales force must charge with sufficient aggressiveness and resilience, like wolves or sometimes even like militant gangsters. They must not waver.

In the command center, however, the decision-makers, advisors, and directors play another game. They typically seek to attain their goals while trying to end the war. They balance and rebalance until a compromise is reached that serves mutual benefits. Of course, such a compromise is based on the uncompromising fight of the frontline soldiers. In some sense, a compromise is the wisest way to achieve the most gains at the lowest cost. It should be still noted that any compromise, or even alliance, is temporary and changeable because it aims at a certain gain. After the gains are divvied up, or a goal is reached, they would enter into a new battlefield where they have to charge and fight again and then try to reach another compromise. Naturally, tactics should change to suit different opponents, but the rule remains unchanged that a war is waged to create peace, and compromise is necessary for mutual wins and lasting peace.

Wang Yukun, a famous management expert, once published a short essay about Huawei, titled "The Middle Ground: Decoding Huawei." It is well written as it defies many conceptual labels that the media have assigned to Ren Zhengfei and Huawei.

One of the "labels" is that Ren Zhengfei does not allow any middle ground or he does not allow his subordinates to make muddled compromises that sacrifice principles. Complaint and moderation are infections deeply rooted in Chinese culture with far- and wide-reaching influences. Yet, Ren Zhengfei does not complain, nor does he follow the crowd or take the middle ground. He has been rational to a fault.

This label was given by Zhou Juncang, an author who worked as editor-in-chief for the internal publication *Huawei People*. As a journalist, Zhou has only seen a flat and superficial image of Ren Zhengfei; he is not able to see a round character. In fact, Ren Zhengfei is a contradictory mixture of determination and flexibility, toughness and softness, sense and sensation, and aggressiveness and compromise. Similarly, Huawei's culture is also a hybrid of East and West, tradition and modernity, and conservation and innovation. According to the law of science, a hybrid species is typically more powerful and resilient.

In an essay titled "From 'Philosophy' to Practice," Ren Zhengfei said:

China has long been influenced by the Confucian doctrine of the golden mean. This doctrine has played a significant role in maintaining social order and stability, but has also deterred the growth of heroes and prevented them from driving society forward with their individual strengths.

Ren Zhengfei said once and again on various occasions that Huawei has succeeded because it had not gone to extremes, and the traditional concept of the golden mean has kept the company from falling apart.

Liang Guoshi, a former employee, wrote a book about Huawei titled *The Breakthrough of Wolves* in which he recorded a dialogue with Ren Zhengfei. In 1996, he and Ren Zhengfei took a walk under a snow-covered mountain in Bulgaria. Ren asked him, "Do you know why Huawei has attained so much success?" He did not. Ren Zhengfei told him, "Because we have followed the doctrine of the golden mean."

As Wang Yukun commented:

> Many people may see Ren as a stubborn man obsessed with disruption and aggressive push. What they do not know is that deviation is not Ren's aim. He pulls back to the path time and again and rebalances along the way. The principle is clear: One can never succeed in life or at work if one just takes a predesigned path without making allowances for deviation.

Theory is gray, while life is always as green as a tree. Theory should be enriched and renovated according to circumstances, however, in order to maintain its life. Ideas are evolving, so we cannot fix them on any existing template. Ren Zhengfei advocates compromise, but he also said, "We do not compromise a bit regarding dedication. We should not allow any employee in the company to remain uncommitted and care only about their personal interests; otherwise a lasting prosperity would be threatened." In other words, values must not be compromised. As the soul of the company, its values should be observed to the letter. In another speech, CEO Ren said:

> Openness, compromise, and grayness may not be as important for the junior employees. Of course, it will cause no harm if they get a basic understanding to better their interpersonal relationships, although I have often observed that they misunderstood them. But they are very important for senior management because we must act like a single body under these principles.

What Ren Zhengfei has not explicitly stated is that, as a way of thinking, the doctrine of openness, compromise, and grayness is also a corporate political culture. If it is well developed and implemented, such a culture would hold all senior executives together in an inclusive, open, cooperative, and mutually enhancing environment. They will not act separately as lords anymore. They will not fragment the territory and create antagonism within the organization. Meanwhile, this doctrine is a strategic basis for business competition. Competitors are not necessarily enemies, and competition can be anything other than a zero-sum game. A business should engage its competitors to achieve mutual wins.

The choice between war and peace, offense and compromise, depends on a pragmatic balance of the company's short and long-term goals. There is no single dictating rule or doctrine.

Section III. It Is Not About One Single Man

Dictatorship Is the Natural Quality of a Leader

Being a leader entails making critical choices. A lot of leaders display apparent and similar characters: determination, assertiveness, or even arbitrariness. And they are sometimes dictators. Steve Jobs once said that collective decision making is stupid as it delays time to market and is a way to shrink from responsibility. In some sense, Steve Jobs was a dictator.

Everybody recognizes that Adolf Hitler was a big dictator. When thousands of German soldiers were fighting against the Allies, Adolf Hitler was biting the carpet in the basement of a castle with great anxiety and dread. As a critic said, "The soul of leaders is soaked with stress." But when he appeared in public, Adolf Hitler always appeared determined, courageous, and unequivocal; he did not allow any doubt.

Founder of Hughes Aircraft Company, Howard Hughes, had led a dramatic and sensational life full of adventure. Named "Hero of the Century" by the American people, he was also special because he had a compulsory personality. At times, he would fly his aircraft around the globe, narrowly escaping death on several occasions. At other times, he would shut himself up in a closed room and not take a shower for prolonged periods, only cleansing his body with tissues.

Business organizations resemble a contingent of troops. There are a lot of similarities: Both require their members to fulfill certain goals or tasks within a certain time window and given environment. So, it can be said that business leaders naturally share a certain idiosyncrasy with army commanders: They defy any doubt. In other words, only those who possess this disposition can assume the role of a leader. This is not hard to see as to why a great number of outstanding American business leaders once served in the armed forces.

Both business organizations and the military need "beneficial autocratic rule" rooted in the natural inclination for conformity and obedience. Conformity is a common phenomenon in the biological world, not just in human society. Wild geese fly in a V formation because a lonely goose would feel insecure; sheep live in flocks; wolves would rather hunt in packs even though they are extremely independent; and ants follow a strict order partly because they are reliant on the other ants and the colony. Organizations have appeared because most individuals lack the sense of security, orientation, or confidence if they are left alone.

Organizations are the inevitable result to provide the necessary vehicle for conformity. But, in fact, to be a conformist does not mean one follows the majority; instead, it means to follow a single individual who leads the majority or the organization. The leader is like the queen bee, the alpha or lead wolf, or the ant commander. The leader must be able to keep a clear mind and point to the right direction, create hope for followers caught in crisis, and lead them through. In many cases, the leader must make the decision alone, unable to depend on anyone else in the organization as everyone else might lose composure during times of crisis. Moreover, at such critical moments, too many opinions would be a distraction, and the best opportunity may be missed if the leader is not assertive enough. Making one or two such mistakes is forgivable, but making continued and repeated mistakes would certainly diminish the leader's authority and reputation, and fewer people would be willing to follow.

In this sense, leaders have become dictators because of the collective noncommitment of the majority of the organization. Whoever dares to make the decision and assume the responsibility can possibly become a leader. This is very apparent in Western corporations. The West boasts political democracy, but their companies implement a totally different culture—"CEO Culture"—in which CEOs have supreme power in strategic planning, personnel appointments, and operational decision making. Therefore, the fate of a Western company often depends on a single person.

Howard Hughes had achieved great success thanks to his arbitrary decisions and gambles, but he had missed a lot of opportunities for the same reason. Steve Jobs founded the Apple Empire with his stubborn autocracy, but it was precisely because he was hard to work with and his excessive dictatorial approach that nearly got him kicked out of the company early on.

In the eyes of journalists, Ren Zhengfei is a mysterious dictator. He seems like a tyrannical leader or an ill-bred boor. He may lash out at his colleagues in public and turn a happy occasion into an embarrassing event. He has also lost his temper even when meeting with government officials. At other times, he would go so far as to nudge his employees in the rear. During interactions with others, he often has little patience and dominates the discussion, turning the conversation into a monologue and continuously interrupting others.

However, Ren Zhengfei is a charismatic and engaging leader. He enjoys exceptional authority and influence among the 100,000 employees at Huawei. He is the highest authority in the decision-making panel.

This is perhaps why he has been assertive and tyrannical, especially during the first 10 years of the company. While he is rather liberal or even gets hands-off in business and people decisions, he at times turns overly adamant in his opinion on appointing or using certain managers. In some cases, his insistence had caused significant trouble to the company.

Putting Power in the Cage

The world is changeable, although it operates by rules. Any individual and organization can be assertive or offer compromises. A good leader should be good at offense but he/she also be able to compromise when necessary. Compromise may not mean exactly the same as passive defense. Compromise is a practical art of communication and a form of democracy, which in some sense means the resonation of louder and weaker voices. At first, everyone is speaking their mind aggressively and loudly; they are trying to get their ideas and emotions across to everyone else irrespective of what others say. Then, they begin to draw comparisons: who speaks louder, whose pitch is higher, whose opinions are more reasonable, and who has a bigger say in the group. In the end, compromise would become the key note of the orchestra. Showy musicians in the band tend to produce cacophony, while those must be respected who compromise to make a resounding performance possible. The most important member of all, however, is the conductor who, in a business organization, is the top leader. The leader can neither rush in conducting the performance nor be a soloist on the stage. There should be a bigger picture in mind, for which the wisdom and strength of other members should be pooled. To achieve the goal of the organization, the leader has to be the first to offer a compromise when needed, in addition to commanding the team to charge. An organization may be powerful only if every member acts in unison under the leadership and compromises in the spirit of rationality. Therefore, the best decision is not often the most appropriate; reasonability is most likely the best choice. This is the efficacy and price paid for compromise—the necessary tradeoff.

George Bush, the former US President, believed the most precious invention of the human race is to tame power and put it in the cage. As the top leader of the most powerful nation in the world, US presidents seemingly possess supreme power. However, in the American political system, any leader is entitled to only a certain amount of power. During the eight years Bush was the "master" of the White House, he was not able to unilaterally make decisions on domestic or foreign affairs. His decisions were subject to the approval of the Senate and the House of Representatives, which are always involved in endless bipartisan debates and disputes. In spite of his cowboy impulse, George Bush had not been able to break free from the shackles of the cage. His hands and feet were tied on many occasions as he wrestled with many actors; he had to make decisions and take actions within the framework of compromise.

Theoretically, politics is different from business. Politics concerns the masses while business is a CEO culture. In practice, however, a business is also subject to a governance system comprised of the board of directors and the board of supervisors. Corporate dictatorship is a myth; so is the idea that Steve Jobs never compromised. Some have even brutally commented that Steve Jobs died at the right time, the argument being that if Jobs had survived for another decade and continued as Apple's CEO, his arbitrary heroism and his closed approach to product development would have ruined the company. Perhaps, and only perhaps, the success or failure of the company would have rested with Jobs. However, this is not a rare case in the business world.

Ren Zhengfei admitted that Huawei used to operate under a highly centralized hierarchy. That implies a lot of risks, and the biggest risk is that the company dies if the man is gone. He said, "We cannot bet everything on the survival of a single man. It is fortunate that I had not jumped from the building; otherwise, I wonder what would have become of the company." Therefore, in the coming years, as he argued, "Huawei must rationalize its management system and operation processes. The company should decentralize its decision making and strengthen its supervision system. The two wheels must go in parallel."

Everything depends on the awareness of the top leader, of course. Leaders must get rid of imperialistic or totalitarian mentalities so that their companies can develop a culture of check and balance. Ren Zhengfei said:

> Personal will [have] to be filtered through collective decision making. A leader must learn to make decisions in an open environment where he is subject to restrictions. He must not be afraid of losing his face, as I believe his face is not the top most consideration.

In that vein, when he meets with disagreements at EMT meetings, he insists strongly on his ideas, but a consensus is reached in the end. Ren once said, "I don't expect all my requirements to be satisfied. I have often met with challenge."

At Huawei there has been a principle that the employment of any executive should be subject to a collective decision. This means no single person in the company, not even Ren Zhengfei, would have the final say about employing any executive; every member of the decision-making panel is expected to reach an agreement or compromise.

On January 15, 2011, Huawei convened a shareholders' meeting during which its new directors and supervisors were elected. After the election, Ren Zhengfei gave a speech in which he described the concept behind the newly established symbolic leader role:

> In order to help our executives grow up better and faster, our chairwoman and I will sit on the board as symbolic leaders. Our role is to veto any solution which we don't agree with and force the board to come up with a better alternative. If we believe the new proposal is still not acceptable we would again reject it and ask them to involve more people in the discussion. In this way, we may not make quick decisions as we did in a small team, but we are able to avoid some major mistakes. Moreover, members in the company's decision-making team can be motivated, and our veto is helping in that sense. …In the future, the chairman will be mainly responsible for impeaching managers, while our managers should still be selected through a complete process. In Huawei's corporate system and culture, I shall play a mere supplementary role. Of course I must remain patient and endure the loneliness in order to fulfill my symbolic role. I know very well that any decision involves a long process. People have to brainstorm before they develop any idea, and the idea must ripen before it becomes a decision, and the decision should be adopted and then implemented. I must refrain from interfering with this process. I will disrupt this process if I keep giving instructions. Loneliness is painful, but will be worth it if it can help Huawei succeed.

As the top leader of Huawei, Ren Zhengfei has conscientiously put his power in the cage, and there is more and more democracy and rationality in Huawei's management. Ren Zhengfei said:

> We are in a great time. …None of our major competitors can implement the flexible mechanisms we have at Huawei, while our smaller competitors do not possess any brand power like ours. We should be able to seize any opportunity as soon as it appears.

Many people care about when Ren Zhengfei is going to retire, and many others, including the journalists, believe that Ren Zhengfei would determine the fate of Huawei. This apparently is not an informed judgment. Huawei's future does not depend on a single man, but a group of over 100,000 people who are fighting together as a team.

CHAPTER FIVE

Grayness: Gathering a Hundred Thousand Intellectuals

Section I. Black and White

Diversity of Human Nature

Twenty years ago, I was a psychology lecturer at a teacher's university. At one of the lectures, I gave a magnifier to some students and asked them to observe their skin and describe their observations. Soon a girl cried out, "Terrible!" The other students were shocked, too.

I told them that no one is perfect. Every person, including great leaders, is multidimensional. They are kind in one aspect and cruel in another; beautiful in one aspect and ugly in another. A good person has imperfections, while a notorious person may have something commendable. Whether an individual is good or bad depends to a large extent on the perspective from which they are observed. Therefore, I concluded: First, you cannot take a clear-cut position regarding anyone; you should not love or hate too easily, or you will lose friends and peace of mind; second, since anyone can be a saint and a devil at the same time, you don't have to look up to any individual, but you cannot look down on anyone either; third, you must understand yourself properly, and you should not appreciate or denounce yourself blindly.

This idea was ill regarded in the 1980s. Even today, without proper context, the argument that we must not tell right from wrong apart is still subject to attacks. To the extent of my knowledge, many Chinese people set themselves apart, harbor hostility toward one another, and suffer tension and anxiety, mostly because we are not tolerant enough. We do not accept differences, including those concerning background, personal disposition, social status, and beliefs. Our perceptions are stereotyped: People fall into definite categories, which is an artistic tradition of the Chinese opera.

Of course, art is different from reality. The reality is that people and their life are diverse. A nursery teacher taking care of dozens of kids and the head of a state governing millions or even billions of people face a similar problem. No two people have exactly the same face or character. The world is diverse and complex. In his New Year address in 2012, Dmitri Medvedev, the then President of Russia, said, "We have all kinds of people, and that's where our power comes from." A villager in a remote area of China sighed after he was elected the head of his village, "The heart of the people is like a deep well. If I can manage this village, I can also manage a county."

Human nature is like the universe—vast but tiny, constant but changeable, regular but diversified. It is constant because human evolution is based on hereditary genes, but every man is rendered unique by his education background, family environment, and personal experiences. Therefore, the most challenging task in the world is to recognize, select, transform, and employ people and put them in certain combinations to attain a particular goal. From a country, to a region, and to a family, any organization must understand human nature, and this is always a tough challenge.

As of the end of 2011, Huawei had 138,000 employees, of which 80 percent were college graduates (including 5,000 with doctorate degrees), and the average age was no more than 30. Unlike other Chinese companies, Huawei has a unique mix of employees: Most are young intellectuals, and they come from different countries. Therefore, Huawei faces a pressing imperative to understand and to manage human nature.

When you go deep into the operational model, management system, organizational structure, corporate culture, and the evolution history of Huawei, you will surely find that Ren Zhengfei is a master of human nature, and the success of Huawei comes not only from technologies, market, or resources, but more from an insight into human nature and its success in managing human nature. Although it is complex and changeable, and any organization consisting of diversified members cannot be put into a template, Ren Zhengfei has tied a knot on everything and given it the name "grayness": If you cannot penetrate it, you'd better recognize it, tolerate it, and even appreciate it.

Huawei Training Center in Shenzhen, China
Source: Wu Yi.

In March 2008, Together with Employees from a Supplier, a Huawei Supply Chain Logistics Manager Went to Survey the Warehouse and Road Conditions for a New Project on Kalimantan Island in Indonesia. Due to Muddy Road Conditions, the Vehicle Got Stuck on the Way to the Facility. All Efforts to Dislodge the Vehicle Proved Unsuccessful Even after Numerous Attempts from the Late Afternoon All the Way till Midnight. After Spending the Night Beside the Vehicle, They Treaded the Mountain Roads for Nearly Two Hours Before They Were Able to Find Some Locals to Help Them...

They Eventually Managed to Get the Vehicle Out of the Mud and Successfully Complete the Survey, Paving the Way for the First Project Deployment on the Island.
Source: Lai Leiyu.

An Ice-capped Base Station in Finland
Source: Zhao Baohua.

Ren Zhengfei at the Red Sea Desert (July 2012)
Source: Huawei.

Ren Zhengfei at the Okavango Delta in Botswana (November 2012)
Source: Huawei.

How Base Stations Are Transported Up Mountainous Terrain in Remote Regions
Source: Jhon Jairo Monedero.

A Project Team Went to Check a Site Located in a Remote area Of Africa. As It Was the Rainy Season, Some Low-lying Roads Became Flooded and Some Even Turned into Channels Carrying Streams of Water. Their Vehicle Got Stuck in the Quagmire and Broke Down. Everyone Jumped in the Knee-Deep Water and Pushed and Pulled, Yet They Could not Free the Vehicle. With the Help of Some Locals, They Eventually Succeeded and Got the Vehicle Restarted. In Spite of Extremely Adverse Conditions, Including Electricity Outages, Water Shortages, Underdeveloped Infrastructure, and Local Conflict, Huawei Persisted in Mobilizing a Wide Array of Resources Over a Period of Eight Months to Complete Network Buildouts. This Tenacity Paid Off as 11 States Were Provided with Communications Services That Were Previously Unavailable, Thereby Creating Turnarounds and Opportunities for Development in This Country.
Source: Liu Yaxiong.

A Base Station at the North Pole
Source: Wang Changmian.

May 12, 2008, First wave of Huawei Engineers Restoring Communications after the Massive Earthquake Hit Wenchuan, China
Source: Luo Tao.

Welcome!
Source: Liu Zhixiong.

Huawei R&D Center in Shenzhen, China
Source: Yang Jie.

Baicao Garden
Source: Chen Tao.

Johann Wolfgang von Goethe, the poet, once said, "Viewed from the summit of reason, all life looks like a malignant disease and the world like a madhouse." Then what if we change the perspective?

Ren Zhengfei said:

> We don't expect the manager we select through the competency review process to be a perfect person. A perfect person is a saint, or a Buddha, or a priest. We would rather pick strong fighters who can form an army. Our competency review is a scientific evaluation process by which we hope to upgrade our management that has appealed more to emotions. But an emotional management system has its merit: It does not require perfection, or rather, we do not demand that everyone should be a perfect person.

At a conference reviewing Huawei's cloud strategy and solutions in 2010, Ren Zhengfei said even more directly:

> In the future cloud of Huawei, you may not tell exactly how many leaders will emerge, leaders that are still invisible today. You cannot deny them; they could be the next Vincent van Gogh or Ludwig van Beethoven. Who knows? We once threw away an instant messaging product. We didn't want it. But Tencent picked it up and has become a giant. Why can't we tolerate anyone else walking a different path? Yes, we are walking on the main road with great confidence, but we should also tolerate those who tread on a narrow path. Can you be absolutely certain that the narrow path won't lead to a much broader main road? I mean we should be ambitious, and an ambitious person has a far and wide inner world where there is enough room for various other people and ideas. If you wish to occupy the whole world you must first accept everything and everyone in the world. You must endure any dissident in the core network business unit.

Scientists seek simplicity. They believe that white is white and black is black. Nothing is white and black at the same time. Entrepreneurs, on the other hand, should not go to extremes. If the executives of Huawei put each employee under a microscope on a daily basis, they would drive themselves insane and ultimately break up the company. Facing thousands of people with diverse characters, the managers must possess an open and inclusive mindset as well as strong nerve.

From the historical perspective, Ren Zhengfei elaborated further:

> The Protestant ethics represent the philosophical spirit of religious reform in the Middle Ages. This is the humanist spirit which later evolved into the

capitalist spirit. It is a liberal spirit that embraces and protects personal differences and human rights. In this way, the capitalist spirit releases and motivates the human potential and drives individual and social progress. Capitalism has two major assumptions: The first is that man is selfish; and the second is that man is greedy. The capitalist social system restrains human defects and sets human motives free.

With such a great insight into human nature, the senior management of Huawei has designed and promoted its core values: customer centricity and dedication as the key to success.

Here, the diversity and complexity of human nature are simplified and clarified. Every person at Huawei will play a certain role in the company as long as they have both material and spiritual motives and accept the principle of "more work for more pay," no matter how many defects they may have.

We could say that management by grayness is an invention of Ren Zhengfei and has been first implemented by Huawei.

Science Is a Lamp in the Dark

What is science? What is reason? According to a Western scientist-philosopher, science or reason is a lamp in the dark that has guided mankind all along. In the vast universe, there are innumerable galaxies, and the Earth is but one cold stone rotating in the galaxy by the balance of gravitation and repulsion forces, while mankind is but a special species living on this big rock. Since it had first appeared, mankind has developed great inventions and creations, which are, however, really paltry in comparison with the unknown. From the ancient past, mankind has been trying to light up the world with the flame of science and reason, but there is still darkness under the lamp: There are relative truths and fallacies.

Therefore, great tribute should be paid to accomplished leaders, scientists, artists, and entrepreneurs. They are heroes of the human race; they are the Titan Prometheus who defied the gods and gave fire to humanity, an act that had enabled progress and civilization. There is some risk with them, however. Any deviation of their reason would push mankind back into the dark, and they would become the victims of history.

The same is true with nations and companies, since both national leaders and business leaders are adventurers who usually bet against unknown risks through intuition and calculation. As Ren Zhengfei said,

"A clear direction is often developed amid gray fuzziness, but the direction is changing as circumstances change. It would sometimes turn indistinct again. The world is not either white or black; it is something of both." Ren argued that the mission of a leader is

> to offer his followers a clear direction and lead them down the road. But where is the road leading to? How can they travel on the road? This is a matter of direction and tempo. And what is a leader? A leader should be one like Danko who saved his people from the dark forest by holding up his own ripped-out heart, burning like the sun. We should play the role of Danko and lead the telecom industry down the road.

Steve Jobs had mapped out the direction for Apple; at least Apple was an invincible aircraft carrier when he was still there. Similarly, the leaders of Huawei have gathered over a hundred thousand intellectuals on the ground of grayness, turning the company into a midsized aircraft carrier capable of navigating most oceans in the world. Now, this vessel is venturing into more and greater unchartered seas guided by adventurous captains with a strategic vision and strong will.

Ren Zhengfei, however, often sighs:

> The business environment is changing too fast and too dramatically. No one knows for sure where the road is leading up to. Take cloud computing for example. We have no idea how far we can go with cloud computing. When I was told that Eric Xu knows, I wondered how he could predict anything. He is not God, anyway. God has created mankind with such perfection that your kids would inherit your complexion and character. But as the creation of God, we cannot predict how the information society will turn out in the future. Therefore, we cannot design a perfect business model.

Ren Zhengfei has, therefore, reiterated, "We must form a strong unity within the company and partnerships along the value chain, so that we can find the right direction together." In this sense, grayness has both internal and external implications.

In this world, there are no enemies; there are only counterparts and competitors. Ren Zhengfei said, "We have turned many friends into enemies during the past 20 years, and we will turn our enemies into our friends in the next 20 years." Enemies may turn into allies under certain circumstances. In 2009, when it was about to take antidumping actions against Huawei, the EU asked Ericsson, Nokia, and Siemens for their opinions. To the surprise of the EU, all the three companies expressed their opposition. This was partly because they had come to regard Huawei as their respected competitor and partly because they needed to work with each other on markets, products, and technologies. In short, they are not engaged in a cut-throat zero-sum game with Huawei but rather a cooperative competition.

This is the only way the captains can let more and more light into the industry.

Ren Zhengfei prefers to explicate this grayness theory with Chinese traditional bagua (literally "eight symbols") trigrams. In the center of the trigrams, there is a circle known as the Ultimate that consists of a black fish and a white fish, also called the yin fish and yang fish, respectively. It should be noted that the white fish has a black eye and the black fish has a white eye. This means white and black contain each other, or yin and yang are interchangeable. This also means, when it refers to an individual, that the person has both strengths and weaknesses, and these strengths and weaknesses complement each other.

This is the idea of change. It is obvious that there is an immense unknown world, but it should be recognized that this immense unknown world is changing. Therefore, leaders, including business leaders, must try to get a clear picture of the indistinct gray world in order to cope with vast changes.

Openness, Compromise, and Grayness

In December 2007, Ren Zhengfei met in Hong Kong with Madeleine Korbel Albright, the former US Secretary of State, who had been considered an iron woman in the international political community and an aggressive foreign minister of the first superpower of the world. At the meeting, Mrs Albright told Ren Zhengfei with rare sentimentalism: "I have read some of your articles, including 'My Father and My Mother' and 'Huawei's Winter.' I am deeply impressed, and I believe that people share emotions." She proceeded to share several stories of her father.

At this meeting, Ren Zhengfei told his guest the history of his company and the logic behind its success. This is the first time that Ren Zhengfei interpreted openness, compromise, and grayness all at the same time. He said he believed they are the secret weapons by which the company has reached its current scale and strength after having started out from nothing. Ren Zhengfei said, "We have been learning from others, including the United States, and in this way I believe we will set new targets and feel the urgency. If we had stayed close-minded, we might have collapsed long ago."

Since then Ren Zhengfei has elaborated on the three concepts on various occasions and asked his corporate advisors to collect relevant resources and conduct further research. On January 15, 2009, at a global market conference, Ren Zhengfei gave a speech titled "Openness, Compromise, and Grayness," in which he said,

> One of the core values of Huawei is openness. A leader should be able to control the direction and tempo and maintain a certain level of grayness. To hold onto the right direction and keep an appropriate tempo is an art, not a skill or method. The key is compromise and tolerance.

Regarding the relationship between compromise and grayness, Ren Zhengfei said, "To maintain a certain level of grayness, we must create a certain harmony among various factors of development within a certain period of time. This process of harmonizing is compromise, and its result is grayness." To illustrate this point, Ren Zhengfei said:

> The managers at Huawei are mostly young and passionate. They don't understand the necessity of compromise, so they meet with strong resistance. In the history of China, reforms have affected the course of social development, but most reformers had not really reached their goals. I believe that, in their own time, they had gone too far and had been too rigid with the resistance before them. If they had taken a softer approach and been more patient, they might have achieved better results. In fact, they lacked certain grayness. The direction would not change, but the course could bend a little bit. It may not necessarily be a straight line; it could be a curve, and at some point it could go around a circle. If we take a step back, we may find that the course leads exactly to the same goal.

In this speech, Ren Zhengfei elaborated fully on compromise and tolerance, but little on openness and grayness, and the relationship between compromise, openness, and grayness was not thoroughly explained. In particular, "grayness" was not touched upon in the third section, even though the section was titled "Without Compromise Grayness Cannot Be Achieved." This miss indeed was a pity.

While we were drinking tea one evening after the New Year of 2012, I proposed to Ren Zhengfei that grayness should be the core of Huawei's management philosophy and the basis of all other concepts. First, I argued that grayness represents a profound understanding of human nature and an insight as to the diversity and changeability of the world. The management of an organization ultimately aims at attracting, retaining, and motivating people. And the key is to bring out their latent positive energy, suppress the idle or evil part of their nature, tolerate their defects and mistakes, and therefore, lead them all, in spite of their differences, in the same direction. Second, Huawei's value proposition that dedication is the key to success is based on a proper understanding of human desire: On one hand, they work hard to improve their life, and on the other, they are committed to helping their company and country grow and prosper. Both desires should be motivated. This means the company recognizes the grayness in human nature. The company does not demand that all its employees be as passionately and selflessly dedicated as Lei Feng. No one in the company is obliged to give up their personal interests. Third, the reason why Ren Zhengfei advocates openness is because he understands the diversity, ambiguity, and changeability of the world in this age. Openness is critical for survival in this globalizing and IT-intensive world. Finally, as human nature is diverse and the global business scenario is changing, bilateral compromise and multilateral compromise are essential for success under such circumstances.

Therefore, each philosophical concept of Ren Zhengfei, be it openness, compromise, or grayness, is relevant to managing both employees and external relationships, including relationships with customers, competitors, communities, and the media. The key issue is how executives of the company understand and apply these concepts. Corporate management is not exactly a science; rather, it is an art.

Ren Zhengfei agreed with me. In fact, Ren Zhengfei has also clearly stated that the grayness of management is Huawei's tree of life.

Section II. Grayness Represents a State of Mind

A Leader's State of Mind

A decade ago, Ren Zhengfei read an article in remembrance of Mao Zedong, the founding Chairman of the People's Republic of China. He was impressed by what Chairman Mao told his assistants: There are no fish in an absolutely clean and clear river. Ren Zhengfei agreed. He also believed that a river, in the real sense, refers to torrents carrying mud and dirt along. Literally speaking, a leader should possess an open and liberal mind. Their duty is to put in place a sound system of rules and mechanisms, or to build up the dam so to speak. The dam should be solid and high enough, and the course of the river should be wide and deep. The torrents would, therefore, be allowed to flow fast. At the same time there should be gates from where water may be let out in the case of flood.

Some believe similarly that a leader should have a vast inner world in which there should be a waste recycling facility: able to recollect, sort out, and process wastes. Any organization is a center of conflicting information and an arena of conflicting personalities. As Yin Luobi said in an article titled "A Private City Under Water":

> People suffer from various psychological troubles in this world, mostly because they have stayed with the same people for too long. They may be depressed, anxious, compulsive, schizophrenic, or delusional, but all these problems stem from one big question: Who am I in the eyes of others?

Therefore, it is the duty of a leader to create a proper evaluation system which can realign personal pursuits with the goal of the organization. At the same time, such a system should both embrace personality differences and keep personal sentiments from impairing the interests of other people and the organization. Another critical factor affecting the well-being of an organization is the health of its subcultures, and the key problem is the spread of rumors or unverified information.

Some entrepreneurs used extreme examples: "When you cannot stop people from shitting or pissing with prohibitive rules, you'd better build toilets." Where should the "toilets" be built? In the inner world of the leaders and managers. A leader must be able to accept the diverse voices of employees, regardless of whether they are wrong, false, hostile, or radical. If a leader cannot accommodate and digest differing opinions, including the ugly and dirty ones, they will overflow into the bigger community.

In comparison, the analogy of being a waste recycler is more appropriate. A leader must listen to the voices of his/her team, but he/she must not cheat himself/herself if he/she can discern between right and wrong. In the words of Ren Zhengfei, "Whatever you resist will rebound." A leader must possess soft ears but sharp eyes. He must be able to sort through the information that has entered his ears and ascertain which is constructive, which is useless, which is harmful, and which is radioactive or erosive. Accordingly, he/she should landfill, incinerate, or degrade the waste, and recycle whatever is useful. This process would both clean up the body and the environment of the organization and enhance its power. To achieve this, the leader must possess a clear mind, an open heart, and strong hands.

There was once a flood of attacks on the Internet about Huawei and its leaders, and everyone could easily see that they had been started by Huawei's employees. These were complaints, discontent, rumors, and "uncovered secrets." Then how should the company respond? After intense debate, the senior management reached an agreement based on the concepts of openness, compromise, and grayness. Ren Zhengfei said:

> Each man is born with a mouth, so he must be allowed to speak. Of course, if too many people speak at the same time, there would be noise. This is inevitable. We cannot stop people from speaking or punish anyone who speaks. If we do that, we would be fanning the flames of hostility.

Therefore, Huawei decided to set up a web forum wherein its employees are encouraged to voice their opinions on the company's regulations, policies, and decisions, and may further engage in free debate without any interference. Several years later, this web community, which was intended merely to increase transparency and appease employee discontent, evolved into an important platform of communication for the senior management.

In January 2012, the opinions of this community forum were collected and organized in a booklet titled *Issues of Huawei* and distributed to each executive. Speaking of the forum, Ren Zhengfei said:

> We were taking a risk when we decided to set up this online forum, but are we are rewarded. This proves that we cannot attempt to lock up anyone's mind or shut up anyone's mouth. The sky will not fall if we let people speak their minds. Instead, if they speak out fully, they can help mend the sky when it leaks. I believe every person has their own goodness, and one is a saint if they can pool all their goodness together. I also believe that everyone has their own insight, and we can make a big decision if we pool together all their insight.

The key is whether the leader attempts to monopolize power, control information, and hold the exclusive right to interpret information. It is essential that the leader has an open mind that tolerates differences.

Tolerance Is the Key to Success

With respect to tolerance, Ren Zhengfei once said:

> Tolerance is the key to a leader's success. Everyone must deal with things and people in their job. One is able to deal with things even if he is not tolerant. For instance, a scientist may be a geek, but he can work very well nevertheless because he deals with instruments in the lab, oftentimes all alone. Similarly, a worker can operate his machine very well and produce perfect products, even though he is not friendly with most other people. Corporate management, however, is a completely different matter. Any manager has to deal with people, and management is defined as a skill to accomplish a task through the hands of other people. If you deal with people, you need to be tolerant.
>
> People are born different. To be tolerant means to accept differences. A manager must show enough tolerance to draw together people with different characters, skills, and preferences in order to create synergy, and therefore, fulfill the mission of the organization.
>
> To be tolerant with other people, one is tolerant with himself. If we are tolerant with other people, we will enjoy a broader space in our life.
>
> To be tolerant is a sign of strength; not weakness. Tolerance, as part of a plan, means the ability to take a step back in order to reach a certain goal but still hold on to the initiative. Of course, it is not tolerance if one has no other choice and is forced to do so.
>
> Only a brave individual understands how to be tolerant. A coward would never tolerate anyone else since it is against their nature. Tolerance is a virtue.
>
> Only tolerance may join different people together. Only compromise may lower the resistance. They lead you toward your goal.

In recent years, Huawei has tried to advocate and allocate oppositional voices. It has even set up a Blue Army organization that serves as an opposition to the Red Army, or the company principal force. Outstanding performers from the Blue Army are appointed commanders of the Red Army. Huawei believes that anyone who cannot find faults with the company has reached the ceiling of their career, while anyone who can see its shortcomings is able to make the company better.

Ren Zhengfei said:

> The Blue Army is everywhere in the company. Every part of the organization includes members of the Blue Army; it does not exist only at the top level of the organization. Our mind is also composed of Red and Blue, and I believe

one is born with Red and Blue inclinations. I have always attempted to deny my own will, and I have always been critical of my own decisions. I believe the Blue Army exists in every field and every process, and the opposition between Blue and Red is always present. I think I can accept oppositional forces in Huawei. We have to accept and unite everyone in the organization, including those who are opposed to our policies. It does not matter even if they form an opposition alliance in the company, as long as they are not trying to provoke dissension with malicious intent but raise divergent ideas on the technology. If we allow diversity in the company, I believe we can motivate wisdom and talent. Opposing opinions are part of our strategic reserve.

The day Steve Jobs passed away, Ren Zhengfei was with his family in Lijiang, Yunnan. When the news came, his youngest daughter, a Steve Jobs fan, proposed that they pay tribute to the deceased, and they honored him with a moment of silence in the outdoor café of the hotel. Ten days later, Ren Zhengfei said,

> China still has no soil for another Steve Jobs. We are not tolerant enough, and we do not protect intellectual properties well enough. Millions of Chinese mourned the death of Steve Jobs, but we wonder why we cannot tolerate Chinese business people? Innovations are only possible on the ground of tolerance. So are great business people.

The connotations of what Ren Zhengfei said are multi-faceted: A nation that does not tolerate any mistake or failure will suffocate its creativity and its elites. Steve Jobs had an eccentric personality. Even though he was addicted to marijuana in his early years, American society accepted him with great tolerance. Tourists visiting the United Kingdom may find a lot of statues along the streets. They include not only great thinkers, artists, and kings but also infamous tyrants and clowns. China, however, remains deep-rooted in black–white duality. For example, the Chinese soldiers who had been taken prisoner in the Korean War 60 years ago were subject to cruel torture on the charge that they had surrendered to the enemy. In contrast, American soldiers who had been captured were honored as heroes in their country.

In the words of an English proverb, "To err is human, to forgive is divine." An ancient Chinese sage said essentially the same, and this idea had been accepted early in Chinese history. But it is surprising that modern mainstream culture does not tolerate those who err once and that black and white are so separate from each other. The truth is that nobody is perfect; if you are unwilling to accept a person as they are, you will be left alone in this world.

A lot of Chinese companies have risen and fallen fast, and the major reason is their founders or managers are narrow-minded or intolerant.

Huawei's executives, on the contrary, believe that one can still be a saint even if one has fallen into a pit, so long as he can get out of the pit and shake off the mud. Huawei would treat any errant employee or executive as a patient and consider it the company's responsibility to rehabilitate them. They will be punished, of course, but the company will not give up on them. The trick is how to strike the balance between punishment and remedy. This is the art of grayness. The company's tolerance is not unlimited, but it cannot set black and white apart so completely. On the other hand, the company should not endure employees who threaten the company. If the company never holds employees accountable for any wrongdoing, the organization will lose its cohesiveness. Unity is essential for companies fighting to survive in the jungle.

This is the key to Huawei's success: tolerance based on grayness.

Leaders Must Surrender Their Imperial Mentality

On New Year's Day 2012, Ren Zhengfei gave a speech to the EMT titled "The Spring River Flows East." The text of this speech was published on Huawei's intranet. Within three days there were 600,000 hits, causing a big stir among domestic media. They wondered: Is this man the mysterious ironman we used to know? Is this the real Ren Zhengfei?

Yes, of course. This is the real Ren Zhengfei, a mixture of pride, confidence, fear, and loneliness. In the speech, he gave an account of his personal experience. In his boyhood, he had heard the story of Hercules from his mother, and also read a great deal on Chinese legends. He had then adored powerful heroes like Li Yuanba and Yuwen Chengdu of the Tang Dynasty. He had also believed in the absurd tale of Zhang Fei fighting against Yue Fei. Later, in his adolescence, he read about Li Qingzhao, the female poet from the Southern Song Dynasty and presumed with adolescent sensitivity that the poet adored Xiang Yu, one of the most resounding heroes in the history of China, as she wrote in one of her poems, "Alive, be a man of men; dead, be a soul of souls." This became the motto of many, and the dream to be a hero inspired young Chinese people to study hard and excel at school.

Due to his dreams of heroism, however, Ren Zhengfei had met with one setback after another. In primary school and high school, he was a solitary student and was denied acceptance into the Communist Youth League. In the PLA, he had not become a CPC member until very late in his military service. Life before he turned 40 was solitary, lonely, and hard.

Ren Zhengfei, who had never led anyone, founded Huawei in his 40s. Much like historical figures who had risen from the grassroots, he had gathered a number of brothers who shared weal and woe. They were not separated by positions in the company; they divided the gains equally among themselves, like the *Outlaws of the Marsh*. He said:

> I founded Huawei by myself, and it was called a self-employed business in China. At that time, to organize a big team was somewhat a dream too big to harbor. I designed the employee shareholding scheme soon after I founded Huawei. I had intended to knit all my colleagues together by a certain means of benefit sharing. At that time I had no idea about stock options. I did not know that this had been a popular form of incentive for employees in the West, and there are a lot of variations. The frustrations in my life made me feel that I had to share both responsibilities and benefits with my colleagues.
>
> In Huawei's early years, I had left our 'guerrilla commanders' alone in managing business operations. As a matter of fact, I didn't really have the ability to lead them. During the first decade, we rarely had any operational meetings. I flew to different parts of the country to hear their reports, tried to understand their situations, and give them the 'go ahead.' I listened to the brainstorming of the R&D staff. R&D was a mess at the time. We hardly had a clear direction, hopping around like a ball in the pinball machine. As soon as we heard customers who demanded improvement, we would exert great energy to meet the demand. Financial management was an even bigger challenge because I had not the least idea of finance. In the end, I had not got the relationship with finance staff right, and, to my regret, promotions for them had been rare. Maybe because I was not capable, I had set the hands of most people in the company free, who have therefore brought so much success to Huawei. I was then called a 'hands-off boss.' I had wanted to be 'hands on,' but I didn't know how. Around 1997, there appeared landlords in the company; various ideas and thoughts existed. No one could tell the direction of the company.

In such plain and sincere words, Ren Zhengfei described the early history of Huawei. Some scholars believe that this is common in the history of China. Most social or political organizations in China were founded with equalitarianism and pristine democracy, such as the Taiping Kingdom of Heaven and the Tung-meng Hui (Revolutionary Alliance) in the late Qing Dynasty. But when they grow big enough, their top leader would become arbitrary and monopolize power. He would be the only head of the organization and any dissent would be persecuted. This seems to prevail in most Chinese organizations today, and even universities, research institutes, and trade associations are no exception.

The imperial mentality is deeply rooted in China, an ancient country with a millennium-long feudal tradition. It is also very common in China's businesses. One might be a common person, like a farmer, teacher, or low-ranking government official when starting up a company, but after the company grows up and gets rich, he would inflate his self-awareness and become a domineering emperor. Personality worship would prevail in the company. The founder would also believe that the company is his personal fortune and forget about the endeavors of his colleagues throughout the years.

The tragedy is that when an entrepreneur becomes an emperor, the company would lose its grayness. White and black are completely separated, and the standard to tell white and black apart becomes the subjective will of the emperor.

When it is controlled by one leader, one voice, or one idea, an organization will turn rigid and vulnerable. Collapse is around the corner.

Does Ren Zhengfei possess such an imperial mentality? Perhaps. It is inevitable in China, and he is no exception. But luckily he is inspired by the philosophy of grayness. He knows that a successful business leader must give up his emperor complex in order to attract as many excellent people as possible to support his undertaking. And, if he is liberal and open-minded enough, he will be able to make even more friends, including partners and allies.

Section III. Defining Huawei's Culture

Neither a Donkey Nor a Horse, Both Chinese and Western

Ren Zhengfei is the unquestionable leader of Huawei, but he is not an emperor. To create sensation, the media would rather give the title of king or emperor to strong leaders. It is usually misleading and biased, though.

An emperor or a king is one who is far above his subjects and is rather detached from the real world. He lives, or rather he is imprisoned, in an enclosure. His or Her Majesty is beyond any challenge: Whatever he or she says is the golden rule. The empire or kingdom under his or her rule, therefore, is strictly governed where black and white do not converge and the atmosphere is intense.

When Steve Jobs was given an emperor's crown, that was a misunderstanding and blaspheme, rather than an extolment, of the technological hero. Aware of this, Ren Zhengfei has been trying to tear away the Emperor's New Clothes that might be put on him, saying that he knows only a bit of everything, or more exactly that he is certain about nothing, and that he is merely a cultural instructor. He said:

> I am half-literate about technologies, corporate management, and financial affairs. I am trying to pick up and learn about these things along the way. So I must gather a number of people and let them play their own parts so that the company may move forward. Personally, I must remain modest, and depend on the collective power.

At a recent board meeting for peer critique and self-criticism, someone proposed to evaluate the boss by a list of questions: Is Ren Zhengfei, our boss, versed in technologies? Seven of the attendants said no. Does the boss understand sales? Again, seven said, "no." Is the boss an expert in corporate management? One of them said, "no," and that man was Huawei's Deputy Chairman Eric Xu. Eric Xu is one of three rotating CEOs of the company, and he is energetic, straightforward, and sensitive to business trends. Some liken him to a clever fox with a keen nose able to detect new opportunities before others. Moreover, Eric Xu understands the importance of cooperation. At a meeting with Xiao Gang, chairman of Bank of China, Eric Xu said that IPD and ISC represent a huge and far-reaching change for Huawei's corporate management system, but the boss knows nothing but the literal meaning of the two terms. Nevertheless, the boss has stood firm behind the change program and put the right people in place. Through this huge 14-year program, Huawei has gained its state-of-the-art R&D competence, end-to-end supply process, and its ability to serve its customers worldwide.

Eric Xu has, in some sense, torn away the façade of the Emperor's New Clothes on the boss and told the true story of Ren Zhengfei who is unique and able to step back in areas where he is not well versed. Yes, Ren

Zhengfei is half-literate with technologies, sales, and corporate management, but he is a corporate management philosopher. To put it in Ren's own words, "Over the past twenty years, I have been dealing with the abstract. More precisely, I have spent 70 percent of my time on abstract matters, and only 30 percent on concrete issues." His task is to learn, contemplate, exchange, and communicate ideas. He said, "Resources will eventually be exhausted, but culture will last forever."

Then, what is the culture of Huawei? It is neither a donkey nor a horse, and it is both Chinese and Western. Any cultural element that is useful for the company's ideals will be studied and adopted. In the eyes of the West, Huawei is following the Eastern logic and playing the game by Western rules. And in the eyes of the East, no one knows whether Huawei is playing Chinese chess or Go, bridge or mahjong. In one word, the corporate culture of Huawei is diversified, fuzzy, and gray.

From Mao Zedong to the Qin Empire

Some management scholars define Huawei as a company ruled with Maoist thought. This, however, is a huge miss.

Mao Zedong called on his comrades to "stick to the right political direction, adopt a simple and pristine work style, and employ flexible tactics." This is an instruction Ren Zhengfei has adored as it fits perfectly with business organizations. No doubt Mao is an organizational Super Master rarely seen in history, and no doubt Ren's ideas deep within have included Maoist and communistic elements. This is the common attribute of his generation, and it is projected into their life and career. According to Ren Zhengfei, commitment to dedication and valuing dedicated employees—or in other words, more pay for more work—are the very values that Huawei has learned from the CPC. In fact, there are many other such examples: It has held meetings of peer critique and self-criticism for more than 20 years, disclosed information concerning managers to be appointed for the last decade, and set up a committee for integrity and ethics compliance.

However, at a deeper level in his philosophical awareness, Ren Zhengfei advocates grayness, or the convergence of black and white, which have traditionally been set against each other. With this awareness, he attaches great importance to openness and compromise. He is opposed to conflicts, but advocates constructive partnership, which clearly sets him apart from Maoist thought. Therefore, the argument is wrong that Ren Zhengfei adopts Maoist approach in the corporate management of Huawei.

Ren Zhengfei once recommended a book to his colleagues: *Hu Yaobang Rectifying Wrong Charges*. He had wanted his colleagues to learn to endure unjust allegations and survive defeat and frustration.

In 2004, when the whole country was commemorating the 100th anniversary of the birth of Deng Xiaoping, Huawei sent an email in the name of its CEO, which recommended an article about the political system of China: "Deng Xiaoping's Thought Must Be Re-understood." According to the article, Deng Xiaoping was both a leftist and a right-wing politician. This political position made a far-reaching effect on Ren Zhengfei, and Huawei has therefore moved forward in balanced waves over the past two decades.

Some former executives of Huawei said:

> The boss is very well read about Chinese history, so the corporate management is much too political. If he really wanted the power, he should not have shared stock equity with his employees. He should have remained the controlling or relative majority shareholder so that he may continue to exert his power and authority.

This is a wrong perception. Huawei's employee shareholding scheme, by which thousands of intellectual workers have themselves become bosses, is a miraculous invention in the business world. This is the soul of Huawei's culture, without which Huawei would not have survived so long. Ren Zhengfei would never agree with them.

Ren Zhengfei is indeed keenly interested in history, but he has often shifted the subject of his historical study to suit Huawei's development. For instance, he loved the TV series *The Qin Empire* and bought hundreds of copies as an expression of his support to this serious historical play. From this history, he realized how hard it is to carry out any reform. It is an elusive art to handle everything in the process of reform, including how fast and how forceful the reform can be pushed forward and where the reform should pause for a while. It demands an awareness of grayness in order to win support and reduce resistance. Shang Yang, the radical reformer of the Qin Empire, had ended up dying a tragic death, but he must be remembered. His death has been a useful lesson for later generations. If he had not implemented the reform so radically and in such a hurry, if he had a historical vision and had aimed for gradual reform over centuries, he would have succeeded. Sometimes, a reform process may last a thousand years; religious reform in Europe is a good example.

Again in 2012, at the 100th anniversary of the Xin Hai Revolution, Ren Zhengfei read many commemorative essays. He said, "The surrender of the Qing emperor is the greatest compromise in Chinese history. He had avoided war and bloodshed. This reflects the political wisdom of the Chinese people."

Ren Zhengfei has also drawn a lot of inspiration from historical movies and programs. For instance, after watching *Emperor Wu of the Han Dynasty*, he started to think about how to handle personal honors and disgraces. Afterwards, he became fascinated by a series of historical lectures aired by Phoenix TV: *Bloody Dusk*. Ren recommended these lectures to other members of senior management. The lesson he learned was that a leader must be flexible under changing circumstances; leaders must be able to take the offensive or hold back, insist on principles or accept failures as circumstances demand. Another program that inspired him was the TV series *Drawing Sword*, which told him that an outstanding general must be tested in the battlefield and that, although young soldiers may have certain shortcomings, the leaders must be able to appreciate their merits and tolerate their limitations.

History is an inexhaustible source of ideas. Any nation has its own history that reflects the national character and wisdom. History also includes the change of organizations, and the state is the biggest organization of all. The rise and fall of a state, including the fate of its leading figures and major events throughout this process, is a spiritual legacy for later generations.

It is impossible for a state, enterprise, or individual to break away from history and start all over. But any organization would never succeed, either, if it lives in the past, unable to criticize or learn from history. The key is to open up its mind to lessons from the past and the outside world.

Between the Donkey and the Elephant

Political cartoonists have been active in American society, especially in its political sphere, for centuries. They have added a lot of humor to bipartisan politics. Politicians portrayed as caricatures do not feel offended; instead, they feel amused or find in them a comic power. The portrayals also help demystify politics and politicians: Politics is merely a profession, and politicians are not saints, either; they are sometimes clowns, too.

The bipartisan politics of the United States has been compared to the fight between the donkey and the elephant. The metaphor originated in cartoons by Thomas Nast, a German political cartoonist who is widely credited with perpetuating the donkey and elephant as symbols of the Democratic and Republican parties. As time went by, both parties embraced their mascots. Even though the donkey may seem dumb to a Republican, Democrats associate the symbolism with intelligence and courage. Similarly, the elephant is flashy and cumbersome in the eyes of Democrats, but is a symbol of dignity, power, and wisdom to Republicans.

Since then the donkey and the elephant have governed the United States with a balance of power. The Democratic donkey, representing the middle and lower classes, insists on increasing taxes on the rich, improving social welfare, and reducing the gap between the rich and the poor; it is essentially a wealth-consuming party. The Republican elephant, on the other hand, represents the rich class and calls for tax cuts to boost economic vitality; it is a wealth-creating party. In general, when the Republicans are in power, the United States enjoys economic boom, but the wealth gap widens. When the Democrats rule, the middle and lower classes gain more benefits and social conflict is relieved, but the economy more often than not enters into recession. This has been the cycle of US politics, economics, and society over the past century.

The clashes between the donkey and the elephant, however, have rendered the American society non-donkey and non-elephant. The country has progressed with equilibrium and a strong vigor acquired through the political scuffles. Then how does it inspire the corporate culture of Huawei?

Huawei hired Mercer, a global leading consulting firm, to design its decision-making processes and mechanisms that contain much Western wisdom. Yet the most critical part of the decision hierarchy, or the CEO rotation, was proposed by Huawei executives out of their understanding of the Western, or more exactly the American, political tradition. The CEO rotation is meant to prevent the company from going too far left or right and to create a balance of power within the company. The passing years have witnessed improvement of Huawei's decision-making through this borrowed mechanism.

Everything is based on pragmatism. Huawei would never label itself as the successor of any single culture. Some argue that Huawei has been able to achieve global success because the company and its senior executives, including Ren Zhengfei, have been westernized. This is in fact another white-or-black misjudgment. There is not a single unchanged totem in the mind map of Ren Zhengfei, and Huawei is a species that has fed on a variety of grains. It has now a wide cultural spectrum. It keeps any cultural element that proves useful and discards anything that is useless, be it Chinese or foreign, modern or ancient.

For example, the value proposition of customer centricity to which Huawei attaches the greatest importance has come from Western companies. Ren Zhengfei has written a number of essays urging his colleagues to learn openness, entrepreneurship, and dedication from the American people, especially from those in the Silicon Valley. Sixteen years ago, Ren Zhengfei passed through Dubai and was amazed. Later, he wrote an essay arguing that "Resources will eventually be exhausted, but culture will last forever," and calling his people to "build a strong Huawei" with "wisdom borrowed from the whole world." In addition, Ren has recommended the films *Battle of Moscow* and *The Long Gray Line* to senior management.

Huawei has a university of its own: Huawei University. It is the incubator of leaders, and a mixer of Eastern and Western cultures. More than 100,000 people have attended Huawei University and taken courses on Huawei's management philosophy, corporate system, values, and code of conduct. They have also witnessed or taken part in clashes of thoughts and cultures. The following list of lectures from 2002 to 2010 may illustrate the origin and evolution of Huawei's culture:

Protestant Ethics and Capitalist Spirit
Returning to the Axial Age
Useless and Useful: Wisdom of Lao Zi and Zhuang Zi
Book of Change and Ways of Thinking
About Nothingness and Abstraction
Particularity of the Law of War and the Nature of War
Guidelines and Strategies for War
Origin, Basis, and Development of Christianity
Modern Western Philosophy
Re-reading *The Art of War*
Buddhism in China: Zen
Comparison of Chinese and Western Cultures
Interpreting Western Art
Aesthetics and Sensational Wisdom
Seeing the World through Paintings
Appreciating and Criticizing Music

On Traditional Chinese Medicine
Fuzziness and Tolerance
Olympics and Greek Mythology
Religious Background of the Current International Pattern
...

Ren Zhengfei calls these courses "eye openers."

Section IV. From the Cloud of Thought to the Rain of Thought

Normative Power and Conceptual Power

Amitai Etzioni, Professor of Sociology at Columbia University, said in his book *Comparative Analysis of Complex Organizations*: "Power is characterized by the means to secure compliance. Such means can be natural, but can also be material or symbolic. There are three forms of power: coercive, remunerative, and normative." He believes that coercive power may cause physical or psychological pain, remunerative power is dependent on material satisfaction, and normative power inspires moral involvement and secures compliance on the basis of rules.

Based on Amitai Etzioni's concept of normative power, David M. Lampton, George and Sadie Hyman Professor of China Studies at Johns Hopkins University's Paul H. Nitze School of Advanced International Studies, raised the concept of power of mind. This form of power creates and disseminates knowledge and ideas to secure support. In some sense, the power of mind exceeds normative power because it covers a range of factors, including leadership, intellectual resources, innovation, and culture.

All the four forms of power coexist in harmony at Huawei, a utilitarian organization. Without the application of coercive power, such as eliminating underperformers, accountability for personal and organizational results, and information security regulations, the company would fall apart. A company is like a troop of soldiers who would be severely punished if they do not follow orders to attack or retreat, or disseminate defeatism. Like an army, a company is a goal-oriented organization for which coercive prohibitions are prevalent to hold the organization together.

Remunerative power is essential for a business organization. To seek for benefits and the idea of more pay for more work are human nature, which any company cannot ignore. Building on this human nature, Huawei has developed and insisted on its core value proposition: Dedication is the key to success. Its compensation, bonuses, welfare packages, and its employee shareholding scheme are all remunerative incentives.

Coercive power and remunerative power are quantifiable forms of power and are based on the black-or-white rules and authoritarian culture. Of course, a company cannot operate without rules or authority, but their effects are limited. They won't create any sense of belonging among the members.

In an age when credibility is diminishing, loyalty is losing value, and idols are falling from grace, the commitment of Huawei's employees is unique. Sure, many people have left, but they have been emotionally attached to this business organization, just as graduates often miss their old school. For two decades, the image of Ren Zhengfei, the "Boss," has never wavered among the people of Huawei. This is another phenomenon.

One may wonder why? The answer lies in normative power and the power of mind. Ren Zhengfei advocates grayness, which encompasses tolerance, openness, and compromise, and, therefore, transcends the traditional black-or-white way of thinking. This philosophy has created lubrication, flexibility, and warmth in the cold business machine and at the same time satisfies human desire for material gains.

More importantly, Huawei's leadership creates a set of totems at each stage of development that form spiritual banners that surpass anything at the material level, and these banners direct every member of the organization. This has caused some of Huawei's employees and their family, friends, and even clients to comment that Huawei employees are brainwashed by the company. "Brainwash" is not exactly right because the company is doing more than washing their brains; it has been trying to change their brains completely.

Every leader is solitary. So is Ren Zhengfei. Why? Leaders are all solitary thinkers. Milan Kundera once said, "Man thinks and God laughs." But the problem is that in this secular world, God is too far away from us, so every organization, whether it is a nation, a company, a school, or a church, needs a leader who keeps thinking and provides direction.

In this sense, leaders are spiritual laborers, puritan travelers in the realm of thought. I have witnessed the journey of Ren Zhengfei in the world of business philosophy and how an idea is formed, reviewed, developed, and systemized. I understand that this is a really tough journey that requires special resilience. Ren Zhengfei likes to describe this process with the concept of cloud. He said, "It takes more than half a year for a cloud to turn into rain." What he means is that after an idea is conceived, there is still a long way to go before it can be implemented. It has to turn from gray to white, blurry to clear, and relevant rules and mechanisms should be developed to guarantee its effective implementation.

The most solitary period in this process, however, is the formation of any cloud in the sky of thought. Most commonly, Ren Zhengfei may get some hints regarding Huawei's management and development while reading a book or talking with someone. These hints then condense in his sky of thought and form spots that gradually link into lines after further reading or talks with different people. Ren would then speak about the same subject on various occasions; the lines begin to expand and he proceeds to piece them together into patches. Afterwards, he presents these patches of thought at executive meetings in which they are discussed and debated until a consensus is reached. The final idea is then publicized in a speech or essay that then stir up ripples among Huawei's employees, much as what happens when a stone is cast into a pond.

Generally speaking, it would take two years or more for Ren Zhengfei to form a cloud of thought, and another half-year for the company to turn the cloud into rain.

Dialectics and Metaphysics

In the Latin quarter of Paris on the left bank of the Seine River there are many cafés housed in classical buildings, and people would be attracted by the fragrance of coffee that permeates through the streets. They would walk into a café and spend a cozy afternoon with a cup of coffee and a book.

In such an elegant, quiet, and yet narrow environment, many great European philosophers have garnered inspiration, including Jean Paul Sartre, Albert Camus, and Alfred de Musset. Coffee has sparked many great ideas that have ultimately changed the course of human development. However, an article titled "Coffee: An Awkward Plant" published in *Life Week* reminds us of the other side of the coin:

> It is less known, however, that coffee and cafés have gone through a bloody history. In the 16th century, the darkest age in human civilization, coffee was considered just as wicked as pagans. Conservative theologians in the Arabian Peninsula destroyed all coffee beans on the streets of Mecca, and

the prime minister of the Turkish Empire put a café owner into a bag and threw him into the Strait of Bosporus.

Times have changed. Perhaps this is a manifestation of dialectics. Beauty and ugliness, warmth and coldness, justice and evil, success and failure, and right and wrong may change into each other over time. Ren Zhengfei said:

> Our faith in grayness and compromise is based on dialectics. With the aware-ness of grayness, we are able to see a wider prospect and stay on course. Our commitment to grayness and compromise does not mean we are weak; it means we are strong. We may have to plan our strategy over a span of 10 years or more, so it can hardly be absolutely clear; there will be revisions or even complete reversion over the course. Such adjustments within the stra-tegic framework would be natural and necessary as circumstances change. But the framework itself has to be broad and gray, so that we can get the direction right, or at the very least, we can avoid heading in the opposite direction.
>
> We don't pursue perfection. There is no perfect strategy or direction in this world. We cannot include everything in our strategy. We can succeed so long as we hold the key. There is no perfect man in the world, either. One changes with time and circumstances. It is not dialectical to consider a man as a saint, or as a devil. We still have to follow the principle of grayness.

Ren Zhengfei encourages senior executives of the company to meet with industry captains of the world while enjoying a cup of coffee. The idea is that they should increase their contacts with the outside world in order to get more information and develop a longer and broader vision. He said:

> You should not only care about things right in front of your eyes. Huawei will not allow either dogmatism or empiricism. If we follow a fixed course, or depend too much on our past experience, we would get lost midway. Similarly, if we rigidly follow a certain theory or dogma we will stumble and get hurt. There are many MBA graduates who cannot run any business. Why? Because they have learned nothing more than the dogma.

Meanwhile, Ren Zhengfei admitted, "I don't mean metaphysics is evil. There are things that are definite and mechanical which we should not bend a bit."

The Germans are the most serious-minded people in the world. Every cell of their brain is encoded with metaphysics and mechanical materialism, which is manifested in their daily life. This is perhaps the reason why Germany has the most advanced and most competitive fine manufacturing sector in the world and has produced the most scientists, financiers, artists, and philosophers. Of course, Germany was also the most dreaded war machine in Europe at one point in history.

In contrast, the British people see farther into the future. They show foresight and a better understanding of grayness in balancing compromise against insistence.

It is sensible to borrow wisdom from the past and the outside world. Huawei has tried to make the best use of every accomplishment from human civilization, attempting to incorporate them into its own framework.

But the question is what should be viewed with grayness and what should remain strictly white or black? Over the past two decades, Huawei has developed its own answer. The company can see gray with its strategy and its people. There can be dialectics. Tactics can be gray to some extent, or they should be adjusted to suit circumstances. Yet the core values of customer centricity and dedication as the key to success must never waver. They are the metaphysical law, or the Bible, of Huawei's 150,000 employees. Ren Zhengfei has led his colleagues to read the Huawei Bible every year, every month, and every day, and the message has been instilled into the veins of every Huawei person.

Meanwhile, people and business operations are treated differently at Huawei. While the people are viewed with grayness, business operations should be handled with exactness in the white-or-black manner. The processes of product development, sales, delivery, and after-sales must be implemented without fault in order to fulfill the commitment to customer centricity. The reason people should be viewed with a certain amount of grayness is that people are growing and changeable, and grayness is necessary to unleash their drive and creativity.

At Huawei's research institute in India, each Indian engineer writes 2,000 lines of code every month, and every Chinese turns out about 20,000 lines. The Chinese employees seem to be 10 times more efficient, but the problem is that each line of code written by the Indian engineers is valid, while for the Chinese engineers only 200 of the 20,000 lines are valid. Apparently, this problem cannot be treated with grayness. Metaphysics, rather than dialectics, applies to scientific research.

This contrast has impressed Ren Zhengfei deeply. He said a nation with religious faith deserves our respect. They have quite a few merits, such as integrity, which we should learn from them. He once recommended to senior executives and customers of Huawei an essay titled "Market Economy with Church and Market Economy without Church" by Professor Zhao Xiao. The senior executives of Huawei, however, are impressed even more by the heartfelt respect that Indian employees have for intellectual property. For many years, Huawei has suffered from theft of technologies by both its employees and external forces. This is a moral and legal issue, and Huawei must not be a bit gray about it. The white and the black should be clearly set apart.

Huawei has set up over 40 research institutes worldwide, and the largest institute of all is located in Bangalore, India.

Ren Zhengfei said:

> The principles of openness, compromise, and grayness are mainly applicable to senior management. People at lower levels can be spared. This is because the decision-making process should be gray, so that the decision-makers can open their minds and learn to compromise. Therefore, they will be able to pool together as much wisdom as possible. People at the lower levels of the organization are mainly responsible for implementing decisions. They must be practical and quick-handed. In short, the decision-making process must be slow or they will make blunders, while implementation should be as quick and efficient as possible.

Commenting on Ren Zhengfei, a senior executive of Huawei said, "For 20 years our boss has seemed very transcendental, but it is amazing that from time to time he may step in and stir up the company. Of course, the organization is able to quickly regain balance. Huawei has developed a self-healing mechanism."

CHAPTER SIX

Self-Criticism: A Sense of Fear Makes Greatness

Section I. Black Hole and the Second Law of Thermodynamics

Metaphor of Lin Chiling's Beauty

In 1854, Rudolf Clausius, a German mathematical physicist, introduced the concept of entropy. The idea is that in an isolated system, molecular thermal motion tends to shift from concentrated and orderly alignment to dissipative and chaotic disorder. In this spontaneous process, entropy keeps increasing. When entropy reaches the maximum level, the system reaches equilibrium in a motionless state. Entropy is the central idea of the Second Law of Thermodynamics. This law also implies that the increase of entropy is irreversible. In other words, entropy is an arrow of time, according to Sir Arthur Eddington, a British astronomer. Time is corrosive, leading every creature in this world and the universe to irreversible destruction.

As Karl Marx said, since they were born, human beings are marching toward their tombs. This is a constant law and dubbed "the irreversible increase of entropy" in science.

One has to guess Rudolf Clausius's state of mind when he discovered this despairing Second Law of Thermodynamics since historical documents show that astronomers and actors have the highest rates of suicide. Most Western scientists, especially Nobel Prize laureates, are turned into faithful religious worshippers while engaged in scientific explorations.

Scientific discoveries have enlightened people, but have also caused them despair. The theory of entropy is one such discovery.

In 1981, a book titled *Entropy—A New World View* hit the United States. The book transplants the concept of entropy from natural science to human society. Even much earlier, English radiochemist and monetary economist Frederick Soddy had asserted that the law of entropy would finally govern the rise and fall of political systems, the freedom or bondage of societies, the movements of commerce and industries, the origin of wealth and poverty, and the general physical welfare of people.

The theory of entropy has no doubt become a philosophical inference about social and human development. One can find that the Second Law of Thermodynamics and the theory of dissipative structure, which will be discussed in later sections, have had a profound impact on the business management philosophy of Ren Zhengfei.

Ren Zhengfei once said:

> One of Huawei's secrets is that we have successfully applied the Second Law of Thermodynamics and the theory of dissipative structure. We have continued to increase and dissipate heat, and in this process we have gained enough momentum that has driven us for over 20 years.

In his essays and speeches, Ren Zhengfei has expressed more anxiety, concern, and self-criticism than pride and satisfaction. "Only leaders who sleep with their eyes open can lead their followers away from danger in this age of change," a financial reporter said about Ren Zhengfei.

Surprisingly enough, however, in 2010, Ren Zhengfei likened Huawei to Lin Chiling, a beautiful lady from Taiwan, after he had "ignored" the company's success for two decades. Why?

Perhaps this is because Huawei has been smeared by some Western media and politicians long enough. Ren Zhengfei said:

> No one can deny Lin Chiling's beauty, however people may slander her. The same is true for Huawei. I don't mean Huawei is very beautiful now, but we are strong and we would never waver in our effort to be stronger. This is also an undeniable fact that won't bend to slander. Ms Lin is beautiful for her looks; Huawei is beautiful, too, for all the years of passion and hard work. Of course, Huawei will get old and lose its beauty. We will also die in the end as some American media seem to wish. But that will happen many years in the future, not now.

He said to his employees,

> Some of you are too soft, but tough guys appear too noisy. The really great people are both tough and quiet. When we talked about Lin Chiling and appreciated her beauty, we just wanted to tell you that the senior management of Huawei has come to a consensus. No matter how much we compromise, our American opponents won't leave us alone. They are too selfish. We have to fight. Why can't Huawei be beautiful? We were not born a beauty, but we can strive to be one.

This speech is full of pride. He did not sound like an anxious crisis forecaster as he had always appeared.

He went on to say, "In the field of cloud computing, you must be ambitious. You are over very soon if you don't want to be number one. We must be tough when dealing with business, but remain humble when dealing with people."

This sounds like a declaration to its American competitors. Huawei has apparently been suppressed too long and too hard. For a decade, Huawei's American competitors attacked Huawei out of fear of the Chinese company. The American government, companies, and media have smeared Huawei's name and tried all means to prevent the company from entering the US market. In response, Huawei has insisted on openness and compromise, in addition to taking reasonable counteractions. Nevertheless, its peacemaking efforts have not brought about equality and acceptance in the US market; instead, the opposition has come even stronger. While a lot of American companies, such as IBM and HP, made large profits from the Chinese market, Huawei and other Chinese companies have been rejected by the US market, and the barrier is turning higher and higher.

Therefore, Huawei was forced to change its strategy from tolerance and compromise to direct confrontation. Ren Zhengfei and other EMT members believed that Huawei possessed enough power to contend with its American counterparts. In a way, this is what Ren Zhengfei was alluding to when he said, "Lin Chiling is a real beauty" and asked, "Why can't Huawei be as beautiful?"

The comparison of Huawei to Ms Lin Chiling, who is considered the No. 1 beauty of the East, has multiple implications: It reveals the popular aesthetic standard of Ren Zhengfei, his confidence and pride in Huawei, and the alignment with key values among the company's executives.

Meanwhile, Ren Zhengfei has a deep-rooted inclination toward self-criticism, which he has insisted on for over 20 years. In this speech, with rare pride, he also said, "We must examine and reexamine ourselves critically so that we may one day lead the world."

That means Huawei is beautiful, but it is not beautiful enough, and if it wants to become more beautiful and make its beauty last, Huawei must be critical of itself. According to the theory of entropy, Huawei must run an open system wherein the increase of entropy is resisted or postponed, or possibly one in which entropy may actually decrease. The contest between Huawei and its competitors will ultimately depend on who possess staying power, or in other words, whose organism ages and collapses slower.

Organizational Fatigue

Every organization has a life, but unfortunately, all living beings will eventually die, including animals, plants, human beings, nations, armies, companies, mountains, seas, and even the whole world and the universe.

The prelude to the disappearance of life is fatigue and aging. One may remain healthy for all his life, but as time passes, his genes will decay, his metabolism will slow down, and his vitality will decrease. A flower is brilliant in spring when it is blooming, but it will wither away in autumn.

This is the same with social organizations. A dynasty may appear robust and full of life in the early period, as the young power still retains the "vigor on horseback." Before long, laziness, hedonism, and corruption will arise and spread. As time passes by, fatigue will prevail throughout the dynasty, although it suffers from no illness (which is hardly possible). The cells would no longer be young, and they would always be sleepy.

Business organizations would decay at a faster speed. Within years, perhaps no more than a decade, a robust organization may suffer from laziness and various negative powers that grab at the company like the arms of an octopus. Why? It is because of their myopic utilitarianism.

Organizational fatigue has not only occurred due to the irreversible passage of time but also because organizations tend to depend on their past factors of success. Adam Smith's invisible hand seemed to play a part after the fall of the Berlin Wall in 1989 and the breakup of the former Soviet Union in 1991. Capitalism was announcing its victory all over the world, and some free-market fundamentalists in the United States declared:

"The world's economy has now entered a stable period." Unfortunately, several years later, the global economy was caught by a whirlwind. As Japanese sociologist Katsuhito Iwai said, "The enemy of capitalism, or the enemy of freedom, is laissez-faireism rather than socialism."

Companies have essentially suffered in the same way. Some of these companies were glorious big names: Bell Labs, Motorola, Nortel, NEC, Sony, Nokia, and Alcatel. However, they have lost their glory and suffered from various ills. The key reason, in addition to some apparent internal and external causes, is that they are too old, and they depended too much on their past experience in coping with modern challenges. In fact, it takes great pains to keep perfectly fit in this changing world.

Organizational fatigue has dozens of causes, of which "history" is the most fatal. Ren Zhengfei is afraid of death, fatigue, and decadence. This is why no "trace of history" can be found at Huawei. Its history of 25 years is full of ups and downs, and includes even narrow escapes as well as grand accomplishments. Huawei has created one record after another, and reached top positions in the world. A number of Chinese and foreign politicians and business leaders have visited Huawei. The company deserves a history museum.

In April 2001, at the museum of Panasonic Corporation in Japan, I proposed to Ren Zhengfei that Huawei should have its own museum. He answered, "Huawei does not need a museum. Huawei should forget its history."

In Huawei, the most impressive place is probably the product showroom where there are only new products and a wall of patents; there is not a hint of history.

History is likely to create laziness, depression, fatigue, and boredom. German philosopher Arthur Schopenhauer said, "The two foes of human happiness are pain and boredom." In this age of information and globalization, idols, stars, and leaders can stay fresh only for a short period of time. Alienation from organization is normal, and loyalty is a luxury.

Huawei is a company with no historical heroes. Ren Zhengfei does not want the company to take on too much pressure from any legacy. As one Huawei executive put it, "The company would not worship anyone in a shrine, not even the boss." Ren Zhengfei pays more attention to the present and the future, and everyone is measured by their present competence and contribution. At Huawei, "the past is a blank sheet."

Black Hole: Evil Eye of the Universe

Ren Zhengfei and I took notice of a report almost at the same time: Two "rogue black holes," as some scientists dubbed them, were observed by astrophysicists, wandering the Milky Way 300 million light years away from Earth and threatening to swallow anything that got too close.

According to the latest report, NASA found an eye in the depth of the universe: NGC 4151. The discovery is a spiral galaxy located 43 million light years from Earth that contains an actively growing super-massive black hole. Gizmodo.com said it was the "Evil Eye" of the universe.

As the news on TV was not elaborative, Ren Zhengfei did further reading on the Internet the next day. He has remained curious about outer space. Several years ago, when the president of Peking University visited Huawei, Ren said that he would like to become a student at Peking University after he retires. He would first study mathematics and then thermodynamics to explore the origin of the universe and the Big Bang. The president was pleased.

Ren Zhengfei often said to his colleagues in the EMT that leaders should possess a wide range of knowledge and broad vision. They should know a bit of everything, including astronomy and geography. And at the same time, they should be able to focus on a certain point, such as the black hole: What would be Huawei's black hole?

It is common knowledge that bees are "matchmakers" among plants. Without bees, the vegetation of the earth, including grains, would be isolated and gradually die out. Then human beings would die of hunger and war. Therefore, the fact that bees are dying in many parts of the world has aroused widespread concern among scientists.

Recent studies show that bees are under threat from tachinid flies. The flies lay their eggs on the belly of the bees, which then lose their agility and sense of direction. Affected bees fly away from their beehives at midnight and die soon after. This would ultimately lead to colony collapse and disorder, or the entire colony of adult bees would disappear all of a sudden.

For human beings, cancer is one of the most fatal diseases. Medical studies have shown that cancer cells are a mutation of normal cells and may grow in any part of the human body. Cancer cells don't age, but continue to grow and multiply. They feed on the nutrients of other bodily tissues until the body dies.

God's creation is miraculous! He seems to have created a single law that governs the universe where there are so many similarities. Black holes are threatening the well-being of the universe. Bees die of fly eggs laid on them. Malignant cancer cells grow due to genetic mutation. And plants are withering away from unknown pathogens within their cell membrane.

Then what are the cancer cells of organizations? They are individual greed and collective unconscious corruption. In the Roman Empire, there were more baths than churches. During the last years of each Chinese dynasty, there was excessive drinking. In any Asian or Western country that had passed its prime, the upper classes usually turned decadent while the lower classes were selfish and cold. To sum up, unrestrained personal desires are the cancer cells of every organization.

Wall Street is now the biggest cancer cell of the global economy. It has first hit Western financial capitalism and is now spreading to every other part of the world, including China. The real economy is being drained, placing global wealth in the hands of financial oligarchs to create a class of upstarts and confrontation in society.

In 2011, China became the world's largest consumer of luxury goods. This is not any good news. It unfortunately indicates that the nation is decaying at shocking speed. The "wealthy class" has barely formed in China over the last 30 years, or more exactly, 20 years. That means that within a single generation, most of the people who got rich first have lost their enterprising spirit; they have turned into a consuming class. In any large or mid-sized city in China, from the very north down to the very south, there are a lot of clubhouses that provide world-class luxury entertainment. Their frequent customers are mostly the newly rich, who had been forced by hunger and scarcity to fight, to take adventures, and to exploit their new frontiers merely 10 or 20 years ago.

Ren Zhengfei is fully aware of the risk. He told his colleagues and subordinates that they must understand why past dynasties have fallen. He said that a new dynasty would take over the power of the previous dynasty at a very low cost since the former dynasty had been weakened by its oversized and greedy royal family. However, the new dynasty would repeat the same story. Each emperor of the new dynasty would give birth to dozens of children, and each child would become a hedonist lord dependent on the national treasury. After dozens of generations, a huge parasitic class would form, which would finally wreak havoc on the dynasty, since the laboring people, who could not bear the burden anymore, would rise up and overthrow the royal family. Huawei must remain vigilant to avoid such a tragic circle. If the company just feeds on what has been achieved, its fall would be a matter of years.

Section II. Dissipative Structure and Self-Criticism

Dissipative Structure and Basic Values

In 1969, Ilya Prigogine, a Belgian physical chemist, proposed his theory of dissipative structure on the basis of the Second Law of Thermodynamics. A dissipative structure is an open system that exists far from thermodynamic equilibrium, with the ability to efficiently dissipate the heat generated for self-sustenance. Entropy production can be minimized or even turn negative, and a higher level of orderliness would, therefore, take form. According to the theory, more orderly dissipative structures would emerge as various systems evolve or degenerate, driving the physical world into growing diversity and complexity. The theory of heat death held by some pessimists was, therefore, shattered.

This is a great discovery. In 1977, as the founder of modern thermodynamics, Ilya Prigogine was awarded the Nobel Prize in chemistry for his contributions to nonequilibrium thermodynamics, particularly the theory of dissipative structure. This shows man's optimism about nature and the law of life. On the other hand, Rudolf Clausius, who discovered the Second Law of Thermodynamics, received little recognition among scientists; he had been harshly criticized for proposing the concept of heat death of the cosmos. Approximately 100 years after Clausius's discovery, the concept of entropy and the principle of entropy increase were recognized as the most fundamental scientific concept and principle applicable to human society as well as nature, but the theory of entropy remained a cold and relentless scientific law.

In contrast, the theory of dissipative structure is much warmer, because it gives human beings courage and hope. It says that so long as we are in an open system where energy is exchanged and released, any natural or human organization may escape chaos and return to order. Therefore, entropy may decrease and the body may be renewed. This is no doubt the best endorsement of human endeavors.

In July 2012, Ren Zhengfei said in a speech,

> Later, my interest shifted from heavenly bodies to social dynamics. I care more about how to keep people going and motivate them to create wealth. This is the source of our reform initiatives. This is also the basis of our core value proposition: Dedication is the key to success.

Further, Ren said:

> So what is a dissipative structure? If you jog every day, you are in a dissipative structure. Why? You are dissipating your energy and turning it into muscle and improving blood flow. If you dissipate all redundant energy, you will avoid diabetes and obesity. You will get healthy and beautiful. This is the simplest concept of a dissipative structure. Then there is another question: Why do we need any dissipative structure? We are saying that we're committed to the company, but most often it is because the company is paying too much. This is not sustainable. Therefore, we must first dissipate such commitment based on excessive pay, and substitute with dedication based on certain mechanisms. There is a difference between working hard to gain the benefit and having something handed to you before hard work. We must dissipate our latent energy and then form new momentum.

Huawei is determined not only to dissipate the commitment of its people, but to also dissipate their pride. Ren Zhengfei said, "We must dissipate blind pride. What are we proud of? Instead, we should feel the crisis. We know the best how hard our life has been." He further stated:

> We have been alternating from stability to instability, from equilibrium to non-equilibrium, from certainty to uncertainty. We are doing this over and over again to maintain the company's vitality. If you eat a lot of beef and don't exercise, you will become fat. But if you exercise hard enough after eating beef, you will become a tough athlete. In both cases you are eating beef, but you end up in a completely different shape, depending on whether you dissipate energy or not. Therefore, we are determined to hold on to this system.

This system is called a "dissipative system." What would Huawei dissipate? Its rich man's disease, its laziness, and its hedonism. And then, hard work will build up tough muscle in Huawei's culture. Dedication is the cornerstone of Huawei's core values, and the gene that has allowed Huawei to grow and mature. As the company flourishes, however, this primitive DNA of Huawei could mutate. In fact, some people and some departments have already lost their shape. In this context, Ren Zhengfei argued in 2006, "When we talk about dedication, it's more of a mental dedication, or always going the extra mile to look for the better, than physical hard work."

It is easier said than done, however. A perfect idea may deform and decay when it is materialized in any strategy and tactics, and a value may be diminished to an empty slogan and finally forgotten. Then how has

Huawei instilled its values across the company and passed them down for so long? While it surely helps that these values are cited and repeated almost every month and every day for over 20 years, the company's insistence on self-criticism is all the more essential.

Self-criticism is an important tool to enhance and consolidate core values. In a turbulent age when people are torn apart between growing economy and declining ethics, companies must try to conserve the uniqueness and purity of their own values, but this is a tough challenge. Therefore, self-criticism is no doubt the best means to effectively suppress increase of entropy in the organization with the least disruption. Ren Zhengfei clearly stated:

> Huawei will insist on openness for the long-term. We won't waver under whatever circumstances. If we don't open up, we cannot absorb any outside energy and grow up stronger. At the same time, we must also insist on self-criticism. We must treat ourselves critically; otherwise our openness cannot last long.

However, self-criticism may not be able to hold back the irreversible increase of entropy, and, therefore, it is especially important to introduce negative entropy flow through radical reform to offset entropy increase. In this way, the organization will be able to escape chaos and regain vitality. Huawei has conducted a number of radical reforms, including process transformation, mass resignation of the sales department, and the buyout of 7,000 people, which have reshaped the organization, dissipated subgroup politics and its hierarchy, and placed people with stronger sense of mission, crisis, or hunger at the forefront of the company.

Self-criticism and organizational reforms have barred reverse selection, or reverse dissipation in Huawei. A healthy and growing organization must first of all possess a strong self-healing and self-restoring power, which means its healthy cells should be able to eliminate and replace decadent and degenerated cells, not vice versa.

From Karl Marx to Louis Kelso

Like a man, an organization in its middle age would often feel tired and diffuse an air of decadence. It is just natural. The organizational fatigue and corruption, as well as the greed of its individual members, may then give rise to some degenerative subcultures, such as subgroup politics, leader worship, collective inaction, treason, and mutiny.

Therefore, leaders of organizations would spend their lifetime fighting against organizational fatigue and corruption. The Roman Emperors, the First Emperor of Qin, Vladimir Lenin, George Washington, Mao Zedong, Margaret Thatcher, Bill Gates, Louis Gerstner, Vladimir Putin, Jack Welch, Silvia Berlusconi, and Adolf Hitler have all experienced and witnessed the craze and fatigue of followers, and of their own. This dramatic change is due in part to the imperfections and faults of the leaders, but the real killer is the fatigue caused by the passage of time.

In history, bloody revolutions and blood-changing reforms have all been intended to punish decadent organizations and conquer the fatigue of nations. The multipartisan political system of Western countries and the leadership transition system of China, from the perspective of organizational psychology, are both based on profound insight into human nature: Everyone is expecting new faces, which will create new passion.

In human history, great thinkers, such as Sakyamuni the Buddha, Jesus Christ, Confucius, Socrates, Karl Marx, Sigmund Freud, Max Webber, and Peter Drucker, were organizational physicians who had tried to examine the health of social organizations (including states and companies) and diagnose and prescribe remedies for their illness. They had reviewed their time, system, society, and country with exceptional coolness and detachment, but in the end, they had inspired and warmed up the public.

For great thinkers, criticism is a sharp scalpel, and the reforms resulting from their criticism have brought organizations away from fatigue and disease while instilling them with newfound life. In the 1840s, Karl Marx, a Western intellectual, published a book, *The Communist Manifesto*, which declared the near death of capitalism with a sharp voice like an owl screaming in the dark. He argued that duality between the bourgeoisie and the proletariat would lead to the ruin of capitalism.

Karl Marx, it turns out, did not kill capitalism; instead, he became a great sweeper for capitalism. His resounding "death knell" declaration had inspired another declaration about 100 years later: *The Capitalist Manifesto—How to Turn 80 Million Workers into Capitalists on Borrowed Money*. The idea was that people could gain income through both labor and capital investment. The book was coauthored by Louis O. Kelso, who is chiefly remembered today as the inventor and pioneer of the employee stock ownership plan (ESOP). Being the man behind the rapid growth of the middle class in the United States since the 1960s, Kelso has helped hold up the sky of the capitalist world.

In 1988, 10 years after the start of China's reform and opening up, a publisher and friend of mine said with black humor, "Karl Marx's *Das Kapital* (Capital: Critique of Political Economy) has been widely read in China, but it seems the real 'capital' was left behind in the West while only 'political critique' was given to the East." In 1992, during his tour to the South, Deng Xiaoping said, "'Do Not Debate' is one of my inventions." For about 30 years, following the principle of "Do Not Debate," China has created the best golden age in its history with miraculous speed. Of course, in this process, China has also acquired a lot of national fatigue and ills.

Today, China seems to be offering more liberty to "debate," while intending to keep real capital at the same time. There is a multifaceted balance to be maintained, and it is a test for the entire nation, particularly for the elite class, including entrepreneurs.

Survival of the Horrified: A Sense of Fear Prompts Self-Criticism

In 1948, Huang Yanpei, prominent educator, industrialist, and politician, who was also one of the founders of the China Democratic League, visited Yan'an, the wartime capital of the CPC. He said to Mao Zedong with near-abrupt frankness:

> For 60 years I have heard with my own ears and seen with my own eyes the rapid rise and fall of individuals, families, groups, and regions. Few have been able to avoid this swift cycle. In most cases, this is because at the start one is focused and dedicated despite difficult conditions. People are forced to fight for life or for a better life. As things turn better with some initial success, they lose their will. In some cases, laziness rises as a natural result of fatigue, and the feeling spreads wider until the whole organization is infected. At this point, no one can turn the table around. I believe this is also true with the Communist Party. You have been fighting for a new life, but I hope you can avoid the deadly cycle.

Mao Zedong answered,

> I believe we have found a new path, and we can avoid the curse as long as we go straight ahead. The path is democracy. If the people are allowed to oversee and criticize the government, the government won't lose its vigilance. If every one of us is alert, our future will be safe and sound.

Mao Zedong was a great man who slept with his eyes open. Throughout his life he had sought to understand the law of the rise and fall of states and political parties. In order to prevent organizational ills and national fatigue, he made a unique invention: movements. Every three–five years, he would initiate a movement to stir up the entire country by involving almost every person at every level of the CPC and China. These movements attempted to awaken individuals and organizations that otherwise would have fallen due to laziness and degenerative ills. In essence, Mao Zedong had wanted to achieve national stability by creating uncertainty throughout the country.

"The peoples of China are at their most critical time." This is part of the lyrics from the national anthem of the People's Republic of China, and has served as a warning call for the whole nation since 1949. During the past years of ups and downs, the CPC, the ruling party, has insisted on the principle of "criticism and self-criticism," and every person and organization has followed this principle through every period of development. This alertness to crisis has served the country well.

As a member of the CPC, Ren Zhengfei has experienced almost every change in China over the past 60 years. He also served in the military for several years. Therefore, in his business management, he has been deeply influenced by CPC governance and culture, just like most of his contemporaries.

Worth noting is that Huawei's self-criticism is a revision of the CPC's criticism and self-criticism. Criticism means to create alertness against danger. In the history of China and the world, many organizations had appeared extremely powerful, but collapsed easily at a critical test. The great Qin Dynasty of China that conquered and united the whole country lasted only 14 years, falling apart at the challenge of ill-armed peasant uprisers. Again, within 30 years of reform and opening up, China has produced a large number of star companies and business people, but how many of them are still on the stage? In most cases, they perished after achieving some success, as they lost their sense of fear and caution and fell short on self-criticism and introspection.

Ren Zhengfei often warned his colleagues that wood turns into ash after it is burnt red. He required his senior managers to read more about Chinese and foreign history, and recommended books, essays, and TV programs that he had read or watched. He asked them to pay special attention to tragedies that have ruined nations and companies due to internal corruption. He said, "The biggest risk facing the company will come from inside the organization. Huawei has insisted on self-criticism; that's how we will conquer our internal crises."

Maurice Greenberg, founder and CEO of American International Group (AIG), is a legendary figure. He is short in stature, yet a financial giant. He once asked Ren Zhengfei, "What is Huawei's key to success?" Ren Zhengfei answered, "Self-criticism. Huawei has been moving forward through self-negation." Greenberg said, "It's a pity I have met you too late. If we had met 30 years ago, I would love to have invited you to work with me."

In fact, the United States, which is the No. 1 superpower in the world, has won this position because for centuries it has cherished an awareness of crisis and has valued the tradition of self-criticism. There have always been critical voices in the country. None of the political parties, politicians, social elites, or presidents have ever relaxed their nerve. Today, however, perhaps because it has been the world leader for too long, politicians and business organizations in the United States have started to get tired, restless, and arrogant.

Huawei's leadership has not copied ideas from books or other organizations. Huawei has derived its corporate values of more work for more pay and its organizational tradition of self-criticism from the CPC. Ren Zhengfei said, "We have learned all this from the CPC." Huawei, however, does not advocate mutual criticism. Ren Zhengfei explained:

> Mutual criticism is likely to hurt each other and create tension in the company. Self-criticism is much better. Everyone can criticize themselves as much as they can afford. While people who dare to reveal their weaknesses and are willing to get help from others will make progress faster, those who are afraid to lose face will become thick-skinned over time and eventually catch up with the steps of the organization.

Ren Zhengfei on Self-Criticism

For over 20 years, Ren Zhengfei has spoken most often about Huawei's core values and its tradition of self-criticism. The core values are the company's spiritual totems to compete and win in the market, while self-criticism is the shield to protect the integrity of its core values. Both are equally important to the company.

When Huawei's Charter was finalized in 1998, Ren Zhengfei proposed to place a stone at the front gate of its new campus with the inscription: "A company's long-term success depends on the continuity of its core values and its tradition of self-criticism."

Let us see how Ren Zhengfei interprets self-criticism. In 1998, he said:

We must continue the tradition of self-criticism. No matter how much we have achieved, we must still insist on self-criticism. The world has evolved through constant self-negation. Whether Huawei will collapse depends on whether our management will improve. And this improvement should be measured by whether our core values are be accepted by our managers and whether we will continue to practice self-criticism.

In a 2004 essay titled "From the Realm of Necessity to the Realm of Freedom," Ren Zhengfei asserted,

In this world only those companies that are capable of self-criticism can survive. In this sense, Andrew Grove, former Intel CEO, was only partially right when he said only the paranoid could survive. One more sentence should be added. One also has to understand grayness and practice self-criticism in order to survive.

This is the first time Ren Zhengfei had placed self-criticism and grayness in parallel as two key factors for a company's survival.

In 2008, Ren Zhengfei gave a speech titled "Those Who Can Climb Out of the Pits Are Saints," in which he systematically elaborated on the importance of self-criticism in Huawei's history:

The past twenty years have told us how important self-criticism is for a company. If we had not insisted on self-criticism, Huawei could not have come so far. Without self-criticism, we would not have listened so attentively to our customers and understood their needs so well, or we would not have paid much attention and learned from the merits of our peers. In short, we would have turned egocentric, and in consequence would have fallen down and out in this changing and competitive market. Without self-criticism, we would have succumbed to any crisis because we could not have inspired ourselves and other members of the organization. Without self-criticism, we would have confined ourselves to an enclosure and missed out on the new ideas which have proven essential for us to become a world-class corporation. Without self-criticism, we would have been blinded by our pride and over achievements and fallen easily into the pits. Without self-criticism, we would not have been able to remove inefficiency in our organization and processes or reduce the cost of operation. Without self-criticism, our managers would not have told the truth, listened to critical voices, or learned the best ideas. Therefore, they would not have been able to make or implement the best decisions. Only those people who have insisted on self-criticism have the right state of mind to accept new ideas, and only those companies which have insisted on self-criticism will enjoy a bright prospect. Self-criticism has led us so far, and will lead us even farther. Our future is dependent on how long we keep the tradition of self-criticism.

In order to institutionalize self-criticism and prevent straying from its intended purpose, Huawei has established a Self-Criticism Steering Committee. At a meeting of the committee, Ren Zhengfei proposed that self-criticism become a key standard for manager evaluation and promotion. He said, "Huawei should change itself from head to toe. We must employ and promote managers who dare to speak up, criticize themselves, and accept the criticism of others. Only such people can fulfill their duties as managers." In fact, he had expressed a similar view in a speech he gave in 1998 on institutional reform and manager development:

Any manager who is not capable of self-criticism should not be promoted. We should carefully examine those who have received no criticism. On the other hand, those who have been subject to harsh criticisms should be classified and treated differently. If they have no ethical problems, we should still give them opportunities. People have a natural inclination toward laziness; they are not born with innovative capability. If our managers cannot criticize themselves from time to time, Huawei would soon fade away. In a few years, we will make it clearer that anyone incapable of self-criticism will not be considered for a managerial position at Huawei.

It was made clear enough in 2006. Huawei had spent eight years in preparation for the forthcoming reform within the organization. This reflects the institutional and cultural character of Huawei, which would not launch any sudden movement. As the ancient Chinese philosopher Lao Zi said, "Govern a great nation as you would cook a small fish; do not overdo it." This is also true with running a company; a delicious dish may be made only through slow and careful preparation.

Most other Chinese companies, including SOEs, are different. Many are afraid of self-criticism. On the surface, their management seems very harmonious, but on deeper levels, they are at odds with each other. In the longer run, the organization and almost every member suffer from "arteriosclerosis," and impurities in the veins and arteries of the organization pile up and transform gradually into plaque. Some other companies adopt self-criticism too rashly, which may cause hostility within the managing board and ultimately lead the organization toward disintegration.

In either case, there have been plenty of examples among private companies: We have seen slow, suicidal decline for lack of a healthy climate for
criticism, and snow-slide collapse from brutal infights.

Huawei advocates self-criticism, but tries to avoid mutual criticism
in its corporate management. Ren Zhengfei believes that a company is
naturally a constructive profit-seeking organization unlike any political organization or government department. It is different from military
outfits and art groups as well. Therefore, he argued, "Self-criticism is not
mere criticism, or intended to deny or negate anything. Our culture of
self-criticism should be constructive. Through self-criticism, we intend to
optimize and further develop ourselves. Our final goal is to improve the
core competitiveness of the company."

This is the underlying purpose for Huawei to hold on to self-criticism.

Section III. Criticism of Consciousness and EMT Declarations

More Like Your Opponent than Your Opponent

Niall Ferguson says in his book, *Civilization: The West and The Rest*, that
the West has risen to global dominance because it has developed six
"killer applications" that the rest of the world lacks: competition, science,
democracy, medicine, consumerism, and work ethic. More importantly,
it has fostered a culture of self-criticism, which Ferguson calls self-
flagellation. "The West is able to find the best cure for any disease. ... In
fact, if any feature is written in the genes of the post-feudalist West, that
feature is public participation and accountability."

Huawei is competing with Western companies in the context of globalization, and the battlefield covers all continents, including the home
countries of its Western competitors, mainly the EU and the United
States. In a sense, basically at par with each other in terms of products
and technologies, the competition hinges upon crisis awareness and
self-criticism. In other words, in order to beat its Western competitors,
Huawei should strive to be more Western than the West and at the same
time take advantage of its inherent Eastern way of thinking. So to speak,
whether the company can combine the skills of bullfighting and Tai Chi
on the ground of grayness will decide the outcome of this game.

The only way to beat your opponent is to be more like your opponent
than your opponent, while possessing special genes that your opponent

cannot copy. Huawei's self-criticism has impressed Westerners, and their comments have been very positive. Western civilization has grown on the basis of continuous self-questioning and self-criticism. They believe criticism is not for criticism's sake; the aim is to improve and optimize the current system. Huawei is following the same path.

In its early years, Huawei had no professional management system or formal decision-making process, and Ren Zhengfei was meeting with customers and listening to reports most of the time. The company had a chaotic diversity of "isms," as each leader was trying to show their power. As a result, it lacked any clear direction or goals. In 1997, when it was marking its 10th anniversary, Huawei was still in a state of chaos, though it remained dynamic and powerful. Fortunately, at about this time, Ren Zhengfei started to advocate self-criticism more often, and its meetings of criticism and self-criticism, the so-called "democratic meetings" which had lasted 10 years, were institutionalized and extended to every level and part of the organization. This is a typical CPC practice for organizational development and has helped Huawei in developing its own managers and teams.

All this, however, is more of an alert than a fundamental recipe. Cliques, hedonism, nepotism, and arrogance had lingered and even intensified in the company.

In short, the 10-year-old company faced two major challenges: One was the conflicting thoughts and goals, and the other was the corruption that had developed along with rapid growth. Ren Zhengfei's solution to the first challenge was typical of Chinese style: He would propose a general guideline or a master idea that governs the consciousness of all people. This guideline was the Huawei Charter, which has played a crucial role in the history of the company. The Charter, drafted by professors from China's Renmin University, took one year to finalize. Thoughts and ideas of all the people were thoroughly expressed, argued, and debated, and in the end, disputes as to the company's future and direction were resolved.

The second challenge was apparently more difficult. Countries, both Eastern and Western, and organizations have had to cope with greed and corruption throughout their history. All have accumulated much experience, but no definite and effective solution has been found. Is it because the challenge is too tough or complicated? Perhaps it is because the challenge evolves over time.

Also in 1997, Huawei hired a foreign company to design and implement a professional system of management procedures. The idea was to change the company's approach to product development from being technology-oriented to being customer-oriented. For this purpose, the company established a Reengineering Steering Committee and set out the principle of "copying, optimizing, and then institutionalizing." For more than a decade, this principle has worked quite well, and Huawei is still optimizing its processes. This Western-styled reform aims to build capabilities to serve its global customers and make Huawei more like its opponents. This reform has produced another effect: It put the power of managers in the cage, so to speak. Of course, when the company shifts from being governed by people to being governed by processes, people with vested interests will be affected and certainly resist such a reform. In response, Ren Zhengfei insisted that "the feet must be cut to fit the shoes."

During the Spring Festival of 2004, Ren Zhengfei took me to Huawei's data center at its headquarters. I was shocked that he could not access the data center with his card. He told me, "Not just the data center and the R&D center, many other locations I cannot get into because I'm not given such authority by the processes." And I came to understand the power of systems. At Huawei, the higher in the decision-making hierarchy, the less power one has in execution. The role of leaders is to build systems and to determine strategic directions. Generals then act on the orders from leaders, and the actual battle is fought at the division, regiment, or battalion level. If the decision makers are too involved in execution, cliques tend to develop and corruption results. Rules and procedures eliminate most problems, if not all.

Ren Zhengfei argues, "We can build up a healthy organization without depending on any individual only when personal authority is negated and self-negation is advocated and enhanced. When processes and IT are into place, the sky won't fall no matter who leaves the company."

Consciousness Criticism: An Inimitable Cultural Code

According to Mao Zedong, China has made three major contributions to the world: traditional Chinese medicine (TCM), *Dreams of the Red Mansion*, and Mahjong. TCM believes in mutual restriction and generation of natural elements, or in the native Chinese jargon, yin and yang check and enhance each other. Therefore, TCM doctors are like philosophers and strategists because they have to attack certain things while defending something else. The classic novel *Dreams of the Red Mansion* is full of intrigue between individuals. Smoke without fire or an explosion without sound would suffocate almost every reader who attempts to appreciate fictional art. And in the game of Mahjong, each of the four players is like a country or kingdom fighting against the others, one versus three. Each player has to play offense and defense at the same time to win the game.

Checks and balances may be the national character of China. This is a wise nation, and perhaps too wise a nation. Therefore, Confucius demanded that his disciples reflect on conduct and consciousness three times a day, and Mao Zedong called on everyone in the country to revolutionize their soul. Apparently, both Confucius and Mao understood the Chinese national character very well, including its merits and weaknesses, and this is why both great philosophers had proposed the same: criticism of the consciousness.

Confessions of Christians are similar to the self-reflections demanded by Confucius, but they are very different from Mao's soul revolution. China has gone through a number of movements on consciousness criticism, the most revolutionary one being the Cultural Revolution championed by Mao Zedong, which had hurt and even distorted the soul of the entire country.

In consequence, over the past three decades, consciousness criticism has failed to make any difference in China because people are afraid and instinctively run from such a movement. At Huawei, however, it was picked up by Ren Zhengfei, and has been used for over 20 years. Every department or division of Huawei convenes a meeting of criticism and self-criticism each month, and every meeting is serious. Each person is supposed to tell their mistakes and problems without blame-shifting or being perfunctory. They are also expected to find the mental cause of any wrongdoing. Other members help criticize in a constructive way, but the company forbids exaggeration, personal attack, moralizing, or any emotional outbreak.

As a result, individual and organizational problems do not plague the company for too long before they are exposed and corrected. Equally important, criticism and self-criticism have not ripped the company apart, but created a dedicated team of 150,000 people. Moreover, the company has not tamed anyone into an obedient Uncle Tom; everyone has a unique, distinctive character. "The boss really doesn't like people without personality and passion. A manager without passion will never get any notice from him, as he thinks lack of passion is the biggest weakness for anyone," said a senior executive of Huawei.

Self-criticism is a tool, but the key is: What to criticize? How? And why? If it is poorly done, such criticism may not unite people or increase organizational power, but produce negative or even opposite outcome. In China, meetings for criticism and self-criticism have been institutionalized in SOEs. Yet, it is not my purpose to judge how effective they are. Private companies, especially those owned by former military officers or government officials, have also tried to purge their companies through such meetings, but quite often ended in failure: Criticisms have led to infighting and division.

Some companies, therefore, such as Hainan Airlines, have turned to religious faith to pull their people together.

Ren Zhengfei said, "Huawei's self-criticism is based solely on its core values. We must not depart from this orientation, and we must correct any step which is not in exact alignment." The core values are rather simple and literal: Do you focus on your customers? Do you stay committed to hard work? Does management value tough fighters? Over the past two decades, this has been the eternal theme for self-criticism at Huawei, and it has naturally made the organization more cohesive.

As a Huawei senior executive remarked, self-criticism, especially criticism of consciousness, is really tough to handle, but how has Huawei managed it? The recipe is twofold: One is the role model of the top management, who are not afraid of losing face, while the second is compromise. This may be known to all, but few companies can make it happen.

It is tough for Chinese companies, and even tougher for Western companies. In the West, or in Christian countries, people only confess to the Lord to redeem their soul, but confession is rare between colleagues or organizations. Anatomy of thought is an invention of China, where there is no predominant religion. In the West, criticism of consciousness may involve personal dignity and privacy, so it is hard to find any such analyses or arguments in their management literature. They would rather analyze human nature from the perspectives of psychology and behavioral science, and would rather depend on institutional measures or Western-styled corporate culture to stimulate people's potential and suppress their evil inclinations.

Huawei appears elusive to the West largely for its culture of self-criticism, reflected most notably by their "democratic meetings."

But Western companies will never really understand how it works, or borrow the practice for their own use because it is a part of Chinese heritage encoded in Chinese culture. In fact, not all Chinese companies are able to fully comprehend or utilize this philosophical tool of self-criticism, and many have yet to westernize their management systems. Therefore, it is not at all surprising that Huawei has been almost the only dark horse that holds the West in awe even as many other private companies from China tried to tap the global market over the past decade. Huawei leverages the best from China and the West, and yet it is neither Chinese nor Western.

EMT Declaration of Self-Discipline

The Maldives is a paradise on earth, where time seems to stand still. The beach, sunshine, seawater, blue sky, and coconut trees help tourists escape the hustle and bustle of the city and business world. It was here in December 2005 that Huawei held its EMT meeting of criticism and self-criticism to discuss and review personal and organizational integrity and self-discipline.

While it might seem odd for such a beautiful and relaxing island to be chosen for such a serious purpose, Ren Zhengfei and his colleagues were resolute and well-prepared.

All EMT members had agreed that, as key leaders of the company, they must be clean and upright and set good examples for other members of the company. Therefore, at the meeting, they approved an EMT Declaration of self-discipline, which demanded that all EMT members, and middle and senior managers, declare and clear their relationships with suppliers. As part of this declaration, all managers will be required to make a public oath, putting themselves under the supervision of everyone in the company.

Two years later, on the eve of the Chinese Spring Festival in 2008, Huawei organized an oath-taking meeting at its headquarters in Shenzhen. Face-to-face with over 200 middle-level and senior managers, EMT members, including Ren Zhengfei, Sun Yafang, Guo Ping, Ji Ping, Fei Min, Hong Tianfeng, Eric Xu, Ken Hu, and William Xu, raised their right hands and declared:

We hereby commit ourselves to integrity, dedication, and diligence by which we shall lead the company through difficulties. We must not allow leaders to set bad examples for their subordinates. We must not allow the organization to crack from inside. We shall honor each and every one of our commitments under the supervision of the company and all employees of Huawei.

After taking this collective oath, each EMT member proceeded to take an individual oath. Ren Zhengfei's oath was

> Since the first day I was CEO of Huawei, I have felt as if I was in the middle of a whirlwind of conflicts and temptations, and I am well aware of the heavy responsibilities on my shoulders. The only way to handle each and every conflict and make wise and determined decisions is through absolute selflessness. This is the foundation for my qualifications as CEO, as well as for anyone who wishes to become a senior executive of the company.
>
> Only through selflessness, can I be fair and just in uniting everyone within the company. Only through selflessness, can I be fearless in insisting on the company's principles, embracing criticism and self-criticism, and correcting my own weaknesses. And only through selflessness, can I be broad-minded in accepting whatever I must accept and taking on every responsibility that I must.
>
> I am determined to resist any and all corruption. I will not allow any of my family members or relatives to enter into any related-party transactions with Huawei, and I will not involve my personal interests in any major decisions of the company.

Then, Sun Yafang spoke her oath:

> I fully understand that, as key members of the company, we will affect the company with every word we speak and every action we take. In my own post, I shall manage myself and those around me. I shall practice self-discipline and follow all of the company's principles. I will not directly or indirectly interfere in any of the company's business activities by taking advantage of the power of my position, or in any way impair the company's interests. I shall be devoted to the company's development, and set an example for my colleagues.
>
> I pledge that during my tenure at the company:
>
> I will not seek personal interests or engage in corruption through the exercising of my rights and duties.
> I will not set up my own company, hold equity in any other company, or engage in stock market speculation.
> I will not allow any of my family members or relatives to enter into any related-party transactions with Huawei.

I will not seek to establish or lead any clique within the company to prevent improper work styles.

I will improve my personal conduct as a qualified citizen of China.

I will strictly observe every item contained in the EMT Declaration of self-discipline, and subject myself to the supervision and inspection of the company and its employees.

What follows is the full text of Huawei's EMT Declaration of self-discipline:

Huawei assumes a great mission and is committed to the common aspirations of all its employees. For 18 years, we have contributed our best and endured tremendous hardships to achieve the company's current position today. In order to continue this success, we must remain dedicated for decades to come.

We love Huawei as much as we love our own life. To sustain our vitality and growth, we will remain alert so as not to fall into the same trap of collapse from within. Hereby, we solemnly declare:

1. We will set a good example of integrity and self discipline. We will derive all our income from Huawei's dividends and compensation and shall not attempt to obtain any income from any other source.

2. We will not attempt to affect or interfere with the company's business activities or seek any personal interests through the power the company has assigned us. Such business activities include, but are not limited to, procurement, sales, cooperation, and outsourcing. We will not damage the company's interests in any way.

3. We will not set up any company, or hold any equity or job in any other company. We shall not allow any company owned by our family members or relatives to enter into any related-party transactions with Huawei.

4. We may help anyone we would like to help, but every penny used should come from our own pockets. Personal and company interests should be clearly separated.

5. We will be honest and selfless. We will not attempt to establish or lead any clique within the company. We will not allow any improper work styles to breed within the scope of our responsibilities.

6. We will restrain and discipline ourselves. We will review our own conduct through self-inspection, self-correction, and self-criticism and develop a self-cleaning mechanism for managers within the organization.

We fully understand that, as key members of the company, we must lead the company forward. Therefore, we will remain united and focused on the company's development. We hereby commit ourselves to integrity, dedication, and diligence by which we will lead the company through difficulties. We must not allow the company's leaders to set bad examples for their subordinates. We must not allow the organization to crack from inside. We shall honor each and every commitment under the supervision of the company and all employees of Huawei.

Within about one month from May to June 2008, every department and subsidiary of Huawei made the same declaration.

Ren Zhengfei had wanted to make the entire company transparent from head to toe, and subject the company to the supervision of its employees. Some doubted Ren's intention, arguing that he has managed the company by launching "mass movements." This is an unfair judgment: Even if it was a movement, in the end it has proved to be an effective means to creating a healthy organization.

The self-discipline declarations for each of the three deputy chairmen and rotating CEOs follow.

Declaration of Ken Hu:

Huawei's success has largely depended on the selflessness of its senior managers and a corporate culture of hard work and dedication. As the company becomes increasingly globalized, this culture is essential for its sustainable development. As a senior manager of the company, I am obliged and willing to practice and promote this value. I hope I can set a good example through my conduct.

Today, I solemnly pledge to all employees of Huawei that I will not set up or hold any equity in any other company, or hold a position in any other company without the company's permission. I will not allow myself or my family to enter into any related-party transactions with Huawei. To honor this pledge, I will start from things that may appear small. I will not bend the rule to accommodate little favor, and will ask my family and relatives to do the same. At the same time, I fully understand, and will help my family and relatives to understand, that the rights Huawei has assigned can only be used to create value for the company, rather than secure my own personal interests.

I am willing to be subject to the supervision of any person within the company, and I will take actions to contribute to the further growth of the company.

Declaration of Eric Xu:

Today, I solemnly declare that, in order to avoid collapse of the company due to internal corruption, I shall consistently and strictly abide by the EMT

Declaration of self-discipline. I will never affect or interfere with any of the company's operations through exercising the rights which the company has assigned me. I shall never allow myself or my family to enter into any related-party transactions with Huawei. I shall never attempt to establish or lead any clique in the company. I shall keep myself active in performing my duties because I believe complacency and inaction are both forms of corruption. I shall insist upon self-inspection, self-correction, and self-criticism.

I hereby sincerely invite everyone in the company to supervise my conduct.

Declaration of Guo Ping:

I hereby solemnly declare that I will be self-disciplined and strictly follow the EMT Declaration of self-discipline.

I understand that the rights and duties which the company has assigned to me are both a vote of confidence and a form of test. I shall not harm the company's interests or seek personal gain while exercising my rights and performing my duties. The businesses I take responsibility for, terminals, strategic partnerships, legal affairs, and information security, are all sensitive and complicated, with profound implications. I hereby pledge, which shall be subject to auditing and supervision, that I will discipline myself strictly and set a good example through my code of conduct. I shall never interfere with the company's operations to seek personal gains; I shall never interfere with the company's decisions concerning procurement, sales, cooperation, and outsourcing. I shall keep my family compliant with relevant prohibitive rules; none shall be allowed to enter any related-party transactions with Huawei. I will maintain my entrepreneurial passion and dedication; I will keep my integrity; I will never attempt to establish or lead any clique within the company. I shall enhance my ability to self-criticize. I will remain self-reflective, and dare to point out and criticize any improper behavior within the company. I will not allow any improper work styles to breed within my scope of responsibilities.

Section IV. The King's Death and Organizational Criticism

Law of the Animal Kingdom: Tiger, Lion, Wolf, and Mouse

One afternoon in 1997, Ren Zhengfei met with an executive of the Hay Group, a global management consulting firm based in the United States. Wu Chunbo, coauthor of this book, who also had attended the meeting, remembered:

During the meeting, they kept talking about animals. Ren said multinationals are like elephants, while Huawei is a small mouse. Of course, Huawei cannot match any elephant, so it has to acquire the qualities of wolves: a sensitive nose, a keen competitive mind, team spirit, and unreserved dedication.

The animal world contains many inspirations for human beings. How had dinosaurs died out millions of years ago? Scientists have never come up with any answer. Tigers are kings of animals; so are lions. They have dominated the animal world and threatened the survival of other animals. Recently, however, both have reached the verge of extinction. Their own survival is threatened. Pandas are even worse off: Their tender and noble looks are always telling the hard truth that the loss of wildness and adaptability is a disaster to all living beings.

Wolves are the perfect combination of nobility and wildness, aggressiveness and team spirit, vigilance and unwavering determination; unfortunately, they are under threat from human beings, and their odds of survival are declining. I am convinced, however, that wolves can still survive in the challenging environment.

Mice are disgusting and dirty in the eyes of human beings, but they possess incredible ability for survival. It is reported that after the 1945 nuclear bombing, almost all creatures had died in Nagasaki and Hiroshima, except mice which proliferated instead. They had survived, and survived very well, feeding on concrete walls and wood. Similarly, 10 years after the Chernobyl accident, scientists found that mice in the area had undergone a terrible mutation.

Louis Gerstner, former CEO of IBM, who was acclaimed for rescuing the "dying dinosaur" and recognized as an American business hero, also said when he was trying to turn IBM around, "If the elephant can dance, then the ants have to leave the stage."

Like IBM, most world-class multinational companies boast a long history and immense size, and they are typically noble industry leaders. They share two common diseases, however: organizational fatigue and corruption.

Huawei shares many of these merits, and ailments as well. With its 20-year history and a team of 150,000 employees, Huawei has risen to a "noble" status and now ranks second in the telecom industry. CEO Ren warned in 1998: "Recently, a handful of people at Huawei have shown signs of corruption. The company will not allow any such trend to develop further. Otherwise, how can we accomplish anything as an organization?"

In his speech at the company's market conference in 2011, Ren Zhengfei noted that past achievement is not a reliable guide to future success. He said,

> We welcome any people who have nothing but ambition. They will be a strong force for Huawei. These people will give us the power to grab more resources, which then would allow us to make more investments. With more investments we can gain even more power. This will turn out a virtuous cycle.

At the end of the speech, Ren said with sensation, "We are like a horse with two wings flying over the grassland. Nothing can stop us except corruption and laziness from within."

Apparently, Ren Zhengfei is afraid that Huawei might one day become extinct like the dinosaurs, or tread to the verge of extinction like the tiger.

The Lucky Bird: Crow or Owl

Animals without natural enemies are often the first to go become extinct, while those challenged by their natural enemies tend to proliferate and prosper. This natural law applies equally well to the human race and the business world. While it grows, any business organization will meet with many opponents. They may pose various threats to the organization, but at the same time, their constant challenge drives the organization forward. When competitors or enemies are standing right in the front, no organization can afford to lose a bit of its aggressiveness, its passion, its cohesion, or the reason and dedication of its leaders. Therefore, a wise entrepreneur would never loathe, but feel indebted to his opponents for coursing his nerve and strengthening the muscle of his organization, thereby enhancing the battle-readiness of the company.

A sense of fear makes greatness. For 25 years, Huawei has lived with fear. Besiege by Western companies and encroachment by domestic competitors has always kept the company alert and proactive.

Natural enemies and their threats are good for a company. Quite often, a great company is made not from an ambitious strategy but from major crisis. This is at least true with Huawei. In less than a decade, Huawei has turned from a clumsy boxer into an adept Tai Chi master who knows how to balance between competition and cooperation, offense and defense. Its position on corporate management in addition to cultural and institutional development has become much different than what it was just 10 years ago. In both cases, there have been major incidents that triggered the change and, therefore, have indirectly driven the progress of the company.

From 1999 to 2006, Huawei had entered a valley. Ren Zhengfei had become so tired that he fell ill: hypertension, diabetes, two cancer operations, and depression.

Psychologists argue that depression in any form not only brings pain, but also sharpens one's mind to realize and confront problems. Anyone suffering from mania could gain tenacity to learn from past failures. In some sense, psychological problems are also early signs of success.

This argument certainly applies with Ren Zhengfei. He once said, "We should not be resistant to criticism from any opponent. We must listen carefully, even if they have gone too far. To beat us, they need to find our weaknesses. We cannot find out all problems by ourselves." A colleague agreed and said, "A crow may be noisy, but no one has ever died from a crow cawing; an owl may disturb the night, but its cry warns us of death. In this sense, both the crow and owl are lucky birds."

Ren Zhengfei nodded in agreement.

Ren Zhengfei divides self-criticism into two categories: consciousness criticism and organizational criticism. Consciousness criticism probes into certain questions: Whether individual and organizational values are safe and sound? Whether the climate is positive and motivating? And whether any individual or team is corrupted? This is a most discussed topic at the executive level of Huawei, and cascades down throughout the organization through "democratic meetings." On the other hand, the company has remained cautious on organizational criticism, as it might involve structural reforms, or real actions. "Reform is a systematic project, and caution is absolutely necessary." Ren Zhengfei said:

> We have emerged from a small company which had scarcely any systematic management. After we implemented a series of reforms, including integrated product development (IPD), integrated supply chain (ISC), and four financial unifications, our management system has evolved from simple and rough to IT-based and fine-tuned. And our company is globalizing. Without self-criticism, we would have been hesitant to change prior policies or statements made by a certain leader, or to revise a process that would cause removal of a certain position. Then how can we build a complete system of business processes? Without the big improvement we have made in our management, we would not have been able to provide lower-cost and higher-value

services to our customers. We then would have possibly lost the chance to survival through today in this competitive market where prices are racing to the bottom. The management system has been subject to self-criticism, as without it we cannot survive in this fast-changing world.

There was once a popular book titled *Small Is Beautiful*. Ren Zhengfei argues, however, "A small piece of grass may be crushed at any time by a big elephant. This is an age of risks, and I believe bigger ships can better survive a tempest." And of course, as Wang Xifeng said in *Dream of Red Mansions*, "A big family has its own problems."

Huawei has grown itself into a large company through constant criticism of consciousness, and cautious but deliberate organizational criticism. Yet in 2008, Ren Zhengfei said, "We shall now shift our focus from consciousness criticism to organizational criticism." But his target this time is a common ill of large corporations: organizational fatigue.

Mission and Fate: When Will Huawei Die?

Throughout the history of China that spans 5,000 years, only four dynasties were able to last longer than 200 years. The average life span of top 500 US companies is 30–40 years, and people draw the inference that the life of a company is about half that of a man. Only one-fourth of Dow Jones companies are able to survive 50 years.

A Japanese management expert proposed a measurement of time: dog years. One dog year is usually considered equivalent to seven human years. Here, I pity my dogs very much: They are so lovely but I have to suffer their early loss of life. Then I may have to pity Chinese companies because most cannot live more than one dog year. Sigh!

For over 30 years after reform and opening up, China has turned out many excellent companies that have been quoted as cases for MBA study, but now 85 percent of them have dropped out. By 2010, the average life of Chinese small and medium enterprises (SMEs) was 3.7 years, while the average life span of European and Japanese companies was 12.5 years; American companies survive 8.2 years on average, and about one-fourth of the 500 best German SMEs survive 100 years.

This is the fate of every organization: They will die sooner or later. But it is the mission of leaders to lead every member of the organization fighting against this eventual demise; they must struggle to live longer and healthier.

As a materialist, Ren Zhengfei is not afraid of talking about death. He said, "One is born to die anyway. What we are doing is trying to let Huawei live as long as possible. We don't want it to die so soon; we don't want it to die in a miserable way, either." To him, the most basic goal of Huawei is to live on.

An Argentine media website reported an exciting scientific discovery from an article titled "We Are Getting Closer to the End of Death." The news said,

> Modern biology has proven that adult stem cells do not age like other cells in the body. That means that before most cells start to age, the stem cells will function regularly. Now we know that stem cells do not age, they can be frozen and kept forever. They can be thawed and reengineered.

The author predicted, therefore, "Some scientists are studying the aging process as a disease, and perhaps in 20 or 30 years we can witness the end of death. The dream of living forever is coming closer to reality."

This news is thrilling, no doubt, although the reality is still far away, perhaps farther than the author had predicted. It has triggered some interesting association though: What and where are the stem cells of Huawei? What is Huawei's nightmare?

No doubt, either, Huawei's stem cells are its core values: customer-centricity and dedication. The two have combined to form an embryo that has grown into the company which is called Huawei. In some sense, dedication is the prototype or gene of Huawei's culture. Huawei would not have survived so long without this gene, which has remained unchanged for over 20 years.

Many people, including those inside and outside Huawei, have associated the fate of the company with its CEO, Ren Zhengfei. We believe it is a mistake. Ren certainly will have his curtain call, as this is a natural law, but the company may not have such an end. Although overall numbers do not look bright, as in the "dog years" argument or the estimated average lifespan of 3.7–12.5 years, there are still long-lived companies. In fact, people's understanding of "organizations" and their creations is still superficial and limited. An organization is a charming but upsetting Frankenstein, and its life cycle is still elusive and vague.

The end of Ren Zhengfei's career is predictable. He has required his EMT members to work in a healthy manner for 20 years. How about the boss himself? Well, he is already 68 years old. However, the organization created by Ren Zhengfei and 150,000 people together may last a century or even longer, or of course it may survive for just another 10 years. The company's fate may depend on external factors beyond its control, such as war and social turmoil, but its own organic problems, such as aging, decay, and middle-age obesity, are even bigger challenges.

Therefore, the key to survival is whether the stem cells of the company can continue to function with vigor and replicate in every system of the organization. In other words, Huawei will die if it loses its stem cells, or its core values, no matter how long Ren Zhengfei stays to lead the company. On the other hand, if it keeps its stem cells healthy and robust, Huawei may still live well and keep growing after Ren Zhengfei leaves the helm.

Since 2008, Huawei senior management has advised many times of its symptoms of being big and warned:

> When soldiers shed blood at the frontline, government officials back at home dined themselves into obesity. That had happened in the Kuomintang army. For us, any one person we add to the back office would mean more work for the fighters at the frontline; that person would surely find some job for himself, and most of the time it is inventing more rules for the frontline to follow. Meanwhile, the rear-end administration has a strong inclination to be lazy. Therefore, we should increase the income of people at the frontline and attract more outstanding staff to the field with higher pay than that of the rear.

Can you imagine an elephant dancing? An elephant is big, but it may not be as clumsy as one might imagine. Life lies in movement. Huawei is still recruiting new employees and continues to expand the organization. Today, it has 150,000 people, and in 5 or 10 years' time, the number may climb to 200,000 or 300,000. The decision-makers of the company will hold fast to its core values and keep exercising its organism to increase its power and vitality. Recently, military terms have been used often within the company: "Moving the command post to the frontline," "Let those who can hear the fire take the command," and "Call for fire." They provide a glimpse into Ren Zhengfei's profound understanding and thorough reflection since 2008 of the common ills that large corporations suffer from.

So what is Huawei's nightmare? When will Huawei die? One day in October 2011, Ren Zhengfei met with Imamura Kazuo, a Japanese businessman and entrepreneur, at Huawei's head office in Shenzhen. At the meeting, after a Japanese delegate finished his speech with a PowerPoint slide show, Ren told the Huawei senior officials at his side, "The Japanese have fallen behind the changing world." After Guo Ping, Deputy Chairman of Huawei, finished his speech, in exactly the same way, Ren sighed, "Huawei is dying. ..."

What does Ren Zhengfei really mean?

CHAPTER SEVEN

Change: Revolution or Evolution?

Section I. Facing the Cold Sharp Blade: Change or Die

Time Passes Like a River

O ver 2,000 years ago, Confucius, a frustrated philosopher, stood on the Yellow River and sighed, "Time is passing like this river, flowing away endlessly day and night."

Two thousand years later, on April 28, 2005, Ren Zhengfei, who compared himself to a passing sage, was thinking about a self-relinquishing revolution to shatter his own glory and create a brand new future for the company.

This day, Ren Zhengfei was invited by the CPC Committee of Guangdong Province to give a speech on Huawei's core values. He said:

> Managing a company is like managing the Yangtze River. We build the dam, and the water flows day and night inside the dam. It is still flowing even while I am asleep. The water flows into the sea and evaporates. The vapor floats in the air and may reach above the Himalayas. At a certain temperature, it turns into snow, and then the snow melts into water which flows into the Yangtze River again. It completes the cycle when the river flows into the sea. After a while, no one remembers the people who built the dam; "the sage mourning the passage of time" becomes invisible while the water keeps flowing. A company is running at its best when no one cares who the founder is or who commands the helm. On the other hand, when the founder is highly visible and worshipped, the company is in danger.

Some media outlets, both at home and abroad, have doubts as to Huawei's fate once Ren Zhengfei leaves the company. It might be universal that once a company is reaching the highest peak, its founder may also be nearing the end. At this point in time, the media and public, as well as its competitors and enemies, would sigh over the fate of the company and draw alarmist speculations.

Ren Zhengfei, accustomed to self-criticism, is keenly aware of this universal law. As a scholar who has served Huawei as a management advisor for many years said:

> Ren Zhengfei is different from most other entrepreneurs. Company founders are generally attached to their company, both physically and emotionally. They believe their company is their child and part of their life, and naturally they won't let it go. Ren Zhengfei is an exception. He believes that a company has its own independent life after it is born. The founder at some point will leave or die, but the company and its management regime may regenerate itself and last. In this sense no individual should be allowed to interfere with the course of its development. At a certain point, a company must cut off its emotional link with its founder.

Huawei had reached this point, and it was waving a knife with a cold sharp blade to cut off the link. The year 1997 was critical for Huawei. The company has since systematically borrowed advanced management experience and practices from the West. Through partnerships with leading consulting firms, including IBM, Hay Group, PricewaterhouseCoopers, Accenture, and Fraunhofer, Huawei has built up its own customer-driven processes and management systems for IPD, ISC, human resources management, financial management, marketing management, and quality assurance.

This has been a tectonic change for Huawei. As Ren Zhengfei said, this was an organizational revolution. Powerful people had lost all or part of their power, and the exercise of power became subject to restrictions. The leader of the revolution would lose power if the change was not well carried out. In history, most reformers had ended in misery because they harmed the interests of too many powerful people. When Huawei was determined to substitute procedural and institutional governance for personal governance, it had to pay the price as well.

For 14 years, Huawei has insisted on its management reform. During these years over a 100 mid-level and senior managers have left the company, or have been demoted or replaced, because they resisted or could not adapt to the change. Many of them had outstanding capabilities or had made significant contributions to the company. But, in order to open up the road for change in the new process governance and operation system, Huawei does not need individual heroes anymore.

Every company has heroes and has gone through such a period of heroism. When a company starts from nothing, heroes are needed and could help the company with their glorious deeds. But in most cases, with their individual ambition and desires, heroes could also make the company a dirty and bloody mess. Moreover, when the startup company grows big enough and transforms into a mature organization, heroes often become hurdles that must be removed.

No doubt, the biggest enemy of reform is people, especially leaders. A reform would be easier and more effective if people yield to the reforms and not vice versa; otherwise, it takes twice the effort for half the results. To some extent, a reform is a revolution since both annul and redistribute power. There are some differences, though. A revolution is often violent and ends in the change of a regime, but a reform is much more reasonable and more constructive. And a reform aims at stimulating the organizational drive, overcoming laziness and corruption, and optimizing the organizational structure.

Unfortunately, in most companies, the leaders prefer violent movements and struggles within the organization to secure their own interests and power when their companies attain certain success. Such movements or struggles never serve to push the organization forward. Instead, an organization is likely to tremble and even fall apart amid such shocks.

Huawei's management reform covers every person in the organization, including Ren Zhengfei himself. Ren Zhengfei admitted:

In Huawei, the top leaders possess less power and command fewer people than lower level managers. For example, a rotating CEO has only an assistant and perhaps a secretary, and does not possess any direct commanding power. The chairwoman and I are symbolic leaders. We have no decision-making rights. We can only veto decisions or impeach other leaders, but we have indeed rarely exercised these rights. They cannot be used often, no more than two or three times a year, or they would lose their effect. Atom bombs provide deterrence as long as they are not exploded. On the other hand, our leaders in the sales or R&D function command 40 or 50 thousand people. They have huge power. Of course, we have instituted a mature monitoring system for them.

Yes, time flows like a river, and a leader passes like time. As Ren Zhengfei said, "Huawei's reform is a process for individual authority to dissipate.

Huawei will become truly mature when it does not depend on a handful of people."

IPD Revolution: Wear American Shoes

China has a long history of raising birds in the cage, while the West takes fancy in taming and riding horses. Birds have little freedom in the cage and are dependent on their master for food and water, and in return appease their master with their voices. Taming a horse is different. Horses have been accustomed to running wild on vast land. People often compare unrestrained imagination to wild horses running free. To tame a horse, one must allow the horse to retain some of its wild nature while attempting to regulate its behavior. In other words, a well-tamed horse runs with belligerent passion but within a certain boundary. The fate of birds and horses is so different, so are the two cultures. This contains a lot of clues and inspirations for corporate managers.

A bird cage represents a certain set of rules and prohibition. And in a vast land where horses run, while there would certainly be a "STOP" sign that the horses cannot go beyond, there is also freedom and imagination. Yet, in the minds of most company managers and employees alike, rules are equal to restrictions. Consequently, company managers tend to pit rules and goals against each other. They falsely believe that rules will make goals impossible.

Ren Zhengfei said, "Huawei's minimal goal is to survive, and of course we shall try to catch up with our Western counterparts in the long run. To achieve this goal, we must wear American shoes." What he meant is that the company should learn the best of its rivals in order to beat them. Zhang Zhidong, a Chinese politician and reform advocate during the late Qing Dynasty, argued instead, "We should depend on the Chinese tradition while drawing on achievements from the West." His reform had apparently failed. Ren Zhengfei, as a latecomer who runs a company at the forefront of globalization, certainly has a broader view of history and of the world.

Huawei's American shoes refer specifically to a set of corporate governance rules that have been well established in the West. They are Tao, in the Chinese terminology, at a much deeper level, rather than superficial methods. In order to enter the Western market, the company must completely westernize its management systems and mix Western concepts with Chinese ones in its management philosophy. This would also be the way to long-term prosperity.

Therefore, the institutional and procedural reform that Huawei had started in 1997 had much deeper implications. It was intended to rectify its "pirate culture" developed in the company's infancy, and would certainly meet with resistance from people and organizations with vested interests. Yet, the tougher part of this reform was the collision, or the desired integration of cultures, ways of thinking, and national characters between East and West.

This is why Huawei was determined to cut their feet to fit the shoes. In most other Chinese companies, such a reform would surely be abandoned half way or cause an organizational earthquake.

When he mobilized the core team members for the IPD reform, Ren Zhengfei said with a stern face:

First, we must dismiss the mavericks with scanty knowledge of the reform. We must also eliminate lazy people without ambition. We would like every one of you to wear a pair of American shoes. We will let our American advisors tell you what American shoes look like. You may wonder whether the American shoes can be adapted. Well, we have no right to change anything; this is at the discretion of the advisors. From now on, you'd better not raise any new suggestion to show you have talent; unorthodox ideas will not be rewarded. Instead, we must try to understand the fundamental idea of IBM's management system, and those with the most profound understanding will get rewarded. Some may ask whether they can make any change if they have understood the system well enough. I would say yes, but not now. You won't be given the go ahead until 10 or 20 years later. I believe at this time we must stay cool and play by the book. Innovation must be based on a proper and profound understanding. There is no point in expressing a new idea before you have fully understood it. I think we should remove any such people from the core team.

We should remove those who cannot understand the IPD reform, too. Membership in this core team is not life-long. I wonder if we can renew the membership every month. I can sign my name 12 times a year for the appointments, and I will not charge you for the signature. This core team should be a revolving club with people coming and going. We will not offer permanent opportunities to those who wish to be mavericks or those with no ambition. A lot of junior managers have complained that Huawei is not fair. I asked why. They said that you, the senior managers, have grown up with the company's resources, and if they could attend those expensive training sessions for which the company paid, they could have been even more competent than our vice-presidents. I think they are right. Many of you have been to those training, but no significant improvements have been achieved. We won't give free opportunities to those who do not improve. Each time I appoint new members to this team, we must take out one or two existing members, even if everyone is doing all right. We should replace incompetent ones with those who have ambition and a right attitude toward learning. Since we are determined to learn from the West, we must try to get a full picture all of the deep-rooted ideas and not just focus on one specific point.

Of course, there are many good management practices, but we cannot embrace them all. One would become an idiot if he attempts to learn everything: Different management approaches lean to different directions, and trying to include all would simply get you nowhere. Therefore, we should hire only one advisor and learn a single model at this time. In ten or twenty years, when we are a US$200 billion company, we may embrace something new. We should not attempt now to invent something new, since we have not really understood this single model well enough. Those attempts at reform over the past years did not work because we were far from focused; we've always wanted to come up with something new or different. This time we must stay level-headed, focused, and pragmatic to only wear this pair of American shoes. We must learn the best from them in order to beat them.

The management reform led by IBM lasted 14 years at Huawei, and it has been a very expensive transformation. IBM has assigned 70 experts to help Huawei, and each charges US$300–600 per hour of service. This is perhaps the highest price ever paid for business advisory services by any Chinese organization.

Then what is the return? In 1997, IBM did a comprehensive review of Huawei's management system and loads of problems were found. The company lacked accurate and prospective judgment of customer needs; it was repeating useless efforts and wasting resources, which drove up costs; while processes existed at each unit, there was no structured cross-functional process, or well-defined and automated process integration; strong organizational silos caused internal friction; lack of skills prevailed and the organization depended heavily on individual heroes whose success could hardly be duplicated; and projects were messy in planning, execution, or change management.

Imagine what the company will become if it does not carry out a fundamental institutional reform. Ren Zhengfei thought of debacle or avalanche! This was a period when Ren Zhengfei was extremely stressed.

Fourteen years have passed, but Huawei has not collapsed. Instead, the company has become a daunting competitor in the telecom world. Vital to this success is the IPD reform, which ultimately led to a modern management system. Through this reform, Huawei has learned how to create a balance: The land is vast, but there is also a boundary; the river is running fast, but torrents are contained within the dam. In other words, in the new system, customer demand sets the direction and the process framework sets the boundary; business operations are made efficient to ensure high-quality delivery end to end.

Even with small earthquakes from time to time, the IPD reform has proceeded quietly at Huawei. Initial success is made, but the reform will still go on.

Section II. Following Established Rules: Conservatism Is Good

From Gangsters to Soldiers

Most companies which die one or two years after birth have died of hunger rather than any disease. They are like pirates who fail to find treasure and are forced to either sail to shore or drown in the icy cold water. Others survive for three or four years or longer in some cases. While business may prosper and the team expands, the gangster, hero, or clique culture that developed early on will only serve to hinder further growth.

During this period, entrepreneurs instinctively seek institutional reforms to end gangster culture and create a new order. This is the basic reform which either as an unconscious and forced act or a conscious and proactive move removes chaos in the organization and fundamentally, or at least superficially, changes the enterprise.

Generally, when a company is unbearably chaotic, the founder would launch a top-down institutional reform to eradicate its primitive passion (or gangster culture) in the hope that the company may take a brand new look overnight. But the result is not always satisfactory, and things get may get even worse. Following radical reform or shock therapy, the company usually faces three possible outcomes: It is struck by an earthquake or typhoon and becomes even more chaotic from open confrontation of opposing forces; or silence prevails across the company, causing a climate that is depressed, passive, pessimistic, cautious, lazy, and perfunctory;

or, in the worst case, there could be a mutiny where the talent jumps overboard.

I have interviewed over a dozen business leaders and employees as to their understanding of "rules," and the answer was essentially the same: Rules are made to restrict behaviors and are generally prohibitive. Imagine a horse galloping at full speed and then suddenly bumping into a solid steel wall. The outcome is certainly tragic.

When they run into the wall, most businesspeople would adapt: They tend to take opportunistic efforts to merely stop leakages. They rush to establish a rule to fix a problem. These rules are then often shelved until a new problem arises, during which time a new rule would be invented. This repeated cycle would lead the organization to internal rot.

Yet still, trial-and-error, opportunism, and resilience have allowed certain Chinese companies to last more than 20 years and achieve notable successes. A handful of them have grown into national or world-class companies. After all, in a country that has virtually no business philosophy or experience, business people can only draw inspiration for corporate governance from China's political culture and the theories of Deng Xiaoping. Over time, they have managed to understand and borrow tried-and-true practices, applying them where necessary and gradually developing a unique culture and system. Lenovo, Haier, Vanke, and Midea are all perfect examples. Although what they have become differs greatly from their initial goals, these companies, after all, have made their mark in Chinese business history.

This is partly attributable to opportunities created by the national drive of reform and opening up, but no one can neglect the wisdom, resilience, vision, and willpower of the company founders during their basic reform. Lenovo founder Liu Chuanzhi, Haier founder Zhang Ruimin, and Vanke founder Wang Shi are not radical reformers or inventors of new management philosophies. Instead, they repeat the same ideas over and over again, ingraining them into the minds of all until such ideas evolve into core values. On institutional reforms, they are willing to compromise and are good at buying-out strategies: They compensate people with vested interests for their submission to rules and their obedience when their power gets restricted or deprived. Of course, they would also apply "capital punishments" to deter ill intentions and protect authority. Critical reforms could be enforced with an iron hand when needed at a critical moment, but generally they are well prepared with contingency plans.

Such entrepreneurs are like turtles that are calm and resilient, but they are also chameleons that camouflage their companies against harm.

Wang Shi, the CEO of Vanke, once said that Ren Zhengfei is a cunning fox. He had perhaps not realized that he was actually painting a picture of himself and his contemporary entrepreneurs.

Basic reform is inevitable for any company (not including SOEs and other companies that depend on resource monopoly; the arguments in this book only apply to market-oriented private enterprises). The key is to build a system of procedures that successfully move away from the gangster-club culture. Such reform is like exfoliation, which replaces the roughness from the legacy of early years with the smoothness of modernization. The methods and tools for reform are important, but the nature of the new system is crucial.

A bad system is prohibitive, much in the same way a cage is for birds or a pond for fish. Under such a system, the eagle loses its sky and the whale loses its majesty. If gangsters are turned into modest gentlemen, how can a company that sets its eyes only on profits last any longer?

A good system is like a race course with clear boundaries or a river with sturdy dams. It accepts individual uniqueness while taming primitive passion, inspires vitality while overcoming apathy. In such a system, bridles are put on horses, gangsters are transformed into soldiers, and guerrilla troops are turned into regular units.

The difference between a bad system and a good system, I strongly believe, deserves the attention of Chinese companies and their leaders that choose to modernize.

This reminds me of fireplaces at Huawei. At the company's headquarters in Shenzhen, a European-style fireplace adorns every reception facility and conference room, which is strange for a subtropical city. In winter, even though it's not really cold, the fire burns when Ren Zhengfei receives a guest; the room is warm and cozy and lightly fragrant with Betula.

Why does Ren Zhengfei love these fireplaces? How can we understand this preference in terms of psychology? Or is it a metaphor?

Revolution Is Tough, but Evolution Is Tougher

Basic reform or institutional development will cause a company to bid farewell to primitive accumulation. In most cases this reform is radical and wide-ranging and garners strong resistance. Leaders and reformers require the courage and vision to take risks and the patience not to rush.

Institutional development does not happen overnight, and there is never a perfect institutional design. A good system is formed through repeated revisions and improvements; as long as the direction is right, the company must move straight ahead until the final goal is reached.

As to Huawei's reform, Ren Zhengfei emphasizes that the company should avoid seven tendencies:

1. Perfectionism
2. Complicated philosophy
3. Blind innovation
4. Partial improvement without overall benefits
5. Officials without overall outlook leading the reform
6. Employees without practical experience participating in the reform process
7. Application of any unproven procedure

Ren Zhengfei said at a meeting in 2009:

> For over 20 years since its establishment, Huawei has never stopped reforming; however, we don't seek dramatic changes in which we will have to pay a hefty price. Perhaps the price is our life. We have moved ahead with gradual, evolutionary changes that you may not notice. We cannot endure dramatic ups and downs. Reform can still be achieved without a hero; we cannot allow heroism to ruin the company.

Earlier in 2000, he had already clearly stated, "Organizational change and development should be gradual and evolutionary. There should not be an abrupt change. We must carry out reform at a controlled and appropriate tempo."

In this statement, he defined change as evolutionary not revolutionary. Why? And what's the difference? Revolution is destruction and total change that is disruptive and very costly. China's history has been filled with violent revolutions, with unrest and turmoil lasting longer than peace and stability. Consequently, China lacks continuity in institutional systems despite its rich cultural heritage. One dynasty overturned the rules and at times destroyed the architectural legacy of the previous. An article in the *Times* (Chuck Your Chintz to China. It's Valued There, February 6, 2012) questioned,

> In China the new is destroying the old, and concrete structures are driving up a ruthless and destructive tsunami. What psychological price the nation

has to pay when concrete structures bury its past? Perhaps the people now are much richer and healthier than their ancestors who had tilled the land with sweat. But if the collective memory is erased, do they still know who they are?

This is the disposition of the nation and will surely penetrate the corporate culture of Chinese business.

Business, however, is unlike art. Artists need to defy and renew themselves, but a business organization, like a nation, needs heritage and continuity. A Huawei executive once said, "A company is a constructive organization. Any radical change or innovation is undesirable. Changes are necessary for growth, but companies must change with caution."

Several years ago, Ren Zhengfei told the story of Xiao He and Cao Can. Xiao He was the first prime minister of the Han Dynasty, and Cao Can took over his office after Xiao retired. "When Cao Can had first taken office, he didn't repeal any rule Xiao He had established, which ensured the continuity of governance. Huawei would like its managers to act like Cao Can. We cannot be preoccupied with innovation all day long." In fact, "innovation" is rarely mentioned in Huawei's documents and is not considered part of its core competitiveness, especially in terms of corporate management. Ren said, "Any innovation has a price, and it will harm the company if the price outweighs the return. Over the years the company has built a rich legacy of management rules and procedures, so any arbitrary innovation would be wasting our past investment."

The antonym of innovation is conservatism. According to Italian painter Jannis Kounellis,

> In Italian, the word conservatism means efforts to conserve everything great from the past. It is not at all decadent to be conservative. Even if we launch a revolution, we are trying to return to our past glory, and then continue the journey on that basis.

This is why the Renaissance, the Italian revolution against the Dark Age, had referred to the classical tradition; it did not cut off the link with history.

Portrayed as an innovative company by the media, Huawei has never agreed that innovation is its soul. Instead, Ren Zhengfei argues, "What's wrong with conservatism? To be conservative is to maintain continuity and stability. Is it really necessary to break all the traditions to be progressive? I don't think so."

In 1999, when Huawei's institutional and procedural reform first began with the support of the IBM advisory team, Ren pledged to "cut the feet to fit the shoes," and took determined measures to eliminate resistance to the reform. At the same time, he remained sober and insisted, "We must develop our management system by improving existing procedures. Such procedural optimization should never stop in order to get infinitely close to being reasonable. Our long-term policy offers big rewards for small improvements."

In recent years, there are frequent reports praising and rewarding heroes that propose or make significant changes to management. Huawei remains an exception that doesn't encourage suggestions for sweeping change. Why? Management is a systematic project where an abrupt change leads to company-wide upheaval. Conversely, minor changes or improvements are helpful for upgrading the system, and are, therefore, more constructive and practical.

To get infinitely close to being reasonable is the ideal progress of reform in the eyes of Huawei's leaders. "Reform is an ongoing process. We should not be too radical. If we make 0.1 percent progress each year, we will achieve 10 percent in 100 years. If we can sustain such progress, our improvement would be incredible."

Perhaps 100 years is too long. By then, Ren Zhengfei and his contemporaries will have left the stage. But Ren does not want to just "seize the day." If the company attempts to do so, nothing will last and the company will have to start over again. This is a common tragedy in Chinese history.

Li Zehou, a famous Chinese philosopher and scholar, argued, quite controversially, that China must bid farewell to revolution. Li explained:

> China spent three-quarters of the 20th century revolting, and revolution became a holy slogan as if any revolution is good. In fact, revolution is not sacred. We are opposed to revolution or deifying revolution. Without it, human society would have progressed even better. The French Revolution lasted many years, but caused France to lag behind the UK, which had developed a stable regime and adaptable political system. The 1912 Xin Hai Revolution delayed China's modernization process, proving in some way that evolutionary reform is better than abrupt revolution.

I don't know if Ren Zhengfei has read Li Zehou's argument against revolution. I strongly believe that Ren would be in agreement with Li Zehou when he said, "Liang Qichao, reformist during the late Qing Dynasty, talked extensively about revolution but he had indeed wanted reform.

Some say that revolution is easier than evolution. I partially agree. I believe revolution is very tough, but evolutionary reform is even tougher."

Ren Zhengfei was born in the Year of the Monkey, which generally implies a restless and energetic character. It is of great surprise therefore that Ren is able to remain calm and patient while changing Huawei from a ferry boat into a mid-sized aircraft carrier; his reform has been solid, gradual, and perhaps conservative, which is antithetical to his Chinese zodiac sign and personal disposition. No doubt it has taken great will to restrain the restless urge.

The bigger challenge is to overcome the restlessness, or the "monkey nature," of his colleagues and the organization. Moreover, he must answer this question: Is evolutionary reform enough? Over time, mild reforms may not clear away the cumulative organizational dirt; if the organization becomes clumsy and slow, is radical revolution necessary? Where's the critical point between progressive and radical change?

Section III. Culture: The Mother of Rules

Mass Resignations in the Marketing Department: Prelude to IPD Reform

Just before the 1996 Spring Festival, Huawei's marketing department underwent a major shakeup that lasted about a month. Managers at each level had to submit two reports: the first, a performance summary of the past year with a plan for the coming year, and the second, a resignation letter. The company would either approve the work report or accept the resignation based on individual performance, growth potential, and business needs.

This was a shocking move. Several years later, an executive of Motorola China recalled the event with sensation. He said only Huawei dared to do it, and it had succeeded. No one can imagine what such a policy would turn out in most Chinese companies and American companies. The turnover rate was high enough among the marketing people, and it took years and a lot of resources to develop a regional manager. It would therefore be a huge loss if they left, even without considering the customer ties that they may take away. No one wanted a single marketing manager to go, but Huawei had asked them, and almost all of them, to resign. Ren Zhengfei was really incredible.

This event, however, had not stirred the company at all. Rather, the massive resignation evolved into a rallying call. Chairwoman Sun Yafang delivered a resignation speech on behalf of the marketing department. She said that the move was a great feat to challenge the tradition of bureaucracy and hierarchy and proved that people at Huawei could really move up or down the ladder depending on their contribution. More than just a stunt, the collective resignation letter inspired a number of marketing managers to speak with determination:

> For the sake of the company, I am willing to sacrifice my own personal interests.
>
> Huawei's culture is characterized by solidarity and growth. As an individual member of the organization, I would love to be a stepping stone for the company's progress.
>
> For the sake of Huawei's lasting success, I shall not drag the company down for individual reasons.

Employees from other departments also spoke with approval:

> Why is Huawei so unique? Because its employees are united as a family and each is willing to sacrifice his individual interests for the sake of the organization.
>
> I've been working here for many years, but I didn't understand the real meaning of sacrifice until today.

The general feeling was expressed by Mao Shengjiang, acting president for marketing. He said:

> I think anyone stepping down from a prestigious position won't feel good; it will take time to recover from the frustration. I'm not convinced if someone says they don't care. If you ask me if I did care, I would say yes. I care about the company's growth and success; I care about the youth, passion, and sweat that we've given to the company; I care about what I can continue to do for Huawei; I care about whether I can still feel confident in my job; and I care about whether I can fulfill the wish of my comrades-in-arms. I don't care about my own face or my position in the company.

For the five years it had existed, the marketing department had made great contributions to Huawei. It was a great asset of the company, or a crack force if Huawei is an army. But why had the company decided to disband this force and build a new one? Decision-makers of Huawei explained:

> Our competitors are so powerful that we haven't seen the limit of their power. We're a mouse while they are elephants. If it stands still, a mouse would be trampled to death by an elephant. But the mouse is nimble and can move quickly. It can even climb up the elephant's back or up its nose. Ultimately, the elephant will become upset if the mouse can always dodge its feet. The idea is that we cannot be conservative, rigid, or static; we must rather have a flexible operation system and organization structure.

Indeed this might be the only way out. Huawei is a private company that started with an initial investment of CNY20,000. Since its first day, it has faced giant rivals waving their fists right in front of its nose. There was no way to success except by working harder than a lion, advancing more bravely than a wolf pack, moving with more power than an elephant, and running as nimbly as a mouse.

This is the daunting reality of Huawei that had lasted for nine years. In other words, the company was forced to shake up its marketing department.

The second explanation is that Huawei was attempting to internationalize itself. Ren Zhengfei said:

> The collective resignation of the marketing department, I think, is more symbolic than real. The spirit it carries is more important. It marks the beginning of our internationalization program. At the same time, it mobilizes our managers who would otherwise feel frustrated, and would turn resistance to our international drive into a catalyst. Now that the marketing department has started, all others would follow suit. Our company won't internationalize without globally experienced managers or international structures. It's normal for managers to move up or down the ladder. Those who have dropped can one day get up again, while those who are promoted may never rise any higher. Anyone without practical experience cannot lead an office; anyone without experience in a related field cannot lead a department. Managers must be deeply involved in the grassroots where new clues to development can be found. Practice is the only test of truth.

Obviously, the collective resignation of the marketing department was only the start. The decision-makers attempted to shake up the whole company, create a sense of urgency in the organization to face the market and customers, and, more important, gear all its managers to the global stage.

At that time, Huawei had already contacted the IBM advisory team.

As said earlier, the IPD reform was a radical revolution for Huawei. Where was the greatest resistance? From those who had lost part or all of their power. The reform has challenged traditional concept of bureaucracy and organization. In retrospect therefore, the collective resignation had been conducted as a prelude to the bigger and wider institutional and procedural reform across the entire company. It was an organizational stress test, a rehearsal before the event. Ren Zhengfei relieved some of the upheaval that the IPD reform would bring so that the American shoes would not pinch too much.

One year later, the 70-member IBM advisory team arrived at Huawei.

Return to the Beginning: Resignation of 7,000 Employees

In October 2007, approximately 11 years after the collective resignation of the marketing department, Huawei once again staged a mass resignation event. This time, 7,000 people resigned in what was dubbed by journalists "Resignation Gate" to represent the seriousness of this event.

Huawei announced internally that all employees who had worked in the company for eight years or longer must go through resignation procedures before January 1, 2008, and then apply to the company for re-employment of one to three years.

According to Huawei's regulations, resigned employees could apply for re-employment within six months, but would be subject to qualification review. Those who passed would be re-employed, sign a new employment contract, and receive the same compensation package as before. The company would retain their shares during the six months, after which resignees would be allowed to cash out if they were not re-employed.

This is exactly the same event that had taken place 11 years earlier, but this time the responses were varied. The previous event caused concerns within the industry only, and some international competitors felt pressure. They believed that a company with the guts to stage a mass resignation and yet have the ability to succeed in the drama must have a formidable management team and a mighty leader. "Huawei will outpace everyone else; it's just a matter of time," an executive of Motorola China said.

But the 2007 event had subjected Huawei to an avalanche of criticism. Hundreds of media outlets, both Chinese and foreign, covered the event with frightening headlines:

Massive Resignation: Huawei Challenges the New Labor Law
China Trade Unions Highly Concerned with Huawei's Mass Resignation
Huawei Fires Its First Shot at the New Labor Law

The Internet was also alive with damning criticism against Huawei.

Huawei was apparently caught in a crisis. Reform is usually a forced option, which Huawei was proving here. Since the IPD reform in 1997, Ren Zhengfei had been emphasizing evolutionary reform and gradual improvement, aiming to optimize the management regime, to get it infinitely close to being reasonable. But why did he launch such a radical change with its human resources management, for which he came to be called a "revolutionary entrepreneur?" He had preferred conservatism to innovation in his business philosophy, but why did he make such a shocking move that made him a radical business leader?

The answer is a change in circumstances. Since 2006, major mergers and acquisitions have occurred in the global telecom industry. Alcatel merged with Lucent Technologies, Nokia merged with Siemens, Sony merged with Ericsson, and Ericsson acquired Marconi. This rattled the nerves of Huawei, which was just about to sit down with a cup of coffee. After 20 years of tussling between mice and elephants, the elephants became sick and had fallen one after another, while the mice had grown to be as strong as the lions. At this time, however, elephants started to hold together, warming each other and attacking competition.

As a Huawei executive remarked, "For 20 years we've had a nightmare almost every day. As long as we remain in the telecom industry, we cannot expect to sleep soundly."

Huawei's Executive Office issued the *Executive Summary on the Recent Human Resources Reform*, which described the competitive landscape and explained the rationale for the massive resignation of 7,000 employees:

Both history and reality have told us that, in the war of the global telecom market, like in any other war, no company is able to win all the time, and the balance can tip or suddenly reverse. Many global giants have been forced to cut jobs in order to survive, and some have fallen during the storm. The prospect is full of uncertainties, and no company can bet on its long-term future or promise its employees a lifelong career. In order to last long enough, a company cannot offer its employees any lifelong guarantees. It cannot tolerate lazy people either, because it is unfair to the dedicated workers and excellent performers, and it's a disincentive for everyone else. No pie will drop from the sky; you must work hard to win a happy future. There is no other choice.

For many years, Ren Zhengfei has been worried that his team would get lazy, and he has sincere hope that the company will remain passionate. He would be thrilled if his staff could all remain tough fighters.

I once had a private dialogue with Ren Zhengfei. I asked, "What's your biggest concern?" Ren answered, "The employees of Huawei are young and rich, and may become conceited and lazy." I asked, "What would you do if they really get lazy?" He answered, "I will sack them." I asked again, "What if most employees are lazy?" He said without hesitation, "I will sack them all and substitute a number of new employees who are penniless but ambitious."

For the rise of Huawei and the fall of some Western companies, the key is the difference in corporate cultures. The institutional transformation of Huawei for over 20 years has focused on this core value: Those who contribute more will be rewarded more.

At this critical moment, however, the new Labor Contract Law of the People's Republic of China was passed. Under Article 14 of this new law, the employer, unless otherwise proposed by the employees, shall sign a labor contract, without a fixed term, with employees who have worked for 10 consecutive years or who have signed two fixed-term labor contracts with the employer.

Entering into a labor contract without a fixed term means one may become a permanent employee. This was no doubt a heavy blow to Huawei, which was implementing its human resources reform. As part of this reform, Huawei adopted a new compensation system in 2006. Its employees are compensated not on the basis of qualification or seniority but on the basis of their duty and contribution by which every job is evaluated and ranked. People are paid for the job they perform and the pay changes if they take a different job. The new compensation system had benefited dedicated employees who had performed the best, while those who were lazy or became complacent because of their past achievements had suffered. Any senior employees who had lost their drive or ambition would be removed from their job. Through this new compensation system, Huawei had expected to preserve the dedication of its employees and motivate them to achieve even more in the global environment.

A more dramatic part of this reform was that it allowed two-way selection: Employees could choose not to work for the company, and the company could let go those contributing less than their pay. In essence, the company had denied any lifelong employment.

This reform was obviously not compliant with the upcoming Labor Contract Law. No one could tell exactly what or how Ren Zhengfei and the other senior executives of Huawei had felt at this predicament. They must have felt anxious and frustrated.

On the one hand, Huawei had entered the most competitive sphere of the global market, and it was narrowing the gap with major Western competitors. Some Western companies were failing and forced to form an alliance that had besieged Huawei, which was fighting alone. In order to win the war, Huawei had to depend on its own dedicated employees, and a flexible human resources policy was crucial.

On the other hand, this attempt at reform would be deterred by the new Labor Contract Law, which was soon to be announced. If it followed Article 14 of the Law, Huawei would have to drop its policy for continuous motivation, and its dream to win the global market by virtue of employee dedication would be shattered.

It is hard or improper to judge whether the new labor law was good or bad, but apparently it only takes into account the superficial interests of the employed and neglected the rights of those who were not yet employed. For a large number of small and mid-sized companies struggling to survive, this new law would be disastrous, which has been proven by the wave of bankruptcies of industrial companies since 2008. If companies fail and workers lose their jobs, I wonder what China, a populous country, may be up to.

Someone made an analogy. The Marriage Law gives people the freedom to marry or divorce. Then, one may find it more difficult to pick a housemaid than to find a spouse. A couple may choose to divorce when the marriage cannot really last, but the employment of a housemaid is likely to become permanent. Therefore, one has to be extremely cautious when picking a housemaid. Appearance, virtue, and housekeeping abilities all have to be checked thoroughly because you would quite possibly be "married" to that housemaid for life.

Huawei was not deterred, however. The company continued its reform and proceeded to conduct the collective resignation. Huawei's lawyers had apparently done a good job. Although media and public criticism surged, the company was not found to have acted illegally.

Huawei had survived another storm.

This storm could have proved fatal; if this institutional reform had failed, Huawei's core value of dedication would have been lost and the company would have died.

Entrepreneurs are typically eager to take risks, but no one would risk being destroyed.

Reform Was Quietly Proceeding

The land was shaking around Huawei, but miraculously, the company, at the center of an earthquake, had remained quiet and calm. Not a single resigning employee had lodged a complaint; not a single dispute had been filed for arbitration or court ruling. Dozens of journalists who had managed to contact the employees in question were simultaneously disappointed and amazed. They had expected the employees to vent their anger or feel bitter about the insecurity of their job at Huawei or wish to defend their job in terms of the new Labor Contract Law.

On the contrary, the resigning employees agreed with the rationale for this reform: As it develops, a company accumulates a large number of senior employees who are well-paid, but have become incompetent and lost their passion; therefore, without this reform, Huawei would have become a pool of stagnant water. Shocked by this reform, Huawei people acquired a sense of urgency, and the company improved its market readiness.

Other employees, who were not expected to resign, became excited. "This reform put an end to the Employee Numbering System. As seniority is scrapped, we are thrilled, and we see a bright prospect." The employee number was once a mysterious and holy symbol in the company. Ren Zhengfei's number was 01. Smaller numbers meant higher seniority, but this system also divided employees, causing new employees to suffer an inferiority complex.

After the mass resignation Huawei rearranged the employee numbers, and now Ren Zhengfei numbers around the 120,000 mark. Since then, every employee is able to compete on a level-playing field, thus creating a dramatic shift in the organizational system.

The change was surely dramatic, since this reform involved a total of 6,687 high-ranking managers, including Ren Zhengfei himself. Ren said in his letter of resignation:

> After I left the PLA in 1984, I couldn't find a good job. To make a living, I incorporated Huawei in 1987. Now, 20 years have passed and this company

has grown into a large corporation with an annual income of US$16.5 billion and a globalized business portfolio, management system, and organizational structure. In the coming years, Huawei will proceed on its globalization journey and continue to grow healthily. Perhaps it won't be long before our sales income will exceed US$40 billion. I am perhaps competent for leading a smaller company with an income of millions of US dollars, but I am afraid I'm not fit to lead such a big corporation. Moreover, I feel I am not physically fit; I am strongly convinced that upcoming generations will be more competent. This is my letter of resignation.

Huawei's sustained development will depend, ultimately, on a scientific and effective system of rules and procedures, and generation after generation of successors who are committed to the core value of dedication. I believe that I shall be the first to follow these rules. And I would like to spare myself from business affairs, so that I can get around to what I really want to do.

The resignation of Ren Zhengfei and 6,686 other managers and employees were approved by the Board of Directors in November 2007. Afterwards, the Board retained Ren Zhengfei as the CEO of Huawei, and re-employed 6,581 other employees; 38 employees chose to retire for age or health reasons, 52 found better career opportunities elsewhere, and 16 others were assessed as unqualified and left the company after friendly negotiation.

It is important to note that some senior managers who were re-employed changed jobs; some were promoted, some were downgraded, while the remainder transferred to other functions. And a number of new and younger faces appeared in the leadership team.

This was indeed a dramatic change that affected the interests of each individual involved. Throughout the process, though, no dispute occurred. There were many discussions externally about the event; the All-China Federation of Trade Unions and the Guangdong Federation of Trade Unions sent investigators to Huawei, but the company was not stirred a bit. This reminded people of two other events: the earlier mass resignation of the marketing department in 1996 and the voluntary salary reduction of certain managers in 2003. These were all radical changes, and people wondered why they had been able to succeed and stimulate passion and drive in the company. What was the secret?

Culture is the mother of all rules and procedures. Looking at the political systems of various countries, one might wonder why the United Kingdom and Japan have opted for constitutional monarchy and France republicanism; most Middle East countries have retained dictatorships, while the United States has adopted a hybrid system of checks and balances. This is largely because of different historical and cultural traditions. Political systems are based on culture, and each change to political systems occurs within cultural parameters. The romantic, radical, and dynamic French won't endure any monarch to occupy the highest position in the country and deter their pursuit for absolute liberty and fraternity. The British are sober, rational, and good at compromise; they naturally prefer harmony and balance amid class distinction and democracy, between the nobility and the commons, and between national symbolism and real politics.

Similarly, corporate systems are subject to something more fundamental. An SOE belongs to the country, and managers are "goalkeepers" delegated by the nation. In China, any SOE or state-owned asset belongs to the people, including its employees; however, no employee can share dividends or exercise power as an owner, such as electing or removing managers. Likewise, managers cannot fire employees at will, let alone instigate mass layoffs in difficult times. This restriction has reduced the competitiveness of Chinese SOEs in the global market.

Conversely, there are often reports of American or European corporate giants or financial institutions firing thousands of employees. This is unimaginable for Chinese companies, including Huawei.

For over 20 years, Huawei has not fired employees on a massive scale. If the company were to one day slide into recession, would Ren Zhengfei and its successor follow the example of Western competitors and cut thousands of jobs? Do they have the guts? Are they ready? Of course, Ren Zhengfei and his colleagues do not lack the courage or spirit of adventure, but the problem is whether the company and its employees would follow the spirit of contract as do their Western competitors, given the special cultural character of China. And would the Chinese government allow such massive job cuts?

But this would happen one day. So in order to delay the arrival of that day, Huawei has continued to transform itself and advocate criticism and self-criticism to enhance its corporate culture.

In Huawei's corporate culture, the core faith is dedication and this faith is evidenced by the employee shareholding scheme. At Huawei, over 60,000 employees hold shares in the company. So why should the shareholders object to any policy that may help the company perform better and grow further? Why should they care if they are downgraded in the corporate hierarchy, lose power, or are transferred to a lower-paying job if there are competent younger people who would create more value for them?

This was the general sentiment at Huawei, where people cared more about dividends and bonus than salary. Their salary was not high, relatively speaking, but the dividends paid each year and the expected growth of such dividends proved stimulating. Therefore, it should not be difficult to understand why the radical, collective resignation of 7,000 employees did not disturb anyone at Huawei.

To put it in a simple way, 6,686 big and small bosses alike were led by Ren Zhengfei, the biggest boss with a mere 1.42 percent share of the company, to revolt against themselves. And the aim of this revolution was to stimulate the organization and motivate each member to avoid the imminent crisis.

In other words, the mass resignation was in fact an act of dedication and self-improvement. Virtually each of them was the company's shareholder. In the traditional term, they were capitalists, and therefore, there existed no conflict between capitalists and workers. In this sense, the media and the public were mistaken.

Section IV. Art of Change: Timing, Tempo, Cost, and Other Factors

No Blind Reform

Reform is the soul of corporate progress, as affirmed by many management gurus. Any company is faced with innumerable unknown risks throughout their progress. Therefore, the core mission of an entrepreneur is to find certainty in the uncertain environment and point to a clear direction in a world of confusion. In this sense, most entrepreneurs are adventurers, or they are gamblers and rebels. They are very likely to get excited about anything new. A time-honored company would have a great number of managers or owners, but only those who dare to challenge or rebel against tradition can lead it toward success. In other words, the success and sustainability of any company rests with its innovation and reform. Of course, innovation is sometimes destructive, and reform may cause disruptions. It is really a critical test for company managers and owners to strike a balance between innovation and order while mastering the tempo and extent of change. Generally, a company must at the same time continue its tradition and mend its system through reforms.

It is only partially right to assert that reform would resolve every problem. The truth is reform has in many cases led to tragedy and death. One must be aware of its risks as reform has become a buzzword nowadays.

Organizational progress or regress is a gradual evolutionary process. Consisting of incubation, accumulation, consolidation, and fixation, this process of evolution creates a unique identity for the organization, or a unique corporate culture. And the cultural identity of Huawei is dedication.

The cultural identity of an organization, however, changes with time. Over time, its identity blurs, and the basis on which the organization survives may weaken or collapse. Time is corrosive, and any organization, no matter how solid it is, will eventually face this decay. Therefore, the long-term mission of any organization is a race against the clock, during which reform is an essential weapon.

Reform, however, is often a double-edged sword. While it eliminates bad cells, reform may also kill healthy cells and organisms. This is common in countries and companies that swing back and forth.

No organization can afford repeated swings back and forth. Any blind reform or innovation is fatal.

In Chinese, blind reform is referred to as *zheteng*, and Hu Jintao, former President of China, urged the country to avoid *zheteng*. This is a great imperative, especially for a nation fancying the philosophy of struggle.

Dragon and Flea

Every idealist is obsessed with the question: Why does a dragon seed ultimately grow into a flea? Or if a baby dragon is born, why does the dragon end up a black sheep? Similarly, many entrepreneurs are puzzled: Why do their companies fail while other companies succeed with management reform? Why are they caught in a chain of miseries while Lenovo and Huawei have become world giants?

While the outcome of reform depends on corporate culture, the methods and skills applied during the reform process are also critical. During the reform movement of 1898, known as the Hundred Day Reform, Emperor Guangxu apparently lacked patience. In less than 100 days, he issued over 40 new orders and regulations and removed dozens of cabinet ministers, which shocked the whole court and the royal family. Regrettably, the reformers he depended on were men of letters and lower-ranking officials without practical power. More unfortunately, they refused to forge alliances or make compromises to strike a certain balance. Influenced by radical men of letters, the emperor became restless and rebuffed the Queen Mother, Ci Xi, who would have been a supporter of change. Therefore, the young emperor was isolated in court; even officials who supported or sympathized with his reform had remained on the back benches. The reform movement naturally aborted, and conservative power was in part to blame for the failure.

About a century later, Deng Xiaoping championed another reform movement, for which he was wise to past mistakes. Although the reform was much awaited and would benefit the whole nation, Deng had demonstrated his great art of reform, which can be a highly valuable source of inspiration for every organizational leader. He liberated and re-employed a large number of ousted officials, turning them into the leading force for the reform movement. At the same time, he started a mind-liberating movement in parallel to create a favorable ideological environment for the reform. He also nurtured a class of intellectuals who justified the reform and called for nationwide support. To guarantee the smooth implementation of his economic reform, Deng reformed the armed forces. At the lowest, but absolutely not the least important level of the country, Deng implemented a household-based land contract system for farmers who were then able to rekindle their sparks of hope. After all this started, he insisted that the process must be gradual. He said that one must grope the stones in the river to cross it, or put one foot on the accelerator and the other on the brake so that the vehicle can traverse ridges, avoid holes, and get around corners. By 1997, when Deng Xiaoping passed away, or 20 years after the reform started, China had made significant achievements in various fields.

Deng Xiaoping has indeed a large number of pupils in China's business community, including Liu Chuanzhi, Zhang Ruimin, and Wang Shi. They share certain common traits: resilience, patience, and vigilance. As the boss of a private company put it, "We are like mice. We hide ourselves in the hole when the wind is strong outside and come out after we know the wind is gone." Moreover, they are tolerant and inclusive. They pull people together and accept everyone, even if they have defects or problems. At the same time, they stand by their principles. They compromise but do not forsake their core beliefs. They have enough self-awareness and hold onto a stubborn faith: As long as they are businessmen, they will never put their fingers in politics.

Interestingly, these entrepreneurs started their businesses around the age of 40 and were around 50 when their companies became engaged in major transformation. For a leader of an organization of a considerable size, this is a mature age. It is true and common in China, at least.

Set the Chicken Flying and Dogs Jumping

Any reform is intended to stimulate the vigor and vitality of an organization. For a company, the biggest challenge does not come from outside; it is neither changes to the market conditions nor the strength of its competitors. A company most often suffers from internal stagnation or rigidity due to organizational friction, laziness, and fatigue. Therefore, reform is necessary to stimulate the organization and delay its decadence.

Any successful reform is based on the insight and prudence of organization leaders. Political or commercial reform cannot be done by one or a handful of people. It requires powerful leadership and a resourceful group of advisors. Reform led by a firm-handed leader with the help of a number of dedicated professionals is much more likely to succeed.

Reform is a systematic project. Any change sets off a chain of events; the goal of reform is to ultimately turn an organization around or give it a completely new face. But it is crucial to prioritize the targets and pick one after another. It is taboo to try to tackle all problems at once. Nothing can be changed overnight. Instead, any hasty attempt would set all chickens flying and all dogs jumping. Literally speaking, the organization would become a complete mess and enemies rise up in all directions. Another possibility is that the organization would assign its resources to all the targets based on averages, but the problem is that any organization has limited resources. If the reform ranges too wide, the end would be miserable or abortive. The Hundred-Day Reform is a bloody example.

Of course, any reform is indeed intended to set the chicken flying and dogs jumping to renew and reinvigorate the organization. But any reformer must observe how such unrest would be organized or directed. Any reform will no doubt hurt some people, especially those who are deprived of vested interests and who naturally jump to reject change. But if such resentment prevails, or even worse, if the chicken and dogs form an alliance against the reform, failure can occur. On the other hand, the reform is more likely to succeed when it is conducted at a right time and in the proper sequence with careful planning.

Huawei's six reform projects started with IPD, then its supply chain and human resources, and in 2007, the change extended to the financial system. At a meeting to present Huawei's plan for the financial transformation, Ren Zhengfei said:

> I always believe our financial transformation should not start with the budget system. If our operation system is still a mess, how can we develop any correct budget? For now our budget system has to move ahead on our own; we must plow the soil and level the ground before our advisors bring us the seeds. In this process, we don't want any skeptical people or those who believe they are wiser than the IBM advisors. We must guarantee that there's proper understanding and consensus, and there must be active involvement. We must eliminate those who think they are smarter than IBM and smarter than anyone else in the world.

Any Reform Has a Price

The massive resignation of 7,000 Huawei employees was labeled as an earthquake by the media, but the world was more shocked by how quiet the company had remained. This was due, in part, to the 7,000 resignees being shareholders and because Huawei had already paid a hefty price for this seemingly radical change. For employees who had worked with the company for over eight years to resign and then apply for re-employment, Huawei adopted an "N + 1" compensation policy, where "N" is the number of years the employee worked with the company. For instance, suppose an employee makes CNY12,000 a month in salary and earns a year-end bonus of CNY120,000, a monthly equivalent of CNY10,000; if he or she has worked 10 years for Huawei, the compensation would be CNY22,000 (monthly salary + monthly equivalent of year-end bonus) times "10+1," or CNY242,000.

This has cost Huawei over CNY10 billion.

This was the buying-out policy which had made the reform possible. Of course, Huawei had made a careful calculation and balance. What is more important and valuable than the sustained vigor of the organization? This is how Ren Zhengfei balanced cost and benefit.

The company's welfare security may also be a factor behind the successful change. Since 2005, Huawei has instituted a dual-track insurance policy, including compulsory social and medical insurance on the one hand and additional commercial insurance on the other. In 2007 alone, the company paid CNY840 million for employee insurance.

In addition to compulsory national and local social insurance, Huawei has purchased commercial insurance from international insurers for all employees to cover personal injury, life insurance, major illnesses, and travel risk. For example, in the event of death while working for Huawei, beneficiaries are entitled to commercial insurance compensation of CNY1 million, in addition to statutory social insurance benefits. Any employee suffering from a major illness is entitled to commercial insurance benefits of CNY200,000; if the employee dies as a result of such illness, the beneficiary is entitled to an extra commercial life insurance benefit of CNY300,000. Considering that social security and medical insurance in many other countries is not up to standard, Huawei has purchased additional medical and travel insurance for its employees working overseas and their families and developed close partnerships with International SOS (ISOS) and other global medical service providers to ensure that any overseas workers and their families would have quick and timely access to medical aid and services.

In 2007, Huawei decided to pay recourse compensation to employees who had died or been handicapped during job performance since its establishment at par with the company's current medical insurance policies. Altogether 14 employees benefited from this policy. Ren Zhengfei said, "In our early years, we couldn't give decent compensation to our employees. Now that we are much better off, we should not forget them."

Self-Criticism Goes Before Reform

West Point Superintendent General David Huntoon pointed out in a recent speech that in the 21st century the core element of successful military leaders is critical thinking. Ren Zhengfei agreed and commented, "That fits very well with our management philosophy. To evaluate the prospects of Huawei through critical thinking, innovative thinking, and a historical viewpoint is the duty of the new generation of Huawei."

Any reform has a dear price, both explicit and implicit. There is also a long-term price: The organization would be hurt if reform is conducted without sufficient prudence. To avoid this, self-criticism is the least harmful tool that can be used repeatedly at the lowest cost. The success of Huawei to date is to a large extent the result of self-criticism rather than innovation or reform.

Criticism is a gradual and progressive tool that keeps an organization healthy. Regular, purposeful, and systematic organizational self-criticism has become a tradition at Huawei. But when criticism fails to eliminate the corruption and laziness of the organization, it would be necessary and effective to implement reform.

Criticism goes before reform as a warning against organizational disease; reform cannot go alone without self-criticism.

Criticism and reform function side by side, and sometimes criticism can clear the way for reform. Anyway, both are essential for any company. Criticism serves to diagnose and make minor fixes, while reform is major surgery on a sick body. What would become of a company that has appeared healthy and robust but suddenly goes in for a major surgery? Moreover, an organization that dares not use the tool of self-criticism can never realize any substantial change or transformation.

CHAPTER EIGHT

Strategy: Fight with Courage and Wisdom

Section I. Ren Zhengfei: Standing Apart

Born in the mountains in Guizhou Province in the 1940s to a family from Jinhua, Zhejiang Province, Ren Zhengfei truly stands apart in the Chinese business community. Some scholars have included Ren in the "Zhejiang merchant" compendium because he exhibits some of the common qualities of that stereotype: practical, committed, and strictly business. But unlike other Zhejiang merchants who tend to huddle together in alliances, Ren has remained an outsider. And his low profile is not a common character of Zhejiang merchants. For instance, Jack Ma (Ma Yun), founder of Alibaba, is a local merchant of Zhejiang, but Jack is one of the most glamorous merchants in China. Some other merchants from Zhejiang Province, like Lu Guanqiu, boss of Wanxiang Group, and Guo Guangchang, chairman of Fosun Group, are high-profile tycoons. And Hu Xueyan, the richest merchant in China 200 years ago, was not only high-key but also deeply involved in politics.

In fact, Ren Zhengfei would rather be considered a native of Guizhou Province. He spent his early years as a solitary and sensitive child in the rainy and remote mountains of Guizhou Province. He grew up in hunger, poverty, and political discrimination in the towering mountains where information was scarce. But the personal relationships were pure and simple, and he had been raised among quite a few brothers and sisters. The natural environment, social background, family setting, and changing times all served to shape his personality. Enduring, and even appreciating loneliness, became a defining quality of Ren's character.

His wife once asked him, "You had no friends in primary or middle school. You didn't make friends while in college or in the military, and now you don't have any friend in or outside of Huawei. Have you ever felt lonely?"

Ren Zhengfei also admitted at a meeting with the company's international advisors,

> I have no personal relations or close business connections with any government official. I don't have much contact with any other Chinese businessmen. Over the past 20 years, I had only met with Liu Chuanzhi of Lenovo and Wang Shi of Vanke twice. I don't have contact with any journalists. My personal life has been painful and lonely. I have not found any playmate or society. I am even farther away from my junior colleagues. I have to take the pains to keep balance in the company; I have to endure the loneliness.

Standing apart is not only a personal inclination or disposition; it also represents his definition of his own social role. For over 20 years while Chinese business people are busy building, worming into and utilizing circles, Ren Zhengfei has rejected offers to enter any business or political circle. He has never sought for membership, let alone leadership, of any association or club. Ren once said, "Neither Huawei nor I need this. We are not obliged, either. Huawei will never budge. Huawei will take its own road. We will focus on accomplishing our missions."

From time to time, financial media would invite Ren Zhengfei, Sun Yafang, or other senior Huawei executives to attend their forums as keynote speakers or guests of honor. Their names would appear on posters, but they have never made an appearance. About this, Ren Zhengfei laughed, "It doesn't bother us that our names become advertisements. The media are running their own business. But our policy won't change. We won't attend any such gathering."

Moreover, for over 20 years, Ren Zhengfei has never been interviewed by any media, either Chinese or abroad. He has stood very firm on his own ground. He doesn't care what the media say about him. To some extent, it was Huawei's corporate strategy for quite some time to keep a critical distance from journalists. No matter what the media say, Huawei is committed to its own goal: to grow up and get stronger.

Even after Huawei changed its communication strategy, Ren Zhengfei still insists on his privilege. He said, "You can respond to any interview. It is all right. But please spare me. I am not fit for hanging out with journalists."

Is it because Ren Zhengfei likes to be left alone? Is he afraid of the sound and fury of the outside world? Or is it because he has other concerns? Ren Zhengfei has never answered the question. But he has often quoted a Chinese proverb at meetings of senior executives: *fu ke di guo*. In English, the proverb means is that one has as much wealth as the kingdom, and the trick rests with the character "di," which means "match" or "rival," and in the more negative sense "enemy." So Ren Zhengfei said, "In China, no matter how rich you are, you must not turn into an enemy of the country." He insisted that one would benefit more by focusing on commercial dreams and refraining from social ambition.

Ren Zhengfei said:

Do I own Huawei? I don't know. I have slightly over one percent of its share. It is not because I don't want more. It is because I dare not have too much. As a Chinese proverb says, a pig will be slaughtered when it is fat and big enough. Perhaps I am right, under the current circumstances in China. Guo Ping, our deputy chairman, once said to me that he envied my carefree life. Well, I don't know how to answer him. I once drove 200 kilometers after dusk had fallen to attend a meeting in the mountains. I don't think any rich people would dare do that.

Similarly, Ren Zhengfei has his reasons for insisting on the nonalignment policy. First of all, as he once asked, "What should I be afraid of, anyway? I am a pure and independent merchant. And our company has paid more than CNY100 billion to the State in taxes over these years."

Section II. Strategic Focus: Doing One Thing for Over 20 Years

Focusing on Business and Keeping Away from Politics

For over 30 years, China has not produced any private company or businessman that possesses as much wealth as the state. There are some monolith-like oligopolies, but they are state-owned monopolies in petrochemicals, finance, telecom services, and military industries. Rich merchants may also arise from competitive sectors, such as manufacturing, the Internet, and real estate. Li Yanhong, Ma Huateng, Zhu Mengyi, Zhang Yin, and Pan Shiyi are rich enough, but they lag far behind the state-owned monopolies. They are still too weak to influence the fate of the country.

This is all due to the history, culture, and institutional design of China.

But there is a puzzling phenomenon in China. As a Chinese-American scholar pointed out, "In the West, politicians tend to think like merchants. They advocate the spirit of contract and make decisions based on numbers. In contrast, Chinese merchants often think and make decisions like politicians. Business management is often political and they would also try to connect with the government." It is strange anyway that politics have remained a keen topic in the business community, even though profound changes have taken place in this country, like globalization, urbanization, ubiquity of the Internet, and rapid economic growth. Most business people do not want to be government officials themselves but remain keenly interested in politics and government affairs. Some would love a political title in addition to their commercial identity. Why? The common explanation is the sense of insecurity.

According to a senior official of the All-China Federation of Industry and Commerce, over 100 private company owners became members of the National Committee of the Chinese People's Political Consultative Conference (CPPCC) in 2008, and 12 private company owners from Zhejiang Province attended the National People's Congress (NPC) as delegates in 2009. According to March 2012 statistics, the 2,987 delegates of the 2012 NPC included 156 bosses of publicly listed companies. Zhang Ruimin of Haier Group was an alternate member of the 15th and 17th central committees of the CPC and received the title of National Excellent CPC Member in 2001. Liu Chuanzhi of Lenovo was a delegate of the 16th National Congress of the CPC as well as a delegate of the 9th, 10th, and 11th NPCs, and once served as vice-chairman of the All-China Federation of Industry and Commerce.

Ren Zhengfei is not one of them, though. As a former military engineer, Ren Zhengfei was a delegate of the 12th National Congress of the CPC in 1982. That was his last political identity, and since then he has never assumed any real or honorary political role, not even as a delegate at the local level. It is not because the CPC or government leaders are not interested in this boss of the largest technology company in China. This is Ren Zhengfei's own choice. Over the course of 20 years, he has repeatedly affirmed his strong faith that a businessperson should be solely concerned with business and should not be involved in politics.

Once a middle-level manager of Huawei told Ren Zhengfei that he had been nominated a candidate for membership in the All-China Youth Federation. Ren gave him two choices: give up the candidacy, or leave Huawei. The manager resigned from Huawei, but in the end he was not granted the membership. The All-China Youth Federation had offered him the candidacy because he was a manager at Huawei.

In the company there is a rule: Whoever participates in protests or makes any political remarks will be fired. Some employees of Huawei's Nanjing Research Institute objected: The Constitution grants every citizen the freedom of speech and the right to assembly, so the company's regulation is illegitimate. Ren Zhengfei responded, "Yes, the Constitution protects the basic rights of every citizen, but it does not guarantee that you work for Huawei. If you exercise your citizenship rights and go to the street, but you cannot be an employee of our company."

Ren Zhengfei has set a bottom line for himself and the company: A business or a businessperson must not get involved in politics or seek any position in the political system. Huawei would be a purely commercial organization and part with the mixture of politics and business deep-rooted in Chinese society and culture.

In the history of China, there were a number of successful merchants who were involved in politics, including Lü Buwei of the Warring States period and Hu Xueyan and Qiao Zhiyong in the Qing Dynasty. They had risen as a result of their connections with political powers but ended up in tragedy due to the same connections. Such tragedies are common in Chinese history and have repeated themselves despite warnings. Ren Zhengfei, who loves to read history books, has no doubt perceived the warning.

In fact, Ren Zhengfei has gone to the extreme. One year, he was named a candidate by China Central Television (CCTV) for the Economic Figure of the Year, and he had more of a chance to win the title than many other candidates. As soon as he got the news, however, Ren urged the communication director of Huawei to remove his name from the list of candidates no matter what it took. His candidacy was cancelled in the end through the intervention of a senior leader of CCTV.

Ren Zhengfei was right. Just look at how the top economic figures selected in the 1990s have ended up. They have essentially disappeared from the stage, except Liu Chuanzhi. No wonder Ren Zhengfei was not at all thrilled; he was even scared by the title. Liu Chuanzhi had dared to accept the title because of his strategic choice and also because he was more capable than Ren Zhengfei in balancing and navigating politics. Ren once admitted, "Personally, I am not fit for politics, especially in the role of a subordinate." Therefore, it was the best decision of his life to dedicate himself to commerce.

Strategy: To Fight with Courage and to Plot with Wisdom

What is *zhanlüe* (strategy)? "Zhan" means offense, expansion, and aggressive progress. "Lüe" means to plot, plan, and design. "Zhan" requires courage, determination, willpower, and cohesion, whereas "lüe" requires wisdom, reason, and judgment. "Lüe" has yet another meaning, which is to give up, sacrifice, or part reluctantly with what one treasures. A spider, for example, surrenders part of its web when danger approaches. This is a unique means to defend itself, and the wisdom is amazing.

What, then, is strategy? To define strategy, one must ask three basic questions: Who am I? What am I able to do? And what am I not able to do? The first question reflects one's strategic identification and positioning. For instance, Ren Zhengfei identifies himself purely as a businessman and positions Huawei as a telecom equipment manufacturer. Fifteen years ago, Huawei had codified this positioning as a provision in its charter and this position has since then never changed. The questions "what am I able to do" and "what am I not able to do" are reflections of the strategic design and direction and the concentration of strategic resources of an organization. Resource allocation is always a critical issue, even when the strategic direction has been predetermined. When, where, and in what context a fight is about to be waged will determine where resources should be allocated. "What am I able to do" and "what am I not able to do" are, therefore, strategic thoughts that change as circumstances change.

On the subject of strategy, Ren Zhengfei has made many observations:

> Huawei's success is a result of its insistence on its "chicken rib strategy." Chicken rib is a paradox: it is edible, but meatless. Western companies have given up the chicken rib, but we have cooked it into a great dish. Practically, we have become No. 1 in network products, and this is our ground for the future. We have been modest on the margin, so we are able to survive, and the narrow margin has compelled us to increase our ability and our management.
>
> Strategic short-termism is the deadly weakness of Western companies. We may never beat Motorola, Nokia, or Ericsson if they were not publicly listed companies. In the same fashion, it would not be impossible for us to catch up with companies like Apple. While they enjoy a superior position, a more solid foundation, and more resources at the strategic level, their shareholders are demanding short-term returns. We are free of this burden.
>
> Don't be obsessed with the idea of becoming number one or number two, or being the first to reach the mountaintop. This is a gamble. It is brutally cold at the top peaks of the Himalayas. One can barely survive at such

altitudes. Survival is the lowest and highest goal of Huawei. If you can survive longer than others, you are successful.

Never consider any across-the-board offensive. We don't have the necessary power. Neither do the Western companies, which are much more powerful than us. Those who did have slid into crisis, as we can all see. We must
take up one thing at a time, and avoid fighting on multiple fronts. Huawei
can't do that. If you can break the wall of Wall Street a bit with all your
might, the whole street can one day be yours, no matter how you break it.

For Huawei, the year 2000 was critical to our strategic transformation.
Due to the IT crisis, all IT companies in the world were collapsing, but we
seized the opportunity against all odds. Crisis is a danger for others, but
opportunity for us. The key rests with our strategic vision and determination.
In the international market, competition is about strategy which depends on
vision, courage, and resources. In the business field, China cannot produce
any strategists like those found in the United States. We must accept this fact
and be at ease with this. We must understand that for a considerably long
time Huawei will remain a follower. We must wait for our competitors who
are wiser and more powerful than us to make mistakes.

We must be able to seize any opportunity in the international market. We
can get on any car that may take us along our road. But we cannot depend
on any strategic alliance. While we befriend someone, we would offend
others. This is a dangerous trick.

So what is a strategist? A strategist is not an opportunist, but he must dare
to bet all he has on the target he aims at. He must follow the main course
and ignore marginal benefits. Certain flexibilities and maneuverings should
be restricted. Flexibility is a tactical concept, but a strategist must be decisive
and determined.

Huawei must not attempt to change the rules of the world, but we must
participate in the rule-making process. Huawei's voice must be heard in
every club that makes rules, and become their important member.

If we open up our mind, we will be able to foster a strategic force. In
2012, we recruited 28,000 new employees in spite of challenging market
conditions. But we believe within just a few years they will grow into 28,000
tigers. They are our strategic reserve.

Strategic Adventure: Natural Mission of Merchants

It is reported that there are three million ships now under the seas worldwide, and the South China Sea, the Mediterranean, and the Caribbean
are three tombs of such unfortunate vessels. This is an exciting but also
scaring fact. Besides the fleet of Zheng He, the Chinese court eunuch and
diplomat who had sailed to show off the power of the Ming Dynasty, the

three million ships belonged mostly to merchants who had adventured to exploit the wealth of the world. Together with their followers, like their captains and sailors who were also adventurous and ambitious, they had come from Europe, America, and Asia.

"About the future, I am in the dark," a Chinese saying goes. This saying is a motto of the wife of Mao Yisheng, the Chinese structural engineer and expert on bridge construction. This is quite true. Where is the bridge leading to the future? Or even if it is constructed, the bridge to the future may fall at any time. This is human destiny; it is also the destiny of merchants and entrepreneurs since ancient times.

Merchants are born to take adventures. It is their fate to identify certainties among innumerable assumptions and find the biggest chance among countless possibilities. A great merchant must be a great strategic adventurer. From the first day of becoming a merchant, and from the first instance in the resolve to accomplish something, they must dedicate all their resources, wisdom, and even life to their cause. If they succeed, they will not only reap flowers and wealth; they will also face endless jealousy, hatred, and struggles for benefits. They have to continue the adventure, during which they many encounter more and more terrible troubles. Any wealth already accumulated will evaporate if the adventure stops. This is why a merchant ship sets sail again after struggling to reach port and will rest only when it finds its spot at the bottom of the sea.

The history of business is also a history of adventures full of the blood and tears of merchants.

Liu Chuanzhi, Zhang Ruimin, and Ren Zhengfei are successful, but they have also traveled on adventures. Their explorations continue, and so it is still too early to know their fate.

Who Are the Sexy Heroes of Today?

In 1984, Zhang Ruimin, a young man of 35, was appointed general manager of the Qingdao Refrigerator Factory. The first thing he did upon taking office was to smash 76 defective refrigerators with a sledgehammer in front of his workers. That marked the beginning of his glorious yet winding business career.

In that same year, Liu Chuanzhi, a 40-year-old official of the Chinese Academy of Sciences and military academy graduate, "plunged into the sea," in the popular term of the time. Together with 11 colleagues, he resigned from his official position and started their business: a computer technology development company which became Legend in 1989. Twenty years later, Liu Chuanzhi was hailed as a godfather of the business community in China.

Ren Zhengfei, who was born in the same year as Liu Chuanzhi, had just left the military, and was working for a logistics supplier for the South China Sea Petroleum Development Base near a fisher village in Shenzhen. Just one-and-a-half years ago, in October 1982, Ren had attended the 12th National Congress of the CPC as the youngest delegate from the military. Other delegates from the PLA included well-known veteran generals like Wang Zhen and Yu Qiuli. By then, Ren Zhengfei had been a CPC member for only two years.

Five years later in 1987, Ren Zhengfei pooled together CNY20,000, including his CNY3,000 severance pay from the PLA and contributions from six other individuals to found Huawei Technologies Co., Ltd. Several years later, Ren went to Beijing to meet Liu Chuanzhi, the founder of Legend. In 2008, Ren and Liu, both captains of industry, met at a beautiful and reclusive villa in the mountains to the west of Beijing. After a very brief exchange of conventional greetings, Ren Zhengfei said, "Mr. Liu, it's so nice to see you again after so many years. I must thank you for the sincere remarks you made years ago; you were very honest and straightforward. What you said has been very helpful."

For over 30 years after China initiated its reform and opening up program, a great number of Chinese merchants and entrepreneurs have come and gone, but few have left any significant mark on history. Zhang Ruimin, Liu Chuanzhi, and Ren Zhengfei are Chinese business paragons and a trio truly comparable with industry captains of the world. By definition of Western management theories, these three Chinese merchants are adventurers who are able to find the path in the dark and lead their followers through. Of course they have taken adventures only in the business world. They are able to clearly establish goals and rules, allowing their companies to possess distinct core values, and these values are so are well-communicated and implemented that they have become their cultural symbols. They are outstanding business thinkers, cultural professors, and preachers of faith. They are business strategists good at "creating something out of nothing."

In a rapidly changing business environment, an entrepreneur depends very much on the strategic vision, and the ability to detect opportunities in the unknown world, and to make the best of limited strategic resources. This decides whether he may succeed, and tells an entrepreneur apart from a professional manager.

Obviously, Zhang Ruimin, Liu Chuanzhi, and Ren Zhengfei possess all the necessary traits of a successful and outstanding entrepreneur. They are all adventurers, business thinkers, faith preachers, strategists, and diplomats. Above all, they have the necessary ability to utilize resources in the best way and the best combination.

This is an age of the Internet. Seemingly unrelated things, messages, inventions, and people have appeared in changeable combinations and relationships that have sparked innovations and even revolutions. The age has gone when a hero decides the outcome of a war and an individual creates the history. This is the new age of creative combinations and assembled civilizations. Resource integrators are darlings of this new age.

An article published November 2011 in *TIME* magazine titled "What Steve Jobs Couldn't Teach Us about Inventing" reads:

> Inventors were once very cool. They were outstanding and romantic figures. Leonardo da Vinci, Benjamin Franklin and Nikola Tesla are rogue geniuses who stole the holy fire of god. But all this has changed. What has indeed happened? Why have inventors lost their holiness and glamour? When is scientific invention not sexy anymore?

Lev Grossman, the author, asserted, "Although I am not at all willing to do that, I would have to blame Steve Jobs, the newly deceased great man."

Who are the sexiest in this new age then? They are integrators of strategic resources, like Steve Jobs.

> Steve Jobs is a genius who has overturned four industries. But he was not an inventor. What Steve Jobs had done was to polish inventions by other people. He merely optimized them. He had ideas and technologies and had a pair of eyes which were as exact as gauges. He had polished and packaged the ideas of other people until these ideas became brilliant and irresistible retail goods. Steve Jobs was not a great thinker; he was a great mixer.

But "who had invented the first electronic music instrument? Who is the inventor of tablet PC? Who is the inventor of smart cell phone? I don't know, and you don't know either. They have never appeared on the cover of *TIME*."

In this age of the Internet, people admire and worship orchestra conductors, strategists, and resource integrators like Steve Jobs, Bill Gates, Ren Zhengfei, Liu Chuanzhi, and Zhang Ruimin.

Diversification: Commercial Opportunism?

Liu Chuanzhi, Zhang Ruimin, and Ren Zhengfei were in the dark as to their future and the future of their companies about 20 years ago when they just started their business career. Exactly as Deng Xiaoping, their mentor and master said, they had "crossed the river by groping stones." To survive in the dark and reach the other side of the river, they had to depend on their adventurism in blazing different trails.

As the Chinese saying goes, one depends on the mountain if he lives near the mountain or the sea if he lives near the sea. Zhang Ruimin, once a worker at the Qingdao Refrigerator Factory, became the general manager, which was his career choice. He later renamed the factory "Haier," which was listed on the Shanghai Stock Exchange in 1994 and had grown ever since into one of the most successful home appliance companies in China and even in Asia.

In 2000, Haier started to diversify. It first took up digital and personal products (PCs and mobile phones) and then ventured into kitchen ware, household appliances, pharmaceuticals, restaurants, insurance, and real estate (Haier ranked 36th among China's top 100 real estate developers). But diversification has proven to be a curse for Haier. Its traditional home appliances lost their competitive edge, and the company has failed to reach the top ranks in any other sector it has entered. Some of the segments have come to a standstill, such as restaurants.

Is diversification really a curse? Liu Chuanzhi also diversified on a large scale at about the same time, more than a decade after he started his PC trading, production, and R&D business. And he had taken essentially the same route: horizontal expansion. The areas Legend has entered include the Internet, IT product distribution, chemicals, mobile phones, restaurants, modern agriculture, the wine industry, asset management, private equity investment, and real estate. Like Haier, Legend (which later became Lenovo) has not reached the top two positions in most sectors it entered, but unlike Haier, Lenovo has established its PC business as No. 1 in China and No. 2 in the world, through the acquisition of IBM's PC division.

About 10 years ago, diversification was a buzzword in the business community as Jack Welch had turned GE into a commercial empire through a diversification strategy and his ideas became mantras among businesspeople in China. Were Zhang Ruimin and Liu Chuanzhi disciples of Jack Welch? Any white-or-black conclusion would be arbitrary. According to media reports, though, the company that Zhang Ruimin admires the most is GE, and the businessman he adores the most is Jack Welch. Liu Chuanzhi has also admitted that his most admired businesspeople are Jack Welch and Bill Gates, and GE and Microsoft are the companies he appreciates the most.

Some scholars argue that Liu Chuanzhi, Zhang Ruimin, and Ren Zhengfei have the biggest chance among Chinese entrepreneurs to become world-class business leaders. It is a pity, however, that Liu and Zhang have opted for commercial opportunism: Their diversification strategies have expanded their businesses, but have also led them farther away from greatness.

This statement may not be completely right. We must understand that Haier and Legend were forced to accelerate their strategic transformation in the late 20th century to avoid disaster due to fierce competition and plummeting margins in the household appliance and PC markets. Diversification was their only choice; it was also risky as it demanded exceptional ability of the leaders to craft the right strategy and integrate available resources. Given the high stake and the daunting challenge, isn't it great if they survive the transformation? Even if they fail they are still great.

At one time, Huawei nearly entered the real estate sector. When suffering from internal and external troubles in 2002, Huawei entered into secret negotiations with Motorola and agreed to sell its hardware systems to Motorola for US$10 billion. Both companies had submitted all necessary documents and were waiting for approval from their board of directors. Chief negotiators had changed into bright beachwear and jogged along Yalong Bay in Hainan; they even organized a table tennis match. But as no one had expected, Chairman Christopher Galvin stepped down from Motorola; his position was taken over by Ed Zander, who didn't approve the deal.

Naturally, Huawei's senior executives were extremely frustrated. But 10 years later, Ren Zhengfei and Huawei should thank Ed Zander a million. If Ed Zander had not rejected the deal, there would have been yet another real estate developer in China, but the world would have missed a telecom giant, and the global telecom industry would have taken a different course—without a strange Asian face and a tough competitor to

Western telecom vendors. In 2011, when the sun was setting on Motorola, there must have been some regret missing the deal 10 year back. The predator relaxed its jaws and the prey escaped; the prey grew into a hunter and nearly acquired part of Motorola's business.

This is the real history: cruel, absurd, and dramatic. During Mobile World Congress 2011 in Barcelona, Ericsson's CEO told Ren Zhengfei that Mike Zafirovski, then Motorola's COO, had shed tears when he mentioned this deal.

Let's speculate for a while what Huawei could have done with the CNY80 billion from selling its hardware systems to Motorola. At that time, quite a few local governments wanted to license land-use rights to Huawei and encouraged the company to develop real estate projects. Ren Zhengfei and some other senior Huawei executives had visited Hainan, Guizhou, and several other provinces. They were contemplating the development of large-scale tourist resorts in remote mountainous areas.

After the deal failed, Huawei's senior management had a long debate on its future strategy and concluded in the end that the company must remain focused. The decision was made to continue in the same business; they believed Huawei could still attain success so long as it focused its strategic resources on a certain target. Clashes with American rivals were inevitable; preparations had to be made.

Ren Zhengfei admitted that, before *Huawei Charter* was adopted, the company was in terrible chaos. They had no strategy, only tactics, and opportunism prevailed. In order to end the chaos, Huawei mapped out a clear and complete "high-level design," *Huawei Charter*, with the help of several professors from Renmin University of China. The charter has offered guidelines for Huawei and has ensured that the company would not deviate from its strategic focus.

Doing Only One Thing for 25 Years

We are forced to make choices every day of our lives. Our choices determine our destiny. We face many temptations and often find ourselves at a crossroad. The key to success is decisiveness: to take only what you need. Giving up can be a great move because so many possibilities exist. These possibilities will not become distractions if one is focused and determined. The majority of people who are mediocre or losers are either too indecisive or too opportunistic. Many people in the business community make mistakes when tempted by opportunity. They are willing to take every chance that is presented, believing that each chance represents a potential gold mine. Therefore, their decision-making processes simply boil down to stimulus and response. They are excited whenever a new possibility emerges, and they would allocate finite resources to infinite possibilities. The result is misery. They fail to accomplish anything, and their life worsens. This is why there have been so many smaller merchants while business tycoons are rare.

To resist temptation is a commercial as well as Buddhist commandment. To focus on one's goal is a secular and necessary faith for anyone who aims high and far. To succeed both would be needed. Nevertheless, resisting temptation seems harder for most people, especially in an age of immense possibilities.

Some scholars sum up Ren Zhengfei's experience over the past 25 years quite simply: reading thousands of books, travelling thousands of miles, and doing just one thing.

It is true, indeed. Over the years, Ren Zhengfei has traveled hundreds of thousands of miles each year. He rarely has any personal contacts, and most of his spare time and flight time has been spent reading and contemplating. Under his leadership, Huawei has done just one thing over the past two decades: telecom equipment manufacturing.

Huawei has never developed any commercial real estate, although many local governments had wanted Huawei to invest, and Huawei itself at one point had such an impulse. It has never tried to speculate on the capital market: It is not a listed company and has never conducted any transactions in the secondary market. Besides telecom equipment manufacturing Huawei has never stepped into any other sector. This is unbelievable for any state-owned, private, or collective enterprise of a considerable scale in China.

This is because Huawei has the determination to resist any temptation, and it has the patience to pacify any stir or impulse within the organization. To some extent, determination and patience are two key factors for Huawei's success.

There is a Buddhist temple in Lijiang, Yunnan Province, called Wenfeng Temple, and in the temple there is a cave where monks meditate and practice Buddhist disciplines. A monk will stay in the cave for three years, three months, and three days, completely isolated from the secular world. Every day, the monk remains silent, alone, and peaceful within a space of no more than 10 square meters; he does not bathe, cut his hair, or even speak. He only kowtows to a statue of Buddha and recites

Buddhist scriptures. In those three-plus years, the monk bows 111,125 times. This is how a great monk comes into being.

Section III. Merry-Go-Round: Huawei's Market Strategy

There Is Not Only One Strategic Rival; There Is an Assembly

In 1999, Dr Kao Ruey-Bin, managing director of Hewlett-Packard's Greater China operation at that time, was working as general manager of the system product department at Motorola China. Among Western business people, Dr Kao was the first to recognize the future of Huawei and also the first to sense the long-term threat Huawei would pose to Western companies.

It is not really "long-term" because Huawei created a "red whirlwind" in the global telecom industry just three years later. Dr Kao expressed his judgment and concerns in confidential letters addressed to the Galvins, but answers were not forthcoming. In the 1990s, the rationality and vision of Westerners were blinded by chronic arrogance and prejudice.

But Dr Kao had insisted on his judgment and managed to meet with Huawei CEO Ren Zhengfei. Since then Motorola began to join hands with Huawei in the Chinese market, first in the area of bundled sales at limited scale.

Several years later, Ren Zhengfei met with Christopher Galvin at Huawei's headquarters in Shenzhen. Motorola was then on the decline, repenting over its technology-led strategy as the failure of its Iridium Satellite project had put an almost an unbearable burden on the company. Galvin was impressed by Huawei's products, saying that they were "good and cheap." He also acknowledged Huawei's value of customer centricity. One year later, Motorola began to sell under its own brand Huawei's GSM/UMTS systems worldwide valued at hundreds of millions of US dollars each year. In July 2006, Motorola and Huawei announced the establishment of a joint venture in Shanghai: The Shanghai R&D Center. "Among the competitors of Huawei, Motorola was once listed as one of the most intimate friends."

Things change over time, however. Motorola had once planned to acquire Huawei with about US$10 billion. But in less than a decade, the tables had turned. In 2010, Huawei came close to acquiring Motorola's wireless network equipment business as it outbid competitors by US$100 million, but the deal was voided due to intervention by the US government.

Almost at the same time, Motorola changed its CEO, and the new CEO Greg Brown decided to file a lawsuit against Huawei with the US court system, alleging that Huawei had stolen its IPRs. Huawei was enraged and was forced to respond. "For eight years, Motorola has been an 'invisible' distributor of Huawei. Our partnership has been very pleasant," said a senior executive of Huawei.

Motorola withdrew its lawsuit on April 13, 2011. Allegedly, the attorney who had urged Motorola to sue Huawei was fired. On July 19, 2010, Motorola's wireless infrastructure business was acquired by Nokia-Siemens at a price of US$820 million.

Following its announcement in January 2011 to cut 3,500 jobs, Motorola cut another 4,000 in August 2011, and in October 2011, the struggling company announced again that 800 people would be released.

That marks the fall of a giant in the international telecom equipment market.

There are no permanent enemies, as there are no permanent friends. This is a universal truth, especially in the profit-seeking business community.

The world of business is a merry-go-round that revolves at dizzying speed. This has been especially true with the telecom sector for over two decades. In retrospect, how many of the once glorious noble or time-honored vendors have fallen in a decent way? How many small companies that sprouted with passion have suffered misery and were ultimately crushed under the feet of giants?

Huawei is no doubt a lucky survivor. When it was founded in 1987, it had virtually nothing: no capital, no products, no talent, and no technology. But they had faced powerful competitors with glorious history and culture, such as Motorola, Siemens, Nokia, Ericsson, Lucent, Alcatel, North Telecom, NEC, and Fujitsu. Meanwhile the living space it had was also squeezed by state-owned or military enterprises like Great Dragon, Datang, and ZTE. Huawei was at a clear disadvantage.

Huawei was encircled, and it had to cross over the walls or break them down. For Huawei's leaders, failure was not an option, but the shadow of failure has lingered and continued to follow them throughout Huawei's progress.

Huawei's success rests, above all, with its ideological strategy. In the early years, Huawei advocated the spirit of the Spartans, the character of wolves, and the culture of pirates. And behind it was an incentive and disciplinary system. The logic was very clear: Dedicated employees would be rewarded and slackers would have to go. This is common sense and natural logic in nature and human society but difficult to implement in real life. At Huawei, though, it has been implemented from the very beginning and has been held as a corporate flag for over 20 years. Almost every mid- and senior-level executive today has endured the cruelty of market tests, and meanwhile they are their own beneficiaries: They have a considerable number of shares in the company and an enviable income.

Then what sets the direction for all these dedicated employees? Customer needs. With customer orientation, Huawei people have been fighting with determination and courage in the Chinese and global markets and have ultimately managed to cut through enemy lines. As Deng Xiaoping said when establishing the Shenzhen Special Economic Zone, one must "blaze a trail for survival even at the expense of blood." This is exactly what Huawei has done over the past two decades.

If a core strategy is needed to explain Huawei's success, there has to be only one answer: to define the right values and have them relentlessly instilled and implemented throughout the organization.

Underlying Huawei's success is an ideological strategy, without which Huawei would have failed.

Huawei's Market Strategy I: Partnering Across the Industry

The history of Huawei over the past two decades is that of a lonely wolf fighting for survival. For over a decade, Western companies have been trying to encircle this lonely wolf and kill it. Inevitably, in the coming years, Huawei will surely face new hunting efforts as renewed fences, rumors, and suppressions in different forms. Since 10 years ago after they recognized the threats of Huawei, as Dr Kao did, Western companies have tried to confine Huawei to the Chinese market. Much to their surprise, Huawei has made it to the global market against all odds. Huawei was not devoured by a tiger or a lion. Rather, it has been able to dance in tandem with them on the international stage, an elegant Chinese traditional dance to the music of the West.

The hurdle, however, has not lowered. If Western giants had failed to contain Huawei in the Chinese domestic market a decade ago, its American rivals are now trying to build higher and stronger barriers, or political walls, to keep Huawei away from the American market.

Huawei's leaders are fully aware that the company's spirit of dedication, aggressiveness, its wolf characters, and pirate culture are essential to its survival. But they also know that mere aggressiveness and a headstrong offense will also drag Huawei into the quagmire. Every coin has two sides. "We must not give up our aggressiveness, but we cannot ignore partnerships either." To wage a war and to seek for peace are not mutually exclusive. They form a dialectical relationship, and both are essential for survival.

During the Warring States period (475 BC–221 BC), the great strategists Su Qin and Zhang Yi traveled around the states and proposed the strategy of alliance to their kings. Their proposals were rejected because the kings believed in absolute power. In our time, a group of Chinese merchants are deploying the strategy of vertical and horizontal partnerships in the global market. "Don't be prejudiced against wolves. Wolves are indeed aggressive, but they are outstanding team players," said a senior Huawei executive. He went on to say, "Huawei has won the respect of competitors through dedication and resolve, but has won even greater success through its open and cooperative commercial diplomacy."

This is true. Huawei has joined hands with almost every major competitor in the world. In 2002, Huawei established joint ventures with NEC and Panasonic to develop 3G mobile phones. In late 2003, Huawei and 3Com set up a joint venture, Huawei-3Com, to develop and sell data communication products. In 2005, Huawei and Siemens formed the joint venture TD Tech. In February 2006, Huawei and Nortel established a joint venture to develop ultra-broadband projects. In February 2008, the Huawei–Symantec joint venture was established. And in December of the same year, Huawei and Global Marine Systems set up Huawei Marine Networks to address the submarine telecom market.

And the partnership between Huawei and Motorola is even earlier, broader, and deeper.

It is common that people embrace each other after they fight, only to face one another the next time. Over the years, as an emerging giant in the international telecom market, Huawei has fought with several well-established giants and has also wedded with some on bundled sales, patent exchange, cross-licensing, joint bidding, original equipment manufacturing (OEM), joint R&D, and joint sales. When Huawei wins a large contract, which often involves more than just one product, it would choose to partner and share the benefits with competitors who have better alternatives on a certain product.

Such a cooperative competition policy has eased the intense rivalry in the international market, and the concept of sharing the world has become a consensus, although it has not yet taken root.

The policy of co-opetition is based on Huawei's business philosophy: openness, compromise, and grayness. Without sufficient openness, Huawei would not have been able to learn from its rivals or join hands while fighting with them. If Huawei didn't have a sense of compromise or if it rushed along with its offense, it would have been smashed by Western companies who would likely have joined hands. But can they really form a transatlantic alliance against Huawei? This depends on Huawei rather than Western companies. Huawei is in fact facing a group of competitors who are not likely to become allies because they represent independent parties of interests. As long as Huawei performs the art of compromise, it can have a bigger room for maneuvering. On the other hand, if it discards the philosophy of grayness when dealing with its rivals, Huawei would fall into the trap of duality to simply classify its counterparts as either friend or foe. In consequence, the company would either seek to join an exclusive alliance or indulge itself in permanent conflicts. In fact, any exclusive alliance is an illusion. Business empires like Microsoft have always remained pragmatic. Likewise, perpetual conflict would also be a rigid dogmatism.

Of course, John Dewey, the founder of American pragmatism, is the ideological mentor of all great merchants. No doubt the decision makers of Huawei are his disciples as well.

Huawei's Market Strategy II: Progressivism

More than 20 years ago, Huawei started marketing attempts with county-level post and telecom bureaus. It then moved up to the provincial level and then went national. Within about 10 years, Huawei had managed to transform from a dealer to a product supplier for remote regions, then a cross-regional supplier, and finally a national supplier. This progress mirrored Huawei's improvements in products, human resources, management, and organization. The perfect competition right in the Chinese telecom market about 10 years ago, especially the presence of multinationals, had been a serious test for Chinese companies still in infancy such as Huawei and ZTE. It was a rare chance for them to face their "tutors" or "mentors" at home who had forced them to learn to fight with enough toughness and skills. They could fall down and out, or hold on and finally rise up as masters themselves. During the first decade of its development, Huawei had moved gradually from the countryside into the city, and this was not a choice. It had to start with the peripheral market because its products, human resources, and management expertise were not good enough.

Western companies in China had forced Huawei to grow up fast. Ten years later, Huawei had taken root in the domestic market and set its eyes overseas. This move, unlike the movement from the countryside into the city in China, was an insightful choice. In 1998, Huawei sold several products to Hutchison Telecommunications Hong Kong, and in 1999 Huawei won its first international contract in the real sense. The buyer was from Russia, where telecom infrastructure was poor. Although the contract value was only US$38, it was still a breakthrough and a milestone. For five years since then, Huawei had been trying to build up its presence worldwide, but with a clear focus on underdeveloped countries and regions such as Africa and Southeast Asia, where Western companies had little interest. Industrialized countries and emerging markets like China were certainly more lucrative. Meanwhile as they had lost their adventurous pirate spirit, Western companies came to find most African markets far from compelling. So far, most of the telecom networks in the most inaccessible regions of the world have been built by Huawei or with equipment from Huawei.

Huawei has fought against its Western competitors with well-planned, progressive steps. It went in the roundabout way before it engaged in direct confrontation. Later, it adopted the policy of cooperative competition. And finally the relationship evolved to a mix of tough conflicts and gentle compromises across the Atlantic Ocean and the Pacific Ocean, and the line in between turned vague. In 2003, Western companies were awakened to the fact that an extremely confident, strategically flexible, culturally different, and fast-growing Asian dark horse had rushed into the pureblooded Western club.

Huawei had penetrated the European market as well. Europe is home to a number of global telecom giants, such as Ericsson, Siemens, Alcatel, and Nokia, but Huawei has unlocked the door. Since 2005, Europe has become a major battlefield for Huawei, generating billions of euros in sales each year. And these are all potentially good contracts because at least there would not be significant aged receivables or bad debts.

In 2007, Huawei entered Japan and has become a mainstream telecom equipment supplier in this country known for its incredibly high standards on quality.

In spite of these advances, however, Huawei has met with resistance from the governments and media, as it did in Europe and India. In the name of national security, these governments had denied the contracts already awarded to Huawei and the media had created and spread rumors against the company. Over time, Huawei came to understand that it must on the one hand become more transparent to present its true image to the skeptics and the media, and on the other hand it must try to improve its relationship with governments, the media, and industry partners. Ren Zhengfei said, "We are operating globally, not merely to increase sales and make profits, but more importantly to invest locally, create jobs, pay taxes, and promote local technology advancement. We want to contribute to the countries we operate and create a business environment where everybody wins."

In 2011, Huawei paid CNY23.5 billion in taxes to the Chinese government, and its total tax contribution worldwide was US$1.5 billion. In Europe, Huawei will be having 26 global centers of expertise, including 12 R&D centers. Huawei will also establish international treasury centers in the Netherlands and Japan for Euro and Yen settlement to expand its partnerships with European and Japanese banking institutions. All these projects are intended to increase the employment of high-quality human resources and the investment in Europe and other regions.

Huawei's strategy for the international market is under a complete overhaul. Technically there is no regional or national identity attached to any multinationals, so it is with Huawei.

Anticyclical Strategy: Making Advance Strategic Moves

Huawei continues to feel increased pressure as it expands its global presence. In recent years, the competition between Huawei and its major rivals has reached a dynamic balance, and nonmarket confrontations with Ericsson, Nokia-Siemens, and other peers are decreasing. Nevertheless, the company has experienced increased resistance from the media and Western governments, especially the US government. As the world's largest superpower that boasts free trade and a free market, the United States has been issuing bans against Huawei, alleging that it is one of the biggest threats to its national security. In fact, Huawei, as a private Chinese company, has yet to supply any network equipment to American operators, or its presence in the American network is zero. How could the company ever threaten its national security?

In recent years, the US government has kept scrutinizing Huawei. They should have known enough about Huawei, but they had not really understood the logic of Huawei's rapid growth.

Huawei is like any Western company in that it has instituted Western practices of corporate management. To a certain degree, the company has been completely westernized, a rare case among Chinese companies. It is unlike most Western companies at the same time. It is not listed on any stock market and as a private company it does not need to deliver short-term benefits to appeal its shareholders. Therefore, it has been able to design and implement its strategy in a time horizon of 10 years or even 20 years. More important, as it has grown up through tests, Huawei is fully aware of risks and more forewarned of collapse and death than any other competitor in the world.

The strategic logic of Huawei is anticyclical. In February 2012, the Vice-President of the European Commission asked Ren Zhengfei, "Why did you recruit so many people when the economic environment was so challenging?" Yes, Huawei did recruit 28,000 new employees in 2011, and expected to add another 10,000 in 2012. Ren responded:

> First, data traffic is exploding, and that means a great deal of opportunities. We believe it is not a zero-sum game, as traffic keeps growing. Second, we're dealing with small-sum consumption, so the financial crisis is irrelevant. People won't spare telephone calls due to the crisis. Third, we are not running a "bubble economy." With so many exceptional people from around the world, we are just making meager profits. Therefore we will not be hit by the financial crisis, unlike those ballooned real estate developers and financial institutions. We can grow even faster. I hope companies in Europe will share this view. If we don't get prepared now, opportunities will pass us by when they arise after the crisis.

In 2001, a technological earthquake hit the United States, and a number of telecom and IT companies, such as Enron, went bankrupt almost overnight. Wall Street was caught by deep pessimism, and the Silicon Valley, the cradle of IT miracles, had suddenly lost its luster. The tragedy sent ripples throughout the world. Stock markets were all hit hard.

Huawei was an exception. It had not only survived the crisis but also reaped exciting strategic opportunities. As it was not a public company,

Huawei was not at all exposed to the disaster of the capital market. But it had been a real disaster for most of its powerful competitors: Their stock prices were plummeting; the technologies and products that once supported their long-term strategies had become burdensome; they were faced with massive job cuts to avoid bankruptcy; and their human resources, once their most valuable assets, were draining away.

This was a sharp contrast. When its rivals were melting and dwindling like snow in the sun, Huawei could have narrowed the gap even if it had stayed where it was. More fortunately Huawei had made sufficient preparations and allocated adequate resources to survive the harsh winter, as Ren Zhengfei, the prophet, had been preaching about the crisis. In the second half of 2001, Huawei sold its noncore business, Huawei Electric, for US$750 million. In 2002, Huawei turned up in Silicon Valley swiftly, but quietly, and completed a series of mergers and acquisitions.

During this period, Huawei started contact with 3Com. One year later, the two companies announced the establishment of a joint venture, Huawei-3Com. Five years later, 3Com bought Huawei's stake in the joint venture as per the contract. Huawei received US$800 million, and 3Com had also benefited significantly from the joint venture.

Both Chinese and Western people like playing chess, and advance moves are necessary and effective in the game; they carry the wisdom and strategic thinking of the player. Yet, in both chess and in business context, what decides the ultimate outcome is the player, or the leader, himself. What is the strategic goal? When is the best time to make a move? How can strategic resources be allocated? What skills are involved? How to strike a strategic balance? Those are all important questions for the leaders to address. And most important of all, strategic leaders must have sufficient strategic awareness, be able to make wise strategic judgments, and dare to take strategic risks.

Section IV. Strategy Generation Mechanism of Huawei

Strategic Brainstorming and the Blue Army Department

The race between the hare and the tortoise is a well-known allegory. The general belief is that the tortoise has won the race because of its persistence and the hare has lost due to its arrogance. This is completely right. But this allegory may provoke other thoughts. The first is about focus.

Once a person or an organization has defined a goal or adopted a strategy, they have the best chance of success if they can focus on this goal and never shift. In the business environment, one should avoid opportunistic diversity. A jack of all trades is a good-for-nothing, and a diversified company is often vulnerable to disease.

The second idea is in relation to speed. The speed of the tortoise is not at all the best choice. A higher speed is preferred in a fast-changing environment. One has to understand, however, that running along a straight line, or a proper direction, can reduce the distance and reach the goal in the shortest time, while it is a waste of time and energy to run in circles at a higher speed. At times, one needs to slow down and then pick up the pace when energy is regained. It is not an exaggeration to say that first-class management gurus are, in essence, similar to symphony conductors.

Last but not least, how about the idea of a tortoise and a hare working together? A tortoise is resilient and persistent, able to stay on course until reaching its goal. A hare, on the other hand, is alert, flexible, responsive, and fast, and sometimes passionate. A tortoise and a hare working together may generate desired synergy through balance and mutual enhancement. Some argue that a strategy should move like a tortoise, slow but stable, while a tactic should be executed swiftly, as when a hare runs.

This is an inspiration from an informal dialogue with Ren Zhengfei in 2009. He said:

> When we were still a small company, I had to make decisions on almost everything, and I used my intuition. My colleagues, likewise, were following their intuition. We seemed to be very efficient, but had wasted a lot of energy running back and forth. In recent years, we have instituted democracy first among senior management, and then the whole organization has become democratic. Decisions are now made collectively. The process is slower, but we have made fewer mistakes. Any idea must be marinated and communicated gradually throughout the company, and we do not expect any change overnight. It will produce great power if it is implemented after being accepted by all in the company.

Indeed, after IPD, ISC, and human resources transformation, or the basic reforms, were completed, Huawei has significantly reduced its arbitrariness. Its decision-making process has been institutionalized. There are the board of directors and the EMT at the top level of the hierarchy, and there are a human resources committee, a strategy and development committee, an audit committee and a finance committee under the EMT. In addition, there are external advisory boards that serve various purposes.

"Major strategic decisions must be made only after they are fully fermented. Senior management should be discussing abstract ideas. They should not care about the specifics of implementation. If you do everything, what should our colleagues down the hierarchy do?" asked Ren Zhengfei. Abstract brainstorming sessions have been a phenomenon in Huawei these years. And a senior executive of Huawei said, "Brainstorming sessions are sources of inspirations for our boss." Whenever they would make a certain decision, Huawei would take a dozen or dozens of people to a beautiful scenic area far away from the city where they can relax. They would be engaged in brainstorming meetings, in the morning for instance, where they express themselves freely. And in the afternoon, the meeting focuses on a certain theme, but the discussion remains open and free. Ren Zhengfei and other EMT members are equal participants in the discussion, and conflicting views are freely expressed. The next day, they focus further on several typical opinions, and finally reach an agreement that is recorded in the meeting minutes. This is not the final decision yet, as the minutes are then distributed to relevant departments for review and feedback. The final decision is made only after repeated reviews and revisions.

"Strategic decisions involve the direction of development. If the direction is wrong, then the faster the company runs, the more likely it runs into accidents." Based on this consensus, Huawei has established a Strategy and Customer Standing Committee under the EMT, to develop guidance, vision, and ideas on strategic and customer issues pertaining the company's mid- and long-term survival and growth. The key mandate is to define the direction, and the committee must avoid getting involved in daily operations. This sets forth the organizational dimension of Huawei's mechanism for strategy generation.

Huawei has also set up a special body under the Strategy & Development Committee: The Blue Army Department. The task of this advisory organ is to play the devil and give the oppositional voice or even alarms that may seem false. The idea is to increase the risk awareness of the Red Force. The confrontations between the Red Force and the Blue Force, like in the real army, will help the company remain self-critical and stay on the right track.

Specifically, the major functions of the Blue Army Department include:

1. To review the company's strategy and technology development from a different perspective, and to think the other way. The Department should identify, examine, and verify vulnerabilities in the strategies, products, and solutions of the Red Army through independent analysis and competitive simulation.
2. To build a system and platform for challenging the Red Army. The Department should analyze and criticize the current strategic logic of the company through debates, simulations, and tactical deduction, and seek for disruptive technology alternatives.
3. To assist business groups (BGs) to establish Blue Army organizations. The Department is responsible for developing and operating processes and platforms for all the Blue Army, and organizing experience and competence sharing throughout the community.

Why Are Spider Webs So Resilient?

On February 1, 2012, L'Agence France-Presse reported:

Scientists said Wednesday they had unraveled the mystery of how spider webs can withstand multiple tears and even hurricane-force winds without collapsing. . . . Once ripped, what keeps the whole web from falling apart? . . . A strand comprises a unique combination of shapeless protein and ordered, nanoscale crystals, they found. When stress increases—the falling branch, for example—the filament elongates in four phases: a linear tugging, a drawn-out stretching as the protein unfolds, a stiffening phase that absorbs force, and finally the breaking point triggered by friction.

The report went on:

Spider threads fall into two categories, and what makes webs so resilient is how they interact, the researchers said. So-called viscid silk—stretchy, wet, and sticky—winds out in ever-widening spirals from the center of the web, and serves to capture unsuspecting prey. But the straight threads that radiate outwards like spokes on a wheel, called dragline silk, are dry and stiff and provide structural support.

The radial and spiral filaments each play a different role in absorbing motion, and the way they are intertwined limits puncture damage to the spot where it occurs, the researchers found. As a result, the web is organised to "sacrifice" local areas so that failure will not prevent the remainder from functioning, even if this is in a diminished capacity.

The report said in the end: "Dennis Carter, an expert on biomechanics at the US National Science Foundation, which partly funded the research, paid tribute to a 'clever strategy' by spiders, which expend precious energy to build their webs."

Coincidentally, Ren Zhengfei had said in 1996, "Spiders are the most respectable warriors in the world. They are always weaving and mending their webs with their thin silk. They won't give up even after they are torn apart or totally ruined by storms."

There are amazing similarities between spider webs and Huawei's organizational structure and strategies. The forces fighting at the forefront are like the spiral sticky silk. They are flexible, responsive, stretchy, and most importantly sticky. They would catch hold of their targets until they are subdued. The dragline silk that radiates outward is like the command center, the advisory department, the logistics department, the human resources department, and other back office organizations. In the upcoming organizational reform of Huawei, the R&D division, which has nearly a half of its employees, will be defined as part of the support system. The support system provides the necessary talent, capital, products, technologies, and solutions. Meanwhile it will deliver orders from the command center: Where should they go? What should they aim at? Should they start an offense? When should they start the offense? These are radiating functions. Of course, how to wage the offense is a tactical issue, and it is the ultimate decision of commanders at the frontline. The support system is also responsible for institutional guarantee, communication of values, and check and balance of rights and responsibilities. These are dragging functions.

The spiral organizations responsible for offense and fighting at the frontline must possess the characters of wolves, gangsters, and pirates, daring to wage one battle after another. They are supposed to weave a big web that catches as much prey as possible to ensure survival and growth of the organization with enough nutrition (contracts). On the other hand, the radiating and dragging organizations, or the back offices, that support decision-making, institutional and cultural development, deliver human and capital resources, and provide products and services must increase their efficiency and responsiveness to ensure that every opportunity is seized. They must also avoid red-tape bureaucracy and personal preferences.

On the organizational spider web, spiral and radiating units play different roles in supporting the organization. They are entangled to limit any external impairment at a certain point.

Entanglement is a great biological philosophy. While human organizations have taken great pains and developed a great number of theories to form any synergy, spiders give their webs immense tenacity by entangling their silk on the web. Therefore, organizational theories should have included organizational bionics.

Then, have the senior executives of Huawei, who are well-known for their learning capacity, been inspired by the spider web?

The organizational structure of Huawei is indeed like a spider web. This is the fruit of constant organizational evolution, and it is to a greater extent what Ren Zhengfei and his colleagues in the senior management team have learned or borrowed horizontally and vertically. Ren once read and was inspired by an essay by Feng Lun, chairman of Wantong Group, "West Point Produces More CEOs than Harvard Business School." Among other things, the essay introduces the US military reform led by Donald Rumsfeld, the 13th and 21st US Secretary of Defense. In this essay, Feng states:

> Now almost every country is increasing their Special Forces while reducing their regular forces. And among the Special Forces, there are new information warfare units and psychological warfare units. What has happened to the costs and benefits following the change? To put it simply, the change is to enlarge the back-end and reduce the size of the front-end. Among the money spent, 70 percent is spent on finding the target and 30 percent% on destroying the target. The front-end units are versatile, and the back-end becomes powerful support for all operations. In the past, a frontline officer cannot order the artillery to fire. Instead, he must ask the command center for support, who would then give the order for the artillery to fire. Now, the back-end support is much stronger, while the front-end fighters are omnipotent. A Special Forces soldier can get the artillery to fire with an email. The location of troops and soldiers is accurately displayed on a large screen before the commander-in-chief in the command center. Can you imagine the special troop that defeated the Taliban in Afghanistan only consisted of 123 soldiers? They were divided into smaller task groups. Each task group had three soldiers, but the back-end support for each group cost US$50 million. The three soldiers included an information expert, a fire and bomb expert, and a combat expert. They understood the expertise of one another, and

were well-trained in first aid. Now, consider how much change has occurred to the cost and benefit relationship. In the past, most costs were spent on arms and ammunition and the deceased. As the bombing accuracy was low, 70 percent of the cost was wasted and only 30 percent% was effective. Now, as cruise missiles are used, 70 percent of the cost is spent on finding the target, through satellite positioning for example, and 30 percent cost is spent on explosives. In modern warfare, the targeting cost is increased, while the cost directly spent on the enemies is reduced.

In conclusion, Feng Lun said, "Military organizational reform is a precursor of business organization reform. Military organizations worldwide are undergoing two changes: Regular units and legal organizations are transforming into special mission units, and illegal or noncontractual organizations are turning into bases."

This essay was highly recommended by Ren Zhengfei and has been widely read within Huawei. Moreover, it has been one of the key references for Huawei's organizational reform over the past two years.

CHAPTER NINE

Balance: Power, Flexibility, and Rule

Section I. Balanced Development: The Law of Nature

Baicaoyuan: Musical Beauty

Ten European-style buildings of between four and seven stories stand quietly among the grass and trees. In the courtyard, one can extend their view and see artistically arranged flora. There is balance between the green space and the buildings. No one feels depressed or dwarfed when they walk between the buildings.

Looking vertically or horizontally, one finds perfect balance in Baicaoyuan. Every space and corner is balanced. There seems to be balance between different parts, and between the parts and the whole.

The above is an excerpt from an essay, "Charm of Balance—Attachment to Baicaoyuan," published in *Huawei People* by Chen Peigen, an advisor of Huawei.

Baicaoyuan is a residential quarter for Huawei's unmarried employees at the company's industrial base in Shenzhen. It was completed in 2000, with a total floor space of 117,851.56 square meters and a total green space of 58,218.6 square meters. The green rate is over 70 percent.

In the essay, Chen Peigen went on:

Subrahmanyan Chandrasekhar, professor of University of Chicago and winner of the 1983 Nobel Prize for Physics, had written a book *Truth and Beauty: Aesthetics and Motivations in Science*, in which he believed the motivation for a scientist to explore science is not logical consciousness, but some subconscious aesthetic pursuit. And he believed there were two aesthetic principles:

The first principle is, as Francis Bacon put it, "There is no excellent beauty that hath not some strangeness in the proportion." In other words, beauty entails proportion and balance.

And the second principle is a definition by Werner Heisenberg, a German physicist, Nobel laureate, and one of the founders of the field of quantum mechanics: "Beauty is balance between one part and another, and between the part and the whole. . . ."

Apparently, Baicaoyuan is balanced and beautiful.

So, then, what is balance? Balance is the symphony of power and flexibility. There is always balance between roaring torrents and quiet streams, round and square, innovation and stability, idealism and pragmatism, pirate culture and institutional civilization, heroes and gangsters, change and conservation, and dialectics and metaphysics. Balance prevails in this world. Buildings of distinctive styles that have developed over thousands of years are the perfect embodiment of balance. Buildings are like fluid music: There is climax, highlight, rhythm, tension, coherence, and even breath. Of every building or every cluster of buildings, however, the beauty rests more with its power and elasticity.

Ren Zhengfei was a graduate from Chongqing Institute of Civil Engineering and Architecture, where he developed a keen, lifelong interest in the art of architecture. Over the past decade, Huawei has built manufacturing bases and research and development campuses in a dozen provinces, and each of them is considered a local landmark and a highlight of the cityscape. For instance, Huawei's Software Park in Nanjing is an open, enjoyable, and practical site and fits in harmoniously with the natural beauty of Zijin Mountain. Science, art, and nature compose a perfect symphony there.

Huawei has never built any facility in a busy downtown area. It prefers remote outskirts where, if possible, there are mountains and water. Huawei's Bantian Base in Shenzhen had been a graveyard, and Huawei's Software Park in Nanjing is located near Yuhuatai Cemetery of Martyrs. Architectural designs are always contracted to the top designers in the world and are always discussed over and over before they are finalized.

Over a decade ago, visitors to Huawei's headquarters in Shenzhen would often be taken to Baicaoyuan, the dormitory quarters nearby. In recent years, however, the visit to Baicaoyuan has been canceled. Obviously, this site which was acclaimed by Chen Peigen as the best example of balanced beauty has lost its charm and luster, because there are now even better sites of balanced beauty.

Ballet Dancers Have Thick Legs

Since 2001, Huawei has been announcing *Ten Management Keys* each year, and however the external environment has changed, the first key is still "sticking to balanced development." Some scholars believe that balance is a core concept in the corporate management philosophy of Ren Zhengfei.

But the problem is that balance is a utopian ideal: Absolute balance is impossible in the real world. A perfect balance means death. Ren Zhengfei said:

> The world is changing, so there is never any exquisite perfection. If you set your goal perfection only, you would have gone to the extreme and ruined everything. If you are perfectly exquisite, you would become a small-footed woman who can never fight. In the past, I had thought that a ballet girl must be slender and have slim legs. In fact, their legs are thick and their feet are large, and they are very strong. The reason Huawei has taken over its Western competitors is that we do not run after perfection.

It is true that ballet dancers have thick legs, and this proves the aesthetic conviction of Ren Zhengfei, a graduate from a civil engineering college: Strength is the basis of beauty. A building may be harmonious, balanced, and therefore beautiful, only when it is built on a solid base and follows the science of mechanics. Similarly, a musical melody, a human body, or a plant will collapse if it loses balance, strength, or support. Without strength, there can be no balance.

Huawei's success depends on its strength and courage, which are key notes of the company's culture. Courage means the gut of Don Quixote to challenge global powers, and strength means, in the culture of Huawei, the willpower to remain dedicated and the capabilities the company has gained and accumulated through its course of development. Ren Zhengfei said:

> We attach great importance to abstraction. Why? We must drag the company along a certain direction. We must define its orientations, including product positioning and human resources priorities. Therefore, we may be able to seize every opportunity that arises ahead of us, and we will match large multinationals in the international market. This is why some have called us Don Quixote. We have matched every product with international trends and standards. We have not focused on the domestic market only; we aim to be a global leader. This is the idea of abstraction. We must seize every opportunity to steer the company along. In this process, we create a new

balance as the original balance is disrupted. After new balance is reached, the company will have a new life.

About 10 years ago, when I first met him, Ren Zhengfei impressed me as an entrepreneur with enormous power of traction. He had the willpower of a soldier and the faith of a fervent religious believer, and therefore, he was able to draw together, inspire, and mobilize so many young intellectuals who were diverse and individualistic. There were at first dozens, and then hundreds, and then thousands, and now over a 100,000 of them, and most of them have now been transformed. A special gene has been transplanted in the organization: It is the cultural gene of Huawei, the dedication to thinking and action. Someone calls this the Huawei syndrome: wolf-like, aggressive, confident, and fearless.

This is no doubt the source of Huawei's courage and power; it is precisely the soul of Huawei, and the natural logic behind the rise of the pirate culture over that of nobility. In the West, most commercial giants had gained their glory by virtue of a pirate spirit, and they have fallen due to the loss of dedication. In Western culture, pirate is not an entirely negative term. Pirates had been the forerunners of the Western expansion during the Age of Discovery. Portuguese, Spanish, and British pirate ships were mostly licensed by kings or governments to explore the seas, and the scope of license was exploration rather than robbery.

Balanced management is not a new idea or practice in Western companies. They have developed well-defined and regulated management procedures that reflect the general maturity of Western companies. It must be noted, however, that quite a number of them have gone too far; they have become metaphysical and mechanical. More appalling is that they have lost the pirate spirit, which culturally and anthropologically refers to the human inclination and commitment to adventures. This is perhaps due to the welfarism that has prevailed in the West for 30 years.

The rise of Huawei and the fall of its Western counterparts over the past two decades, to some extent, reflect the balance of beliefs and cultures. Ren Zhengfei believes in power and simplicity. He said, "Beauty rests with simplicity. Anything is beautiful so long as it is simple and its functions are simple while it fulfills the same goal." On the other hand, Western companies are getting finer and meticulous with the management procedures that are more and more quantitative. They are indulged in procedures that are often games of numbers and entail a complicated philosophy.

In the headquarters of Apple Inc., there stand two flags: One is the company flag, and the other is a pirate flag featuring a skull. That means Steve Jobs understood the soul and mission of a commercial organization. Ren Zhengfei also understands that numbers are the result of dedicated fights rather than mere calculations. This is true with a ballet dancer. You can see their beautiful dance on the stage, but you may not realize that it requires lasting tough training behind the scene and the most important part of the training is to strengthen their muscle. Therefore, each ballet dancer has thick legs and large feet, without which any flexible and soft move, or any dynamic balance, would be impossible. Isn't it true also with a dizzying skyscraper?

Of course, indulgence in muscle and power can prove disastrous. A single-dimensional pursuit may help a company grow quickly, especially during its primitive accumulation. The company may therefore survive and develop some power and muscle. But if it charges blindly, the company will suffer from external frictions and internal conflicts that will also build up. Therefore, balance in a certain period would become the key issue for organizational management.

Balance, however, depends also on power in any circumstances. Ren Zhengfei has been forced to embrace balance by the reality: A black widow will surely be surrounded by enemies, so Huawei must be flexible. This is also the result of its efforts to learn from the West. In some sense, Huawei's emphasis on balance after 2001 marks an end of its wolf culture and its local identity, although this new management concept is still based on its culture of dedicated fight.

Seeking Balance Between Order and Chaos

Balance is the highest level of organizational management. It is, however, a relative and temporary concept, while power is a lasting pursuit. Balance and imbalance are dynamic and interchanging. If an organization keeps going ahead in imbalance, some parts of its body will wither with disuse, while some other parts are overused and worn out, and therefore, the whole body collapses one day. If every part of the organization grows in balance, the organization will gain power and strength. On the other hand, it must be realized that long-term balanced growth may result in the loss of passion and competitive power, and the organization is highly likely to suffer from the growth of entropy: laziness, equalitarianism, cliquism, and corruption will rise and prevail, and the organization will finally die quietly of organizational fatigue and leadership fatigue.

Therefore, balance is always a critical issue for organization leaders. They have to refrain from radical moves and disorder, and shortly after the organization strikes a certain balance they have to give the organization enough stimuli to keep it away from conservatism and avoid any indulgence in unchanging order. Political and business leaders are all engaged in such a pendulum, swinging back and forth. They have to take risks sometimes to keep themselves safe from bigger risks. Mere leftism or rightism belongs to poets and philosophers only; they are not fit for business leaders. Almost all leaders are contingentists, although some successful leaders are idealists as well. The success of historical leaders, in the final analysis, has depended on a rule: to seek balance between chaos and order. This rule also applies well to organizations of all types, including universities and churches. Ren Zhengfei said:

> What has been our focus over the past two decades? We have focused more on R&D and sales & marketing and paid little attention to organizational balance. This is why we have met with so many troubles. The marginal systems have been neglected. The past 20 years has passed away, and we cannot do anything with it. What we can do is to achieve more balance within our organization and in our development over the next 20 years. Our relationship with the media will be part of this balance.

Saying that the media is part of this balance, Ren Zhengfei meant that Huawei is a business organization that has grown on the philosophy of openness, but it is not open enough to the media. Instead, Huawei has resisted the media which have to guess what Huawei is doing. There are natural misunderstandings and even rumors. Huawei had meant to avoid distractions by keeping the media away, but the result is more disruptions. Therefore, Huawei would better open itself up to the media from now on. Ren Zhengfei said:

> Huawei will try to attain order within the company within five to ten years, and give itself more power of expansion. Order is not meant to restrict the company's growth, or let it indulge in expansion. We would like to see that it is orderly but not dead, lively but not chaotic. The company should follow certain rules.

"What are rules?" Ren Zhengfei asked, "Rules mean standards, procedures, and formats. But they are not rigid."

The years from 1997 to 2005 were a critical period for Huawei's organizational and governance reform. From 1997 to 2003, in particular, Huawei had created a totally new framework for itself. First, it adopted Huawei Basic Law and then completed its organizational procedure and logistics reforms, including IBM's IPD and ISC reforms which had made Huawei's primitive management culture obsolete. As said much earlier in chapters on reform and self-criticism, an organization often faces some fatal risks when it is trying to eliminate its gangster or pirate characters: separation or at least dramatic fluctuations. The solution of Ren Zhengfei is: first copy, then institutionalize, and finally, optimize. This process is intended to brainwash everyone involved in this process, including its leaders.

By 2005, Huawei's procedural reform had produced satisfactory fruits. The procedures were essentially mature and institutionalized. That means Huawei has passed the critical period and become a balanced and orderly international company.

In 2006, however, Ren Zhengfei started to think about how to disrupt the balance and address the ills of large corporations. He said:

I told the people in our UK office that Huawei must refine its management. By that I mean we must try to put an end to the chaos and seek order. But I had not mentioned the need to disrupt the balance for further expansion. Some people have therefore misunderstood me. That's why I recently told our people in the Mexico office that marketing is not like painting or embroidery. We cannot be satisfied with refinement. We must also develop a clear direction for advancement. We must understand and follow the underlying trends of the market. To enter tier-one carriers, we need to develop sound strategies and plans. Breaking through the wall requires right strategies and effective plans, as well as strong willpower, determination, and the persistence of leaders at the critical moment. The leaders must also remain dedicated.

The purpose of refined management is to keep our expansion in order. We have never thought of closing our gates. We do not mean to stop expanding. We must stand up to competition. We must have the courage to win, without which we won't be a winner of the game. So I don't think there is any conflict between refined management and expansion; we must effectively combine them. As a Chinese saying goes, we should muddy the water before we go fishing, but only the most skillful fishermen can catch fish in troubled waters.

Philosophically speaking, any balance will be broken someday, which will give rise to new life. We can then move forward with renewed balance. It is much similar to the balance of our life. We will one day die, and when we do, a new balance will form because the next generation will continue.

Death is never a taboo for Huawei's leaders. "Huawei will die someday, and all our efforts are intended to postpone that day." This is absolutely true. Balance is effective to prevent organizational collapse, but it is necessary to break a certain balance to prevent the organization from dying in quietness. An organization will collapse and fall apart in disorder, but it may not until it dies in rigid balance.

Section II. Dance of Ideas: Thinking Systematically

Idealism Versus Apocalypse of Crisis

Business management is essentially a process of managing crises. A company must face and overcome crises throughout its lifecycle, whether it survives decades or hundreds of years. The Titanic hit an iceberg and sank to the bottom of the sea because its designer, builder, and captain had failed to sense any crisis due to blind faith in its perfection. Likewise, the death of organizations, including states and businesses, is above all the result of the arrogance and blindness of their leaders.

On every wall in Mitsubishi Electric in Japan, in the offices and corridors, there is a picture of a vessel running into an iceberg, and the caption says, "Only you can save the ship." This picture and caption had shocked and also inspired Ren Zhengfei.

Ren Zhengfei is no doubt the most apocalyptic business man in China. He has given more warnings of crisis than most other Chinese business leaders. Some scholars argue that he has "institutionalized" crisis warning.

He gave the most influential warning of crisis in 2000. At that time, people were rejoicing at the arrival of the new millennium, and the IT industry was booming like flowers in the spring. IT elites were optimistic to a fault, as if the IT industry was about to dominate the world. The annual sales of Huawei this year amounted to CNY15.2 billion, and its profits hit CNY2.9 billion, ranking first among electronic companies in China. Huawei could have joined the festive noise. But Ren Zhengfei, instead, warned with a cold tone that winter was coming for Huawei!

Ren Zhengfei's forecast was proved right. In 2001, the American dotcom bubble burst, and the 3G dream in Europe shattered before long. The IT industry entered the Ice Age. More frightening, the IT industry has no summer or autumn. For decades, it has always passed directly from spring to winter, and its spring is always short-lived. This is due to the inherent characters of the IT industry.

Four years later, in 2004, the IT industry experienced a warm winter and Huawei had just freed itself from a chain of both external and internal shocks. At this point, Huawei could have relaxed. In fact, the IT industry was recovering from the crisis, and IT stocks were transforming from Cinderellas back into princesses in the Wall Street. By the end of the year, Lenovo acquired IBM's PC business. Spring seemed to be just around the corner.

In the third quarter of 2004, however, Ren Zhengfei warned again that Huawei should get ready for the coming winter. He said, "We must inform every one of the real difficulty. If we fail to predict the challenges ahead, we would be backed into a corner." This warning was indeed surprising because Huawei's global sales revenue had reached US$3.827 billion in 2004, a record-high in the company's history.

In 2008, Ren Zhengfei picked up his forecast of crisis. He said once again that winter was coming. He cautioned, "Huawei must get seriously ready for the tough and cruel challenges brought about by economic globalization and market competition." Ren further stated, "Senior executives must be fully prepared if the economy would slide back into recession. The situation will probably worsen in 2009 and 2010."

Some media houses seemed to notice a coincidence: "Ren Zhengfei is reminding his employees of the winter at a regular interval of four years." This is interesting but not exact, however. In fact, since the establishment of the company, Ren Zhengfei has kept talking about crisis every year and almost every month, and he has spoken of policy crisis, market crisis, capital crisis, cultural crisis, human resources crisis, management crisis, regular crisis, and contingent crisis. It seems that crisis is omnipresent, and Huawei has reached so far against so many odds.

In 2010 and 2011, Ren Zhengfei repeated the same warning to the middle-ranking and senior executives, "Crisis will arrive. We can wither a bit, but we must not fall apart."

There is a problem with the warnings, though. Will the team get bored with the warning? Will they lose their sensitivity to the warning if it is repeated for 20 years? Will they take it as a false alarm like the villagers in the Aesop's fable: the Shepherd Boy and the Wolf? In the fable, the boy who felt dull attending to a sheep flock kept calling "Wolf! Wolf" for fun and laughed at the villagers who came to help him. But when the wolf did come, no one came to help him no matter how hard he cried "Wolf! Wolf!" because the villagers thought the boy was trying to fool them again. In the end, the wolf killed all the sheep. Now, Ren Zhengfei has been crying "Wolf! Wolf!" But the result is different: Each time he calls his people would become alert and excited. Why? This is because there is really wolf whenever he calls, and more than one wolf has come. There is a gang of them. Therefore, Huawei is able to summon enough defense whenever the wolf comes. As a senior executive of Huawei said, "Our apocalyptic boss has kept us excited and alert all along."

There is yet another problem. Will people get distressed and helpless if he mentions crisis every day? Will they doubt the future of the company? Will they take it for granted that Huawei will collapse sooner or later? Will they lose their dedication since the company has no future? And why should they still forge ahead since they will meet with one crisis after another? This is the conflict and duality that Ren Zhengfei has to resolve, and it is also one of the secrets of his management philosophy.

Ren Zhengfei likes to stress a belief to the extreme, but at the same time he would put forward a different or even diametrically opposite idea. It is amazing that both ideas well supplement each other like yin and yang in the Chinese philosophy. This is a perfect balance, and a model of systematic thinking that has been constantly preached to senior management of Huawei. For instance, Ren Zhengfei would keep talking about crisis, but he remains an idealist. He would not only preach apocalypse and fatalism but also paint a brilliant picture of the company. In some sense, the brilliance of Huawei's future overwhelms the dark fatalism, and he insists that the company will finally become a global industry leader and every people of the company will fulfill their dreams if they work with consistent dedication and overcome every crisis.

In 1990, Huawei had only 20-odd employees, but the boss had managed to motivate them by telling them thrilling stories. He had given them enough faith in their future. Ten years ago when Huawei was going global, Ren Zhengfei inspired his colleagues in much the same way. He said:

> In this age, a company needs a global and strategic vision just as a country must depend on global resources in order to prosper. A company cannot keep growing if it does not become part of the global business eco-system,

and an employee may not enjoy any successful career if he does not possess a wide vision and adaptability.

This statement had moved his "generals and soldiers" to tears. One year later in 2001, Ren Zhengfei wrote an article titled "Spring of the Northern Country" in which he said, "Winter will be gone and spring will surely come. We'd better acquire and accumulate strength through internal transformation during the winter. When snow melts and the stream starts to flow, Huawei will be able to enjoy the bright spring days." Again in his New Year's Message 2010, Ren Zhengfei said with great sensation, "We've heard the thundering canons of the New Year. They are inspiring us to win new battles. As long as we keep our tradition of self-criticism, we will surely go from victory to victory. Nothing can stop us, but corruption from within."

In 1994, Ren Zhengfei made a forecast which was ridiculed as a fantasy. He said, "In 10 years, Huawei will be a top-three player in the global telecom market." No one took this quixotic fantasy seriously, but this forecast, which was indeed a vision and a belief, has burned in the hearts of Huawei people for over 20 years. Today, this forecast has come true, as Huawei ranks second in the global telecom market.

Idealism and crisis awareness are the key notes of Huawei's philosophy. They seem to be mutually exclusive, but they indeed support and supplement each other. Both are extremes which interact with each other and, therefore, form a synergy that keeps the scale in balance.

Ren Zhengfei is a crisis prophet. He is also a wonderful story teller, and it seems a special gift of leaders to tell inspiring stories.

Notion of Balance Born in a Tight Space

Masaaki Imai, Japanese management guru and the founder of Kaizen, the philosophy that focuses on continuous improvement of processes in manufacturing, engineering, and business management, asserted in an article "Western Business Management Philosophy Has Failed":

> One belief holds that a company's mission is to maximize the share owner value, while another belief is that the company should be committed to satisfying customer needs. This difference requires more deliberations. ... The management of Western companies is obliged to create shareholder benefits, and boost the price of their stock. But stock prices go up and down in the market. Therefore, in order to prevent their stock price from falling down,

the management is inclined to adopt policies that support short-term goals. In this way, they won't be able to develop long-term goals which are essential for corporate development. ... Most Western managers have failed, and their management philosophy has failed as a whole, too. It is because they have stopped pursuing long-term goals. They do not focus on products that support the company's long-term development. Last but not least, the leadership of Western companies has failed also ethically. What makes a good leader? Who are real change leaders? In the East or the West, a successful leader must have a burning desire. If he pursues his goals with such a burning desire, the company can be the best in the industry.

What is the burning desire of Huawei's leaders? It is to become a top-three player in the global telecom industry. Huawei has made it about 20 years after the fantastic forecast was made. Why? Twenty years ago, private companies had essentially no access to any resources. What they could depend on is a burning desire, an impulse to survive, and their readiness to take risks. On the other hand, they were faced with winds from all directions. In the telecom market, in particular, their rivals were Western giants who were all armed to the teeth and boasted abundant or even redundant resources. So why has Huawei emerged from the jungle? The key rests with the core values that Ren Zhengfei has insisted on and institutionalized in the company.

During the long run that lasted over 20 years, Huawei has unconditionally followed the principle of customer centricity, and therefore, developed low-cost products that have met customer needs and offered customers the best service. Moreover, Huawei has remained faithful to this principle, which has built a level of trust with its customers in forming a "community of destiny." As senior Huawei executives put it, "Customers are the only reason Huawei exists. The customer is God. If we don't believe in God, who will save Huawei?"

Huawei's rivals, on the contrary, do not have any faith in their customers. They believe in the Wall Street, their shareholders, speculative investors, and the managers who own large shares of their stock. In some sense, they are slaves to stock charts. It is not because they lack common sense or vision, but because they are situated in a short-termist environment where people opt for radical strategies while customer needs and future are ignored. Huawei has won the game because it has taken the opposite direction: It is committed to customers and the long-term future. It has planned its business and corporate development by the decade.

Ren Zhengfei argues that the company could not fulfill its ambition if it becomes a public listed company. The problem is this is an age of the capital market. Without the incentive of speculative gains, how can Huawei attract and retain so many excellent people? People, or human resources, are critical for survival in the IT industry, and the most powerful weapon to win excellent people is the so-called "gold handcuff" stock options. But Huawei has given up the gold handcuff. According to Ren Zhengfei, people would lose their dedication once the company is listed, and that would be a disaster for the company. The wings burdened with gold simply cannot fly.

Huawei has designed a "silver-handcuff" incentive system: the employee shareholding scheme. This is a long-term virtual stock option, for which only dedicated employees are entitled to participate, and the shares cannot be traded on the stock market. This means that the shareholding structure is extremely decentralized but extremely closed at the same time: Only those who remain dedicated to the company and have made continuous contributions can benefit from the scheme and receive dividends from the shares they hold. Anyone who leaves or is no longer dedicated must give up their shares. Huawei does not allow any pure speculators to benefit from the labor of the dedicated employees. It does not mean Ren Zhengfei or the corporate is cold-hearted. This is due to the challenging environment of the industry and the mission of Huawei.

Huawei lets its employees benefit from its growth, but will not allow them to feed only off dividends. Huawei likes its employees to work hard and remain dedicated, but would never let dedicated people suffer. This, again, is Huawei's philosophy of balance.

Huawei's core values form a closed balance. Customer centricity is the goal and soul of the company. It is the basis of its survival. But how can the company attain this goal? Dedication. Every conduct and belief of the company and its employees must be dedicated to its goal. Then how can the company keep so many intellectual workers, more than a 100,000 of them, dedicated? The answer is to share the benefits of dedication. Ren Zhengfei has repeated once and again that the company won't "let Lei Feng wear worn-out socks." Therefore, they form a dynamic close circuit, a complete chain in which each link connects with and depends on the other, and this circuit has given Huawei abundant power for growth and success.

Of course, Huawei has faced many internal and external challenges on its way to success. In the early years, the company had suffered from the lack of capital, talent, products, and government connections. In the latter years, it lacked management experience, sound procedures, and solid rules. In the past decade, Huawei encountered encirclement and obstruction by its Western counterparts. Moreover, for over 20 years, there have been serious internal challenges. First, Huawei has more than 60,000 shareholders, and none of them owns a relative control. The number of individual shareholders and its scattered holding structure are both rare for any company in the world. At the same time, Huawei has refrained from diversification and opportunism. In consequence, Huawei's management has been forced to make choices within a very limited scope. They must not make any major mistake on business strategy, management procedures, product and technology direction, human resources development, and selection of future leaders. Its major operational policies, too, are subject to harsh internal and external tests which, however, have forced the leaders to develop an art and philosophy of organization and business. The philosophy of balance has been developed, modified, and finally perfected in such a narrow space.

Black-or-White Is a Metaphysical Assumption

As water overflows if it is too full, one stumbles if he has too much faith in himself. In history, a huge number of heroes had ruined themselves with arrogance. Only those who have tasted the bitterness as well as the sweetness of life and have been forced into moderateness by frustrations can succeed and remain successful for a long time. Therefore, moderateness is a virtue. Likewise, it is an indispensable character of any organization. For an organization, there must be a goal, but there are various means to fulfill the goal and the process varies as well. For instance, it cannot force its rivals to the corner because the rivals would fight back with unexpected force if they are pushed too hard, especially when their survival is threatened. At this moment, the organization will meet with a crisis. Therefore, why don't you seek for coexistence? Similarly, an organization surely needs rules and procedures, but it should pay more attention to incentives and communication with good faith. While business may be judged in a black-or-white way, grayness is essential, particularly regarding people. One cannot be treated or measured with too much precision. A flower is the most enjoyable when it is half blooming, and wine is the most sweet when you're half drunk. This poetic rule of thumb applies equally well to market competition and organizational management.

It is interesting to note that quite a few leaders love driving and cooking. When you sit behind the wheel, you may from time to time step on the accelerator or the brake and you may turn left or right according to the traffic on the road. It depends on your experience, intuition, judgment, and response. Cooking is equally enchanting. A dozen or dozens of different natural and chemical ingredients would be transformed very soon into a delicious dish by a cook who seems to be playing a magic. It depends on knowledge and experience, but a blueprint in the mind and systematic thinking are also indispensable. Moreover, the cook has to time the cooking process precisely and artistically. No wonder Lao Zi, founder of Taoism, said, "Governing a large country is like cooking a small fish."

Isn't managing a company like cooking a small fish as well? Ren Zhengfei said, "Grayness is a normal state, while black-or-white is a metaphysical assumption. I don't want our company to go to extremes. I would like it to possess some systematic thinking." "Huawei does not allow empiricism or dogmatism," said Sun Yafang, chairwoman of Huawei, in her essay "Small Wins Depend on Wisdom, Big Wins Depend on Virtue." This is true. But we cannot completely deny experience or dogmas so long as experience does not translate into rigid empiricism and dogmas do not turn into rigid dogmatism. Ren Zhengfei believes that the past is the basis for future development and that it is wise, rather than idle, to remain on the "golden mean." This belief has been confirmed by the history of Huawei. Before the IPD reform, Ren Zhengfei demanded that anyone who doubted or resisted the reform must go and that he would remove any member from the reform-leading panel who "were too active in thinking." He insisted strongly that they must "cut their feet to fit the shoes" and that the procedures should be first rigidified, then institutionalized, and then gradually optimized. Apparently, he had believed in "dogmas," that is, procedures and rules. But dogmas cannot metamorphosize into dogmatism, and procedures cannot keep dedication away. So when they become too rigid and lose their compatibility with the core value of dedication, procedures must be reformed. This is why Ren Zhengfei has made some shocking remarks in the recent years: "*Huawei Charter* has become obsolete. The management expertise of IBM is not totally fit for Huawei. Their mission is over."

Huawei is a commercial organization extremely strong in execution. Although IPD and ISC reforms had met with resistance 10 years ago, procedures may easily become rigid once they have been deployed, and optimization would be much harder. This is a paramilitary commercial troop, which is why systematic thinking and the philosophy of balance must be advocated among its middle and senior executives.

A business organization is a complex, dynamic, and multipolar chain. Every link, including internal and external systems, interacts and drives one another back and forth. There is no one road that is always suitable. It would sway a bit between left and right, between radicalism and conservatism, and between stability and change. It keeps revising direction by correcting its mistakes. Many dualities, for example, exist at Huawei, including dualities between the employee shareholding scheme and the decision power, between criticism and construction, between nondiversification and limited diversification, between democracy and centralization, between competition and cooperation, between openness and closure, between offense and compromise, between leaders and heroes, between action and inaction, between construction and deconstruction, and between dialectics and metaphysics. These dualities are severe tests for senior Huawei executives. They are far beyond the operational issues that ordinary business managers face; they are philosophical questions. Therefore, Ren Zhengfei has been arguing for many years that Huawei's mid- and senior-level managers must possess broad cultural backgrounds.

Ren said, "I believe, in the future, our managers must have a broader cultural background in addition to their market experience and insight. By a broader cultural background, I mean they need to know a bit of everything. Moreover, we should rotate our officials dynamically, so that they may have the opportunity to learn from each other and broaden their cultural vision."

What does "a bit of everything" mean? Ren Zhengfei may mean they need to have some knowledge about history, philosophy, military affairs, geography, from among many other areas. He has been trying to get the idea across to his colleagues for over 20 years, including the senior executives and the clerks.

If one reads books on different topics, more cultural insight will be gained. If one also faces and handles complex situations, a more systematic and multidimensional way of thinking will be developed. Then one would not be limited to the stance of simple, mechanical, or black-or-white attitudes toward any issue. Thinking with grayness is the most precious quality of a leader.

Ren Zhengfei loves driving; he enjoys controlling the wheel. He also loves to cook. It is said that he is good at cooking spicy dishes, but he is also good at tempering these creations to satisfy moderate tastes. This is the same as his leadership style: He may seem to go to extremes, but he has never produced extreme consequences.

Section III. Strategy Is Straight and Open While Tactics Involve Tricks

Operations and Management: Saying No to Opportunism

Business operation and management are two key issues confronting business organizations; they are also two popular terms that are often mistaken for each other. In fact, the puzzlement is the result of misunderstanding of some basic concepts.

For any business, operations are intended to maximize benefits, as businesses are profit-seeking organizations. "In this world, the most shameful businesses are those that make continuous losses, and the most disgraceful entrepreneurs are those who create deficits for their organizations because they have defaulted on their natural obligations," said a famous management scholar.

Operations are customer-centered. A business cannot generate any profit from within the organization. It will reap benefits only after its products and services are accepted by its customers. Therefore, Huawei argues that customers are the only reason for its existence, and its value rests with serving its customers because they are the source of profits. If it expands its operations, the company would be able to offer products and services to more customers.

On the other hand, management is intended to support operations. Internal management may not earn money for the business but it offers the necessary support for money-earning operations. Good management means high efficiency. In some sense, management is a tool to overcome inefficiency.

Business operation and management complement each other like yin and yang in the bagua diagrams. If they are well-matched, the business will benefit from high efficiency and reap satisfactory rewards. Nevertheless, balancing operation and management does not exclude focusing on just one of the two. In a certain period, a business might focus on either operation or management to create balance at a higher level.

During the first decade, Huawei had focused on business operation. This was a wise choice for the newly born small company because survival was the first imperative. Since 1997, Huawei has shifted its strategic focus to internal management, trying to improve its efficiency and profitability by introducing a world-class management system.

As Huawei accelerated its globalization drive, it redefined its mission, vision, and strategy in 2005:

1. Serving customers is the only reason Huawei exists, and customer needs are the driving force behind Huawei's development.
2. With high quality, good services, and low operating costs, Huawei prioritizes satisfying customer needs to improve their competitiveness and profitability.
3. Huawei will continue its management reform to ensure efficient process-based operations and high-quality end-to-end delivery.
4. Huawei will develop with its counterparts as both competitors and partners, create a favorable business ecosystem, and share the benefits of the value chain.

The above statements indicate clearly that Huawei has taken both business operation (Statement 1) and management (Statement 2) into account and has paid attention to both external environment (Statements 1 and 4) and internal development (Statements 2 and 3). In this sense, Huawei's strategy, which is based on its business philosophy, is a strategy filled with balances.

Strategies are fundamental schemes. They should be straight, open, systematic, and multidimensional and should exclude opportunism and attempts to cross the river by groping the stone. Anyway, Chinese companies, including Huawei, have been in the market for about 30 years; we can no longer simply follow our heart or move forward through making and then correcting mistakes. We should have acquired a long-term memory of experience and lessons; it is unwise to forget about them completely. Meanwhile, we should learn management from the West and give up our speculative and opportunistic preferences. The immature market economy has offered Chinese companies too many opportunities, so Chinese business community has paid exclusive attention to market operation and neglected organizational management. The problem is that market competition has become increasingly fierce and cruel, and the queue before the window of opportunity is getting even longer. The real challenge that Chinese companies face is to improve organizational management and build a dynamic balance between operation and management.

Unlike strategies, tactics are tricks and often changeable. Chinese merchants, who have grown up in the Chinese philosophy and most probably have read *The Art of War*, have tactical wisdom in their blood. Therefore, Chinese companies, especially smaller ones, have won battles in the international market with their tricks, but they have been subject to widespread criticism and distain.

In the past two decades, numerous Western and Chinese companies have risen and fallen. Their fall seems to tell a law: Western companies fell because of dogmatism, while Chinese companies fell because of empiricism; Western companies fell because of rigid tactics, while Chinese companies fell because of strategic loss and myopia; Western companies fell because they ignored customers, while Chinese companies fell because they ignored organizational and cultural development. In short, prolonged systematic imbalance is accountable for the fall of many Western and Chinese companies.

Balance of Terror: Innovation as a Factor of Self-destruction

Innovation is a mantra now. When a business gains some success, innovation may be quoted as the key factor, and when it falls they would be criticized for insufficient innovation. Apple Inc. and Kodak are extreme examples of the importance of innovation.

Is innovation really the key factor behind the rise of Apple and the fall of Kodak? Is innovation really so magical? Weren't there numerous examples of innovation in history that were disruptive and destructive? Bell Labs, once the national pride of the United States, fell 10 years ago due to excessive innovation. Motorola is basically dead, and the murderer is technology supremacy. The disaster occurred to the IT industry at the turn of the century because technology had lost its holiness, and since then innovation worship has been ridiculed by the market.

Ren Zhengfei said, "You are destroying yourself if you embrace innovation, but if you reject innovation, you will be destroyed by others." Over the past two decades, global competition in the IT industry has been the cruelest. A large number of tech giants have fallen all of a sudden and even smaller tech startups have died halfway during their rise, either in emerging countries like China or in industrialized countries like the United States and Japan.

Quite a few factors account for the fall of Western IT giants. The leading factor is short-termism from capital worship and shareholder centricity, while blind innovation is also a pandemic killer. Smaller companies, especially new startups, have not died of insufficient technological innovation. They have died because their innovation is not aligned with the market or customer needs or they suffer from the shortage of some critical resources. The same problems have troubled Chinese tech startups. However, Chinese companies were imitators, not innovators. Even among the mid- and large-sized tech corporations today, some still suffer from technological gaps and poor R&D capabilities.

Like Lenovo, Huawei started as a trading company, but Huawei had developed its own products within just a few years. Since 1991, Huawei has invested 10 percent of its sales into R&D each year, and this percentage did not change in 2011 when its sales amounted to CNY203.9 billion. As a senior Huawei executive said, "At Huawei, any cost can be cut except the 10 percent invested in R&D. The head of R&D would be 'killed' if he failed to invest this 10 percent!"

Huawei's R&D team is the largest group within Huawei. It accounts for 48 percent of the workforce, and in October 2012 there were more than 70,000 R&D employees in Huawei. With this largest R&D team in the world and a total investment of US$4.5 billion in 2011, Huawei has been creating three to five patents each day. Huawei has registered 36,344 patents in China and 10,978 patents overseas and has made 10,650 international PCT filings. Of the 23,522 patents that have been awarded, 90 percent are invention patents. With all these fruits of innovation, Huawei has not only improved the competitiveness of its products but also entered into partnerships with international competitors through patent exchange. As Ren Zhengfei said, "A fragile balance of terror has formed between Huawei and its Western counterparts." Of course, this balance has formed on the basis of Huawei's general strength, but the decisive factor is Huawei's technology and product development capability.

The word "innovation," however, rarely appears in the "management dictionary" of Huawei and is seldom mentioned in the speeches and articles by Ren Zhengfei or corporate documents of Huawei. Why? As Ren Zhengfei said, "Huawei holds the belief that we should lead the industry in terms of product technology innovation. But we should keep just half a step ahead because we would be the martyr if we were three steps ahead." Ren Zhengfei explained in 2005:

> We were once engaged in blind innovation. We were technology worshippers and cared little about customer needs. We simply tried to sell our

products and systems to customers, but wouldn't listen to them. In consequence, we had virtually lost the next-generation switch market in China. We realized later that we were wrong and we have changed our practices. Now, we have caught up and become the world's number one in the switch market. Blind innovation has accelerated the death of many Western companies. We therefore believe that the market is our priority. We can succeed only when we meet customer needs.

Ten years ago, Ren Zhengfei had a meeting with experts from Bell Labs. One of them asked, "Why has Huawei been so successful?" Ren answered, "It is because we understand the needs of Chinese customers." There is another question for Ren Zhengfei: Will the fragile balance between Huawei and its Western counterparts break several years later? The answer is SURE. The outcome depends on multiple factors. It depends above all on the bilateral or multilateral balance of strategy and tactics, which certainly includes the ability to make the right innovation at the right pace.

Section IV. Huawei: Success of the Management Philosophy

The Success of Dialectics

Before concluding this book, it is necessary to sum up the ideas in the previous chapters.

Chapter 1 "Common Sense and Truth: Customer Centricity" and Chapter 2 "Common Sense and Truth: Dedication Is Key to Success" are about the core values of Huawei. To some extent, common sense is equal to truth. It is a common sense that almost all the successful companies in the world are customer centric. Huawei believes that customers are the only reason for its existence, but this belief is not Ren Zhengfei's own creation. This is a basic law of the business world for centuries and can perhaps be referred to as the basic business ethic. Disappointedly, this ethic has been blurred and even given up in this new age when people worship capital and technology. Now the shareholders, instead of customers, are priority number one, and technology assumes supreme power.

Huawei has succeeded because Ren Zhengfei keeps his common sense and insisted on the truth of customer centricity, which has been dismissed as obsolete by the global IT industry. To some extent, customer centricity has been played by Huawei as a secret weapon to fight for survival.

In Europe, America, and China alike, many high-tech companies have been pushed by private equity investors and the greed of their founders into the capital market and have since then been driven by the capital market. On the other hand, Huawei is able to make decade-long plans for a customer-centric future. Therefore, Huawei's success is in a way the success of its core values. It has been able to catch up with and exceed its Western counterparts simply because their values have become misplaced.

Huawei's success is also the success of dialectics. The core values of Huawei, customer centricity, dedication, and sharing benefits with dedicated employees, form a dialectic chain. Customer centricity depends on employee dedication, and it is a common sense that employees may keep dedicated to the company on the condition that they can share the benefits of their hard work. In the Chinese language, "salary" means "fuel," and, therefore, to increase the salary is equal to adding fuel to the fire. A more generous incentive may drive employees to work even harder. And the most generous incentive of Huawei is the employee shareholding scheme, which is tank of oil that has fueled the dedication of its people. The flames have lighted up its past and will light up its future too.

In short, Huawei's core values have formed a dynamic and organic balance among a pull (customer centricity), a thrust (dedication), and an engine (benefit sharing).

Chapter 3 "Openness: A Matter of Life and Death," Chapter 4 "Compromise: The Law of the Jungle," and Chapter 5 "Grayness: Gathering a Hundred Thousand Intellectuals" form the second module of this book. Ren Zhengfei often mentions "openness, compromise, and grayness" together and these terms form the philosophical basis of this company and shaped its course leading to excellence. If it has only core values, Huawei may build a powerful organization, but this organization would not be very elastic or flexible. In the global environment, a flexible company is often more competitive than a powerful one. In the last two decades, Western companies have been losing power, but Chinese companies are turning rigid. Fortunately, Huawei has achieved the balance of power, flexibility, and rule. Openness is the highest level of flexibility. Huawei has survived and achieved so much success because it has implemented a fully open policy with regard to its R&D, marketing, human resources, organizational reform, and institutional development. "Openness" is on the tip of Ren Zhengfei's tongue.

"Compromise" is the philosophy of contingency. According to Ren Zhengfei, it is the means to survive in the jungle. The market is much like a jungle where the fittest survives. But the fittest may not remain the fittest all along or get even stronger, and the fiercest may not be the king. The tragic fate of tigers and dinosaurs is a warning for businesses. Compromise, a flexible art, can save them from extinction. For over 20 years, Huawei has applied the dialectical balance of offense and compromise to its business operation and organizational management and has, therefore, created the vitality and harmony within itself and a balance of terror with its Western competitors.

"Grayness" is mentioned last because we believe the concept of grayness is the cornerstone of Ren Zhengfei's business philosophy. It deserves special attention.

Chapter 6, "Self-criticism: A Sense of Fear Makes Greatness," and Chapter 7, "Change: Revolution or Evolution," are the third module of this book and present an instrumental philosophy. If core values and the concepts of openness, compromise, and grayness are engines of Huawei's business philosophy, self-criticism and change are guardians, correctors, cleaners, and monitoring and balancing systems. The core values and philosophical concepts are definite standards. It is wrong to deviate from customer centricity and dedication, and a company will suffer if it is deviates from its core values. Similarly a company won't live long if it is not open. On the other hand, self-criticism and change are not values; they are tools. When a train overspeeds, the brake system has to be activated; when the train is overloaded or underpowered, the control system will fan up the flames in the boiler. The train will also go a bit left and then shift to the right in order to keep balance. This is the dynamic balance of power, flexibility, and rule.

On the philosophical map of Ren Zhengfei, however, self-criticism is more highlighted than change. In recent years, "change" has been given a sacred mission that is unbearably heavy. It seems change is the key to any problem of any company or country. Change is a tool, but it has gradually become a value. Hasn't Barak Obama won the presidential race through an incessant repetition of his promise of change?

Ren Zhengfei has repeated, however, that a company is a constructive organization, so any change should be avoided until it is absolutely imperative. As a systematic project, change is a double-edged sword which may hurt the company if it is not handled without enough caution. Change is also a magic box. There is an angel, but more often a devil comes out when it is opened. Huawei has gone through several dramatic changes, and they are successful because the leaders have kept very cautious in the process. They have taken everything into account and rejected any reckless or ill-advised move.

Ren Zhengfei prefers gradual improvement and self-criticism. In essence, self-criticism is a means to gradual improvement, and therefore, an effective tool to maintain the core values of the company constructively. When it becomes a conscious habit in the thinking and conduct of managers, self-criticism will play a significant role.

Change and self-criticism are twins. They support each other and check each other in a balance. Self-criticism is the precursor of change, and when self-criticism fails to uphold core values, change will take over the key role while self-criticism will become a supplement.

Chapter 8, "Strategy: Fight with Courage and Wisdom," is the last module of this book. It maps out and illustrates the strategic thinking of Ren Zhengfei, including his ideology strategy and market strategy, his strategic focus, strategic balance, strategic resources, strategic adventures, strategic conflicts, strategic partnerships, and the mechanisms for strategy generation. They contain a lot of useful insights and inspirations.

Grayness, Balance, and Pragmatism

American novelist Theodore Harold White once remarked, "The United States is a nation based on notions. Notions, rather than the land, make the government." This remark fits Huawei extremely well. Huawei had nothing at the start except a handful of rash Prometheuses. What does it have today? Tangibly, it has several artistic parks, or clusters of buildings, plus millions of electronic equipment. The really valuable assets of the company are the intangible intellectual properties, and the most valuable asset is the people who have internalized the business philosophy of Huawei. This is the basis for Huawei's future and hope. Business philosophy, the notion, underlies everything else. Without business philosophy, Huawei is an empty body that will wither and die soon.

Then what is the fundamental philosophy of Huawei? What is the cornerstone of Ren Zhengfei's ideas? It is grayness. The title of Chapter 5, "Grayness: Gathering a Hundred Thousand Intellectuals," has merely revealed Ren Zhengfei's philosophy with regard to people. In fact, grayness has much wider coverage and plays a much bigger role. Without grayness, Huawei's core values won't remain on a long-term stable balance. For instance, the relationship between satisfying existing and stimulating potential customer needs, the relationship between sharing benefits with dedicated employees and the company's long-term goal, and the relationship between spiritual dedication and hard work are likely to turn rigid without grayness. If any core value becomes a rigid "truth," the balance among customer centricity, dedication, and benefit sharing with employees would deform and finally break.

Grayness also underlies the courage to open up. Huawei is a rare open business organization in China, which is a result of the industry dynamics and the idealism of Ren Zhengfei. Openness is the only approach for Huawei to rise from the bottom and enter the club of leaders at the top of the industry pyramid. Huawei must become a sufficiently open and cooperative organization which is able to learn the merits of its counterparts. If it had insisted on telling the white from the black and dividing the industry into friends and enemies, Huawei could not have grown up so fast and achieved so much success.

Grayness represents the value judgment of people and circumstances. Gray is a natural color, so through a gray lens, one can see that every people, every organization, and everything in the world is multifaceted and cubic. The negative side coexists with the positive side in a coin. And every people or organization may be offensive sometimes, but they may compromise when necessary. In the early years, Huawei had extolled the wolf character and insisted that the people of Huawei should become a pack of aggressive wolves. As circumstances change, however, Ren Zhengfei has opted for the gray way of thinking and resorted to internal and external compromise. This is proved a wise choice.

Grayness has also maintained the constructive character of self-criticism and change. Many business organizations have failed to inspire passion through organizational changes. Instead, changes have resulted in destructive disruptions. Why? A key issue is the leaders of self-criticism and change think in an extreme way: For them, things are either black or white. They tend to dismiss the past and other people and easily lose patience when improvement is slow. They want to see change overnight. Under such circumstances, failure is predestined. With his insight into grayness, Ren Zhengfei advocates self-criticism rather than cross-criticism; he is cautious about change and insists that any change must be gradual.

Grayness is the root or the cornerstone, and balance is the highest level of grayness. The law of excluded middle is not gray or balanced. Therefore, *Huawei Charter* is full of ambivalent statements, such as

"We shall not only ... but also... ." They are paradoxes but they are balanced against each other. Ren Zhengfei's speeches and articles over the past two decades are also full of seemingly contradictory but essentially compatible remarks, and the key rests with the actual circumstances. For instance, its strategic positioning must be clear and definite so that all frontline and back-end warriors have a clear goal and direction. But as circumstances change, the strategic position must change. The relationship between democracy and authority is another example. The former implies vigor and creativity, while the latter represents order. Neither of them is dispensable, and the problem is how they can be balanced. There should be rules, while the leaders should be able to take contingent actions as necessary. A company would perhaps become stagnant, spiritless, and lifeless, if there are a number of middle and senior managers who see gray, but there are few passionate heroes who can tell black from white easily and are committed to single-dimensional success.

A company is a utilitarian profit-seeking organization. Like a politician, a businessman is changeable in popular perception. It seems changeability has become a distinct label of organizational leaders. This is because any organization has a certain goal, and the leader must lead a group of people to reach this goal. Various appeals, therefore, would influence the decision-making process, or perhaps even the belief of the leader. And the changing circumstances inside and outside the organization will also affect the leader's perception and judgment. Therefore, it seems defining competence of excellent organizational leaders to change according to circumstances.

Idealism is the power that pulls an organization and its leaders along, while pragmatism is the basis for organizational strategy and actions. To achieve any idealistic goal, an organization must take realistic actions that suit actual circumstances. Sometimes they must be radical enough to break the balance, while at other times they must remain prudent in order to maintain and enhance the balance. The United States is an idealistic country with its American Dream, but the pragmatic philosophy of John Dewey has been the spiritual cornerstone for its progress and development.

Organizational leaders are changeable, but they hold on firmly to pragmatism and core values. From a short-term perspective, they may appear changeable or even capricious, but in the longer term, you may see excellent leaders are unanimously balancists.

This is the beauty of grayness.

Epilogue

*T*he *Huawei Story* has taken us nearly six years to complete, from conceptualization, to framing, and finally to publication. The book's authenticity and reliability are backed by the information from a 3 million word corpus of documents Huawei has released internally or publicly (including meeting minutes, Ren Zhengfei's speeches, corporate resolutions, and articles from the internal periodical *Huawei People*) as well as more than 1 million words in article text concerning the global telecom industry and the course of opening up taken by the Chinese business community. The book's authenticity and reliability is also guaranteed by my frequent interactions with Huawei's former and incumbent executives, including Ren Zhengfei, over the past 10 years. The first draft took more than one year, after which it was revised more than eight times based on opinions and suggestions from various sources.

The simplified Chinese edition of this book was published in December 2012. The traditional Chinese edition was subsequently published by *Taiwan's Business Weekly*, followed by the release of the Korean edition. A total of 250,000 copies have been released as of the time of this afterword, creating far-reaching impact on Chinese and Korean readers. Over 100 media outlets have reported or commented on the book. This work has also prompted the business, management, and media communities to study Huawei in a frenzy of enthusiasm. We have been invited to give more than 100 lectures at universities, companies, financial institutions, government agencies, and academic institutions across China.

This is not a book about Huawei's history. This book focuses on the logic behind the legendary globalization process of a Chinese company. What are the factors that have transformed a private Chinese company into a global leader in the communications industry in a short span of 25 years? Is its success derived from political associations, its corporate culture, its philosophies, its management systems, or other elements? This book attempts to reveal the truth and "genetics" that have contributed to Huawei's success and discusses the trajectory that Huawei is likely to take to either decline or achieve greater success.

About the Authors

Tian Tao is a member of the Huawei International Advisory Council and Co-Director of Ruihua Innovative Research Institute at Zhejiang University, Hangzhou, China. In 1991, Tao founded *Top Capital*, the first Chinese magazine on private equity investment, and has served as its Editor-in-Chief since then. He worked as a publisher of *Popular Science* (Chinese Edition) from 1995 to 1997. In the past 20 years, Tao has started a number of businesses in advertising, publishing, and media industry. He also co-founded two IT companies, Beijing Umessage and Hillstone Network Co. Tao is a lover of several sports, including swimming and golf.

Wu Chunbo is a Professor and PhD Supervisor of Renmin University of China, Beijing. He earned his PhD in economics from the same university in 1998 and has served as a dean of the Institute of Organization and Human Resources, School of Public Administration, Renmin University of China. He has been serving as a Senior Corporate Management Advisor for Huawei since 1995. Playing tennis is his favorite hobby.